MAKING SENSE TOGETHER

HUMAN HORIZONS SERIES

MAKING SENSE TOGETHER

*Practical approaches to supporting children
who have multisensory impairments*

by

Rosalind Wyman

A Condor Book
Souvenir Press (E&A) Ltd

*Dedicated with love to Emily and
to her parents, Jayne and Koji*

First published 1986 under the title
Multiply Handicapped Children
by Souvenir Press (Educational & Academic) Ltd.,
43 Great Russell Street, London WC1B 3PA

This new edition, retitled, completely revised
and largely rewritten, published 2000

ISBN 0 285 63510 7

Typeset by Rowland Phototypesetting Ltd.,
Bury St Edmunds, Suffolk

Printed in Great Britain by
The Guernsey Press Co. Ltd., Guernsey, Channel Islands

Acknowledgements

This book represents the efforts of a great many people, especially parents with whom I have worked. In particular I must mention Norman Brown, Christine Taylor and Suzanne Todd, whose thoughts and writing are quoted in the first chapter. I am indebted to these parents for permission to reproduce their work. Thanks are extended to colleagues who have allowed me to quote from articles which first appeared in *Talking Sense*: Judith Peters, 'Motor Skills'; and Jo Franklin, 'Testing hearing: adapting the Distraction Test'; and to Doreen Norris for very practical advice.

I would like to express my appreciation to David Brown, Head of the Family Education and Advisory Service, Sue Evans, Deputy Head, and all the team at the Sense South East Family Centre, Ealing. The quality of the Family Education and Advisory Service team's work is an inspiration to colleagues and plays a vital role in the lives of many families having a child with multi-sensory impairment.

As well as people within the Family Advisory Service I would especially like to thank Rodney Clark, Chief Executive of Sense, for his encouragement of the original project, and Eileen Boothroyd, Education Officer, Sense, for all her professional support. Thanks go to Sense colleagues: Jenny Fletcher for her diagram about resonance boards; Mary Guest for advice regarding Usher; and Jessica Hills, Sense Chairperson, for being there.

I am particularly grateful to Beverley Mars, Bedfordshire, Judy Armstrong, Principal Psychologist, and the Sensory Teachers Team in Lewisham, and to colleagues in Greenwich, Kent, Surrey and other Local Education Authorities with whom I have had the pleasure of working in recent years.

I am happy to acknowledge the University of Texas at Dallas,

Callier Center for Communication Disorders, for permission to quote from the Callier Azusa Scale, and the State of Michigan, Department of Education, for permission to quote from the *Manual for the Assessment of a Deaf-Blind Multiply Handicapped Child*. Thanks are extended to Robert J. Smithdas for permission to quote from his poem *Shared Beauty*. All allowed publication of their work in the original book and it has been reproduced again here.

Thanks are due to Phil Grey for all photographs, to Gail Prout for her line drawings and to Joanna Gomm for additional illustrations in this edition. Margaret Gomm provided invaluable secretarial help in the original publication, *Multiply Handicapped Children*. Jayne Koji has given not only of her time by providing secretarial help in the writing of this book, but also personal assistance with further suggestions and ideas as Emily's mother.

Most of all my thanks go to Al and Emily who have been excellent teachers for their parents, giving knowledge to them about the needs of children with visual impairment who have additional needs. Some of that knowledge is represented in this book.

R.W.

Contents

The children
'A child is multisensory impaired when s/he has a degree of combined visual and auditory impairment which can cause communication, developmental and/or educational difficulties.' (Sharing a regional approach. Report of the GEST project. Education provision for deafblind children 1992–1995).

Definition of deafblindness that has been adopted by the Nordic countries
'A person is deafblind when he or she has a severe degree of combined visual and auditory impairment. Some deafblind people are totally deaf and blind, while others have residual hearing and residual vision. The severity of the combined visual and auditory impairments means that deafblind people cannot automatically utilise services for people with visual impairments or with hearing impairments.

'Thus deafblindness entails extreme difficulties with regard to education, training, working life, social life, cultural activities and information. For those who are born deafblind, or who acquire deafblindness at an early age, the situation is complicated by the fact that they may have additional problems affecting their personality or behaviour. Such complications further reduce their chances of exploiting any residual vision or hearing. Deafblindness must therefore be regarded as a separate disability which requires special methods of communication and special methods for coping with the functions of everyday life.'

Extracts from the Education (Special Educational Needs) Regulations 1994
'The knowledge, views and experiences of parents are vital. Effective assessment and provision will be secured where there is the greatest possible degree of partnership between parents and their children and schools, LEAs and other agencies.' (Code 1.1 fundamental principles.)

'The value of early information and support to parents cannot be overemphasised. The better informed and the better supported parents are the better they are able to contribute as partners to the assessment of their child.' (Code 3.12 assessment.)

'LEAs should ensure that parents have the fullest possible access to information and support during the statutory assessment process and that they are fully involved in contributing to their child's statement.' (Code 4.69 statement procedure.)

1 The Parents' View

The birth of a child who is disabled inevitably alters the life pattern and expectations of his or her parents. They have to adapt, throughout the pre-school, school and post-school years, to circumstances that they may never have envisaged. Their entire lives will be affected.

Traditionally people expect to live happily ever after when they settle down together, although most of them go through times of adjustment to living as partners and becoming parents. Certain expectations about being parents are often fulfilled, but for some all does not go so smoothly. They have a child who is disabled. From the moment their child is born, circumstances and feelings beyond their control may overwhelm them.

When they are told about their child's condition these parents may feel as though they are being stretched on a rack. All too often they receive the news under very difficult and traumatic circumstances, sometimes not even in privacy. Many break under the strain. Even today, some parents have to face an intolerable burden of emotions alone. Sometimes misinformation and misinterpretation creep in. It may take many years for parents to find out everything they need to know; time and again they may have to reinterpret details that they first heard under severe emotional stress.

They may well be surrounded by a dozen or more 'well-intentioned' professionals who are strangers to them, and they may feel unable to express their grief and anxiety, or to ask questions of the person whose task it is to give them the essential details about their child's condition.

Deep resentment and anger can result from the way they are given the news at this crucial time. Information should always be conveyed in a dignified and sensitive way, and parents should be encouraged to ask questions and to come back and discuss things whenever they feel the need. Parents who have been told about their child's condition under less than ideal circumstances almost invariably recount feelings of isolation, grief, confusion and hurt for many years afterwards.

Christine writes:

At first he wouldn't breathe—then he did and was cleaned up to be given to me. When I held him he was so cold, so skinny; then he opened his eyes. They were pale blue. To me his eyes were something like in a horror film. He is blind—my baby will never see me! It's all so vivid even now. What do I do? I think of white canes and dark glasses. He is so cold and thin. I cannot express how I feel; my mind, my feelings of shock, will not let me speak. The midwife fusses around us. My husband keeps walking up and down, saying over and over again, 'He is so thin, so pale, like a skinned rabbit.'

I hold Paul, trying to get him warm. I wish he would stop looking at me with those staring eyes. The midwife phones for a doctor and he arrives half an hour later. He examines Paul and is very concerned about his heart and his breathing, yet says nothing about his eyes. Paul makes no sound at all. All I want to do is hold my baby. He is so cold, but he is wrapped in a blanket and put in his carry-cot. I just can't take in all that is happening. I start to feel numb, my mind will not accept what is happening to us—this numbness will stay with me for the next few years, whenever something painful happens to Paul. If I had been left alone with him for just a while, maybe I would have let go and cried for both of us, and it would have helped me later when I was told about his disabilities.

The doctor tells me, in best bedside manner, that he is going to take Paul to the local special care unit for further examinations. I cannot go with him, I'm told, because I've just given birth, and anyway he will be home in about a week's time. The doctor keeps going on about Paul's heart, but to me then, at that moment, it is his eyes that matter. I wish someone would explain to me about his eyes. They take Paul away to hospital: it's windy outside, the time is 4 p.m. I hope they take good care of him, and please, please, God, let me hold him soon.

Very few of those involved can recall instances of parents who say that they were given the news, however potentially devastating, in as delicate, careful and kindly a way as possible. But gradually, conveying news about a child's disabilities is beginning to improve. Many teaching hospitals have acquired much more experience of working with the parents of children with disabilities, and they now consult parents' organisations and share information about how to work with parents in a positive way.

Sarah Jones's recent experiences highlight this improvement. She was taken into a private room to be told about her child's disabilities, and it was clear to her that the paediatrician had set aside time for them to talk together. Sarah did not feel hurried through his explanation of the diagnosis and was encouraged to ask questions about her little girl's condition: the doctor had lots of illustrations, diagrams and photocopied articles to hand, and was ready for Sarah's questions, positively encouraging them throughout the conversation. He indicated that he was available at the hospital if she wanted to telephone him any time during the week, and made sure that she had another appointment to see him within seven days.

The next time Sarah visited the hospital she was told about voluntary organisations that she could get in touch with, and books and pamphlets were available. She was also given the telephone number of a help line. Like many parents, Sarah kept a file for all of this information, so that she could take up offers of help as she became ready to do so. In addition, each time she returns to her child's teaching hospital, she knows that more information can be made available from the hospital's database. It is so important for all parents to acquire as much information about their child's condition as possible, to look back over and use as he or she grows and matures. It's also important to realise that parents' needs change just as much as the child's.

Well informed parents, however sad and angry they may have been, will usually be able to take positive steps towards helping their child; whereas parents who are agonising and still hurting emotionally and have *not* armed themselves with the necessary information are less likely to see anything positive about their child.

If diagnosis does not happen at birth, parents may worry, together or separately, about their child's development; they may hide their anxiety from each other, or may tell one side of the family but not the other. I have heard of parents taking their child to a paediatrician or to a diagnostic assessment unit without telling their partner, and I have known several mothers who have attended developmental play sessions with their child without telling the father.

*   *   *

Norman and Christine both have children with multisensory impairments (msi) and have been members of Sense (see page 33) for many years.

Norman's son was nineteen and Christine's was five at the time they wrote down the following thoughts. Both boys are profoundly deaf, with very limited sight, and they communicate through gesture. Both parents live their lives with a heightened awareness that they sometimes wish they did not have about the medical conditions affecting their children. They know that, however much they love them, they wish they were different.

Norman writes:

I am moved to write not because I have solutions, but in the hope that my slowly increasing understanding—mostly the result of hindsight—will be of help. I merely bear witness to one experience, and you must modify it with yours. One other qualification I would make: I cannot speak for every family, but only for a family with a member who has little or no formal communication. I think this is important. There are many people with disabilities with whom I have shared a full and rich communication that cheers the heart. Many points of which I write come from the daily experience of continual care and contact without the blessing of exchanging views, information and general chitchat with the person being cared for. I would not like anyone, least of all any people with disabilities who read this, to think that having a disability in the family automatically leads to the considerations I shall note. I write for the families such as mine, with a child who, for whatever reason, is called a non-communicating child. I use 'non-communicating' to mean those who cannot use words or signs to convey or receive abstract thought. Here I paint a picture bleaker than I hope you find it.

When I consider the life of our family, the problem areas fall under four main headings—time, guilt, grief and stress.

The needs of the parents vary as the child grows, partly because the needs of the child change, but also because the parents are growing as well, with strengths and wants that alter. But one consistent pursuit of mine has always been the pursuit of time—time to understand and adapt but mainly time to recover and time in which to capture moments that are just my own.

When our child first arrives, time flees. We are launched into an immediate and wearying race to claw back space in which to do the right things so that no one in the family suffers.

There is a fivefold quest in the first five years: for knowledge, diagnosis, treatment, rights and placements. We are desperate for knowledge. What is wrong with my child? Why does my child not do those things? Why does my child do these things? Where can I go for help? Who will understand?

The truth usually unrolls slowly. Few of us grasp the full picture straight away. Revelation leads to suspicion, to confirmation, to another suspicion, and so on, as our quest for knowledge becomes a quest for further diagnosis as well and we whirl our confused way through a series of shocks. As each fact is stated, and even as we pursue the next, we are seeking treatment for the previous one; and sometimes we take steps that later prove futile, leading us into cul-de-sacs, because the *whole* picture is still unknown.

Christine:

The white coats went into a huddle. A sister came in and said she was going to take some blood after all; she said the problem might be rubella. This was the first time that word was said and I didn't know what it meant or why she had said it. I was given an appointment to go back in four weeks.

Sunday 25 March was Mother's Day that year. What happened that day changed me from a normal 'run of the mill' person to the mother of a child who is profoundly deaf and severely visually impaired.

Parents occasionally talk about losing a child or mourning for a child they did not have as an essential period of readjustment. They speak, too, of needing time to begin to hope together, so that eventually they can rethink their perspectives and adapt their lives to accommodate their new situation. This time of adjustment may take anything from a minute to a year and some parents may never adjust. But over time, in most families, parents are able to become involved with their child, knowledgeable about his condition, interested in his education and realistic about his future.

Norman:

It is a period of immense confusion compounded by the fact that each thing we need to know is in the realm of a different specialist, and the multiple journeys start. Those agonising waits for the appointments for which we arrive on time, after the most enormous hassles, only to find a crowd of others waiting, who have all been given the same arrival time. Consequently, when the specialist is finally seen, our child is so distressed, and has so distressed us, that any coherent dialogue is impossible. All we want to do is escape, as does the child. No tests work, the right questions are not asked, anything said is only half remembered, and we come

away with only one concrete outcome—another appointment, when usually a different person will see us and require
briefing from scratch.

Not only is there the problem caused by the treks out,
there is also the problem caused by the treks in—of other
people coming to our homes. These visits become more
frequent as we move from considering knowledge, diagnosis
and treatment to encompassing rights and benefits, and
begin the quest for placements. The health visitors, the
peripatetic services, the social workers, the advisers, the
checkers of claims, all beat a track to our door and, if our
problems increase, so do the visitors. We welcome them all,
for we need their help, but we are often pinned down and
vulnerable within our once safe refuge, our own home, subject to invasion when it suits others. The very response to
outside agencies can be draining, and the duplication of
effort immense. I have spoken to one social worker who
stepped in to become the buffer between a mother and
these agencies, and found that she had a list of twenty-eight
people likely to call or needing contact. At only one a day
and once a month, that would leave not even the weekends
free.

And all this is happening when we ourselves need time,
in particular that all-important time, the time to accept; the
time to realise that our child is still a child, a child with
special needs, for whom no miracle cures can be awaited:
just herself, just himself, with potential to be explored, love
to be given or awakened, and a dignity and life to be safe-
guarded.

Norman's experiences are echoed by many parents. One father
told me that there came a point when he wrote to all his involved
professionals to explain that if he and his wife were ever to
become real parents of their child, they needed time to themselves. The professionals had to understand that on each occasion
they visited they were taking up the child's time as well as the
parents', and it was leaving everyone exhausted. Luckily, all
seventeen involved professionals understood!

Norman:

It took me seven years to accept—and I am still caught out.

Parents need time to accept a new perspective, a new way of life; and time to accept other people's attitudes and to learn how to cope with them.

Christine:

Paul is in an oblong plastic box—something I've never seen before; I always call it a coffin. He has a breathing pad under him which bleeps all the time. How that bleep frightened me when it stopped at different times. I do wish parents were told why they are used—we didn't find out until after it had stopped the second time. The fear of that pad is still with me now.

A young student nurse stands beside Paul all the time, like a prison warder. I ask if I can hold him. 'No,' I am told, 'he is far too weak.' She then begins to tube-feed him, without telling me what she is doing. The shock of seeing this happen—the only thing it brings to my mind is force-feeding, and I have never seen anything like it before. A sister comes in and tells us that the paediatrician will be seeing Paul tomorrow—no doctors have seen him yet. My arms ache to hold him; I touch his tiny blue hand, it is so cold. The student nurse says we must go now.

At home our other son starts to cry. 'You promised me my brother would be here when I came home—why isn't he, when can I see him?' How do we explain to a three-year-old? We sit and hold him and try to explain.

Services that offer immediate practical assistance, both in the hospital and in the community, need to be coordinated. Help and advice should be on hand so that parents can help not only their child with disabilities, but also, if necessary, their other children, to cope with the news. Grandparents and other family members, too, may need help in understanding and coming to terms with what is happening within the family. Offers of advice, home teaching and therapy require consistent and delicate planning, so that parents have the choice of opting into these services when they are ready.

Norman:

We can forget how to relax. We can also forget how to fill our time—our own time. When the child starts attending school, one parent may suddenly realise that dedicated concentration on the child has emptied life of all other contacts and activities. Suddenly there is nothing, and the buzzing mind has only itself to turn upon—a strange backlash that even the working partner cannot share, not experiencing that gap. We must be sure that our child does not become the only thing in our lives. We drive ourselves hard, don't we? We drive ourselves to do our best for our child, and we can also drive ourselves to avoid the issue, to block out the pain and shout down the doubts. But our child's problems do not release us from all other problems; these merely become deferred or avoided until they can be avoided no longer.

Christine:

I pick up Paul, he looks different—drunk. His pale blue eyes stare at me even more. A doctor tells me that Paul has been given a massive heart stimulant; if he lives until morning he will be sent to a different hospital, as they can do no more for him. My whole being wants to scream. No one said anything about dying, my baby won't die. They still don't know what is wrong—why? They are doctors, why don't they know? I can still see Paul now as he looked then; my memory won't let it fade. I know in an instant that my baby is disabled, that the doctor doesn't give him much chance of survival. I lay Paul back in his plastic 'coffin' and run out of the hospital. If ever I needed to believe in God's existence I really did that night.

Norman:

How much time and how many words are currently spent on personal relationships. An average day's reading or viewing could convince you that nothing else exists. Yet in our family there is not time for such distractions. We can often forget that we are ordinary people underneath, because we are not supposed to function as such. We are the pivot and focus of myriads of involvements, all child-centred. Perhaps it is all background to my next point—the potentially divisive effect of the child. It is true that he or she can draw families together, marshalling one parent's protective instinct and the other's care in a concerted effort to move mountains—and the mountains can move. But underneath, other forces are at work. If we are not careful, marriage becomes a serious business and the humour dies.

Christine:
Every other day we went to hospital. My husband gave up work and signed on the dole.

Some parents feel 'dictated to' by professionals—they are given appointments, told to visit a bewildering assortment of clinics and specialists—and they may feel that they play a very small part in the life of their child. Many parents, however, are beginning to reap the benefits of a shift in attitude, knowing that they are important and vital members of their child's team. They often act as coordinators and feel that they can and should participate as equals with a real role in the ongoing treatment of their child. Sarah Jones, for example, said that initially she was very vulnerable, letting the doctors do whatever they wanted, never once questioning *what* they were doing. Now, however, she is 'a little wiser, and I know not to accept everything that people put to us. We have learnt to challenge their words and to ask questions such as: what is that for? why are you doing that? what will that test prove?'

Norman:
How hard it is to face up to the problems in a relationship and discuss them. How easy it is to mistake the problem or defer the discussion when your child is assumed by all the world to have the overriding call on your attention. How difficult it is, even when you are willing, to find sufficient

time and energy to tackle that discussion. How easy to feel your own problem is not worthy of note and, therefore, that neither are you. But, unattended, the problem will fester until it becomes paramount.

The progress can be subtle. Amid the turmoil and the weariness, the good times grow scarce. The needs of the child are such that on most occasions at least one parent must be on hand. Child-minders can be arranged for special occasions, but for many meetings and social events such cover cannot be found, especially as the child grows older. Thus, such occasions are often refused or attended by one parent only. Before long an insidious process begins. If one's only contact with the outside world is when one is solo, a subconscious feeling can emerge that good times are associated with absence from one's partner, and one's partner is associated with stress and strain. Very destructive. To this is added the fact that most professionals work office hours, so their visits to the home are usually to see one parent only. However much that parent tries or intends to convey what s/he has learnt, s/he remains more in the know and more able to build upon that knowledge and upon his/her contact with the child. This can lead to the partner feeling redundant, with a sense of inadequacy compounded by rejection. So the partner withdraws further, turning more and more to the supportive role.

Professionals need to see themselves as partners in the parents' team, working together to obtain the best possible services for the child and his family. The parents know the child, have assessed his abilities, and have observed him (often minutely) over a longer period of time than the professionals. Parents know how the services they have already received actually work, how efficient they are, and the need to build on them. They know their present situation very well, too—where they live, what toys they have, what equipment they would find useful, their own abilities and how much time they have. *They know their child*, and they have specific hopes and plans for his or her future.

Parents know their child.

Christine:

Two therapists came in, and one said to the other, 'Oh, look, he isn't as bad as we expected.' What they were expecting I don't really know; but it put me on my guard straight away. The therapists showed me how to strengthen Paul's trunk and, hopefully, his weak muscles. Paul cried the whole time, every time. But as the weeks went by his muscles did become firmer, although he still held his head back all the time. I was told that his neck muscles were very floppy and I remember trying to make him hold his head up all the time, even when he was asleep. It became a 'thing' I kept doing all the time, but it made no difference—his head stayed back.

Many parents report a feeling of being overtaken by 'things to do'. Sarah Jones was able to involve relatives in her little girl's care, but she said that there were many occasions when they undertook her exercises but did not play with her. Turning Sophie's head so as to straighten her neck obsessed them to the point where they retained an over-zealous interest in her diagnosis but not in her progress.

Christine:

One evening, after Paul had brought his feed back at me again after I had taken three-quarters of an hour to give it to him, and with him still not responding to me, I shouted at him, 'Why are you like this? Look at me! You are supposed to be a baby, not a rag doll! I want you to live, to grow up and be someone.'

Paul cried, and for the first time ever he let me cuddle him, and I felt him respond to me. He was five months old and at last he felt as if he was mine, all mine. I had felt, up until then, ever since he came home from hospital, that he was a stranger. We had never had the time to be together. I had never tickled him, heard him laugh, seen him look for me around the room—all the little things I had done with my other son when he was a few months old. I never fell in love with Paul. I was always too busy feeding him, exercising his body, giving him drugs, trying to interest him in toys—with no response; and always I was so tired.

Now I cried the tears I would have cried if he had been allowed to stay at home with me in the beginning and not been taken away from me one hour after birth. From then on, although things were up and down, I slowly grew to love him as a baby and not as the rag doll I was looking after so automatically.

Parents can often see their successes, week by week, but they may need help in charting their child's achievements. A goal-planning method can be a useful and constructive way of working. As parents gradually see their child attaining the goals set, this often leads to the realisation that they are becoming very effective teachers of the child. Realistic goal-planning in partnership with specialist teachers and therapists is a positive and useful intervention mode that is occurring more and more throughout the country. Parents who feel able to contribute to their child's all-round developmental achievements also feel able to change or modify the methods they are using and to suggest solutions to their professional co-workers.

Parents have abilities. Planning with parents helps everyone, particularly the child, to achieve so much more.

Norman:

One can give a great deal to a job if one has a secure base to return to. If conditions at that base are stressful and require continuing effort, both job and home suffer in the long run. The partner at home cannot look for relief when the employed partner returns—and indeed feels guilty at needing that relief instead of being able to provide it. The employed partner is coming home to a new shift rather than to relaxation, and feels guilty at being unable to fulfil expectations. Both are looking for respite, even from one another; but the presence of the partner constitutes a constant though unspoken cry for help, and weariness is mistaken for reluctance to provide that help, even by the weary other partner.

Thus isolation closes in, as the world, already small, contracts to what we can cope with, and we shrink away, even from one another, or tire of our own complaints, until we feel that in each other's eyes, and in our own, too, we have become some kind of monster.

The world turns over, but those times to which outsiders look forward—the festivals and the holidays—become the times we dread, for our periods of greatest stress are when everyone demands a show of happiness. So we pretend, and move a little further away.

Our dreams on ice, we feel our energies must go exclusively to the child. We seek an appropriate programme and then try our best to make it effective. Recognising the need for consistency, we make our home into a school. For some time it does not matter; this is what parents do, for any child. Labels and signs appear, the furniture changes, ornaments and books move further up the walls, toys are scattered everywhere. But for how long can you keep this up? If your home is a teaching environment, when does it become your home again, and how do you become just Mum or Dad?

I am not so naive as to say, 'You must make time to be together and talk together and have fun together', because I know that often it really is impossible. Making time is easier said than done, especially when you are living at so many people's mercy. All the same, capture it when you can.

Christine

My health visitor agreed that, at about nine months, Paul should have some help from a peripatetic teacher, as whatever I could do for him was not enough. I needed some help.

A teacher came on the scene. She was marvellous—a peripatetic teacher for children who are visually impaired. She came once a month and we all looked forward to her visits. My other son would wait at the front gate and, when she drove up, would help her in. She always had a large laundry basket full of toys and used to chat away to my older son, asking him how he had got on at playgroup that day.

Her theory was that if Paul could not get to the toys, then the toys would have to come to him. She introduced him to all kinds of 'feels', every texture; she had a book of carpet squares and would very gently encourage Paul to touch them. She showed us how we could make our own toys rather than use plastic all the time; she told us about books we could read and told me about the Disability Living Allowance.

How we loved that hour. At last someone was helping us to help Paul. The time passed so quickly, and when she left she always left two toys for Paul and an 'unofficial' one for my other son. He used to help the teacher put everything back in her car, which was full of toys, and we would wave goodbye, longing for the next time she called. Her guidance really started us on the road to helping Paul learn to play.

She treated him as a child who needed help, never a labelled 'rubella child', as some of our professionals did.

Although there are factors that place the parents of children with disabilities in a unique category, it is invidious to group them all together. Every parent is an individual and deserves recognition of his or her personal value. Parents need to be seen as equals—equal co-workers with their children, equal to their advisers and potentially as able as anyone else. Both professionals and parents have certain specialised and generalised skills, which they can use in their interactions with each other for their mutual benefit. Professional people need to adapt and adjust just as much as parents are asked to do.

Some years ago there was a child born to Hindu parents who was unable to tolerate milk, and was slowly starving to death. Realising that the mother was very devout, the dietitian called in to help solve the problem said, 'I know you are a Hindu, but the only formula that I can find to keep your child alive has beef extract in it and you do not eat beef.' The mother replied, 'God has given me this child, so God will have to readjust his thinking. Give her beef.' And the child thrived.

Like so many parents, this mother was able to adapt to meet her changed circumstances. We must always remember that the parents of children with disabilities have had to make tremendous adjustments in their thinking and their aspirations. We should not expect them to match the convenient stereotypes of 'parents'. Parents have different hopes, different fears and different needs. Recognising and acknowledging all these needs and differences should enable parents and professionals to work together more positively. Truly equal co-workers treat, care for and educate children effectively and efficiently the more they cooperate.

Norman:

I think of parents as ordinary rather than as specially chosen, although I will allow that going through the fire may refine us a little. We have our own talents, strengths and weaknesses. Sometimes a parent who might otherwise have chosen to work with children with special needs has such a child, and finds a rich fulfilment in his or her care and education. Sometimes, as in my case, a parent's talents seem all to lie in other fields and nothing seems to come naturally, so that the child's rearing becomes a learned and arduous process. Sometimes the force of circumstances, together with personal and family composition, makes it impossible to manage—and the difference between survival and breakdown can be only a hair's width. Yet the strength of love may be equally strong in all cases.

Thus we cannot judge one another. Love does not conquer all, it endures all.

Christine:

I have always felt guilty that my body did this terrible thing to Paul.

Working with young children with disabilities and their families can often involve intensive parental support and education, so that in the vital early years parents are given enough back-up and guidance to re-establish themselves in their own eyes as effective and worthwhile. Some parents need to be helped to see that they can be confident educators of their own children.

Christine:

I longed to meet other parents with children like Paul. I longed for my older son to have the opportunity to play with children who had a brother or sister with similar disabilities, but I was told by everyone that Paul was the only child affected by rubella in my town. I felt so alone. I felt that if Paul had had a disability that was more commonly known we would have found a kindred spirit. We felt cut off from the world, and so we cut ourselves off even further. We only mixed with people who would not stare if Paul held his head back or behaved in an unusual way. At times I used to smile to myself when under-fives threw temper tantrums in shops or in the street. I felt that nobody stared at those children, but that everyone stared at us. I felt I was no longer one of the crowd, but always slightly out of step.

Sometimes I longed to be like a sheep in a field. Anonymous. Ordinary again.

Norman:

The decisions to be made on the way are grievous and may cause divisions. They are another cause of stress, and may even make us feel cut off from other parents who have followed a different road. If you have doubts, you must learn to forgive yourself as you would forgive others in a similar plight. Some would say that between the child's needs and the parents' lie the brothers' and sisters' needs, putting back even further those of the parents, and providing fertile ground for further guilt and worry. How do the other children react to having a brother or sister with disabilities? What effect will it have on them and their future? The question 'What are they missing?' becomes 'What am I depriving them of?' Can they take second place in my time and not feel they are taking second place in my love? Will they suffer through not having a normal life? What is normal? It is what I perceive as the standard, drawn from press, television and books, or the comments of friends. For a child, what is normal is what I am used to, and it is only when someone points out how different I am that it touches me.

Christine:

Paul has shown me a new meaning to life. The natural world now looks so different to me. The goals that Paul took so long to achieve, like sitting up, feeding himself, walking, I treasure more than mothers of children without disabilities.

Norman:

They take some hard knocks from us. We come to expect much from them, and they from us. How often do we struggle through the day until at last our child is at peace? And the second you breathe that sigh of relief, the brother or sister appears with a pain or a problem, silently saying, 'It's my turn now. Now make an effort with me', and you have no effort left. Suddenly your young ally becomes your enemy and you snap back, seeing the hurt in his eyes and overwhelmed by the waves of your own misery and guilt. But children are not built by such moments. They are built by the others, when your arm is around them and the bedtime stories are being told, when the laughter rings out and silliness reigns, when the tears are shared and the interest shown and the tired parent, after the snap, gives that little extra special time that heals all. Such times do happen. But it's hard to grow up in a situation in which you cannot compete, where, no matter how strong the case for attention you

Brothers and sisters have equal needs within the family.

present, there is always another more pressing demand. It is harder still when you are in competition with someone you love.

Christine:

If Paul goes anywhere, we all go together. As a family we cope together. I have seen couples destroyed by the demands of the child. It is not going to happen to us.

Norman:

I do not know whether it is easier to be the older or the younger brother or sister of a child who is disabled. Does the period of undivided attention you received before the arrival of your young competitor give a stable base on which to build, or does it merely make the trauma worse when such a powerful rival appears? Does a younger brother or sister find it easier to accept the situation as it is found? It is pointless to speculate because we have to deal with situations are they are.

Christine:

If the tension gets too bad we talk it out.

Norman:

As they struggle to make sense of the world, they must also absorb the effect of a brother or sister with disabilities in that world. Earlier than most children, they will become aware of the fallibility and vulnerability of parents. Although striving for their parents' attention and time, they will also begin to share with their parents some of the hurt and pain that can lead to resentment of their brother or sister. Yet resentment is forbidden them. You can fight with your brother and let natural resentment escape that way—but not if he has disabilities. All must be sublimated. Confusions may manifest themselves in an over-solicitous concern or in withdrawal. It is a lot to handle . . . They love their brother or sister and feel so helpless—indeed, are often pushed away. They love us and do not like to see us so consumed. Their own needs are but part of the whole. Their outbursts are against us because there is no one else to be against. If you are supposed to love everybody, at whom do you scream about the injustice of it all?

Christine:
We at last found a haven, somewhere where we didn't have to explain about Paul. We met parents like ourselves for the first time. We now knew that we would be all right. We could get all the help we needed and could relax for the first time in five years. Now Paul has a chance. Now it is up to him. We think he will make it. The pale, cold rag doll who was so weak and tiny is capable of growing into a strong, communicating person. He has potential. He has life. He is willing to learn. He wants to be part of this world.

*   *   *

What lessons can be drawn from the stories of Norman, Christine and Sarah? Most parents realise that they will have to make long-term decisions about the way they will bring up their children, how they will be educated and what their lifestyle will be. These choices will vary from parent to parent. Parents of children with multisensory impairments may feel they have no choice offered to them. They are faced with a bewildering number of facts which they are asked to absorb. They are told that their child is going to need the care and treatment provided by professional 'experts'. Sometimes their image of themselves as adults capable of bringing up children immediately shatters. They have to learn to work with people whom they had never imagined encountering. They feel isolated because of their child's disability. They may then search for other people with whom they can identify. The brothers or sisters of the child with disabilities may need even more attention and love because they feel that they have lost importance in their parents' eyes. Many parents ride the storm and families do stay together, despite the enormous pressures that they are asked to cope with. Many partnerships, however, do not survive.

The child with multisensory impairments needs the support of parents, and they in turn need the help of the community.

The way others view their children can become a further burden, making some parents feel strangers in their own locality. When Christine allowed someone else to look after her son Paul during a summer holiday she reported that, even though he was not with her when she strolled along the beach, she felt 'disabled'. People who work with the parents of children with disabilities must never lose sight of their unique situation. Giving them help and support whenever they need it is one means of ensuring that they do not break under the strain. Parents who have confidence in the availability of support will usually succeed in their endeavours.

Throughout the country there are many parent-partnership schemes which offer positive help, advice and guidance to the parents of children with special educational needs. Some of these schemes run parent groups, while others provide information from a central office. Many parents find that discussing their needs with the parents of children with similar needs can be helpful. Others prefer to 'go it alone', and opt into services as and when their child requires them.

When professional people are working with parents it is essential that they see them as individuals with individual needs. Asking them to undertake activities with their children that they don't have time for will usually result in frustration for both parties. The following ideas about working together with parents are the result of parents' suggestions. As an involved professional:

Do
- Talk directly to parents, and face them sitting where they can see you clearly.
- Establish that you and the parents understand each other's language and are on the same wavelength.
- Listen attentively to what parents are saying, and leave space for them to follow up with other questions.
- If you need to take notes, ask permission first, explain what they are for and who will see them. Share them with the parents.
- Take note of cultural differences. Treat all parents as capable and autonomous individuals, and when you need interpreters talk directly to the parents, using the interpreters to translate every word spoken.
- Remember that parents have other commitments and are often unable to spend more than short periods each day engaging in specific activities with their child.

Don't
- Use jargon or abbreviations in conversation—for example, 'LEA' can sound like 'elleeay' and will not have meaning unless parents have heard the abbreviation before.
- Talk more than you listen, thereby missing some of the vital information that the parent is giving you.
- Cut across the important emotional issues that are affecting

the parent and that influence the way she is able to respond
to and interact with her child.

- Let your attention wander to the next thing on your agenda—
always say at the beginning of the discussion if your time is
limited.

The changing needs of the child as he grows and develops, and
of his family, are vividly illustrated here in a letter from Richard's
mother:

> I remember the day Richard was born and the feeling of joy
> at the arrival of our first child. But this was quickly followed
> by a whole host of different emotions—fear, uncertainty,
> hope, and then despair as we were thrown into a world we
> were totally unprepared for. The following months passed
> in a haze of hospital visits, diagnosis and rediagnosis—
> confusion as we tried to find our way through the maze of
> medical jargon and decide how it would actually translate
> into our day-to-day lives with Richard . . .
>
> This month Richard becomes a teenager, and the uncer-
> tainty and worry will always be with us—both from the
> medical angle and in the ongoing battle to ensure appropriate
> provision. However, we also realise what tremendous joy
> he has brought into our lives, showing a courage and deter-
> mination to get on with life that have been a lesson to us
> all. He has also enabled our paths to cross with those of a
> great many dedicated and very caring professionals.
>
> Richard was four years old when we made our first visit
> to the Sense Family Centre at Ealing. I had mixed feelings,
> because I felt that we had done more than our fair share of
> sitting in waiting-rooms in order that some part of Richard
> could be assessed! As the front door opened and we were
> warmly welcomed into the 'big house', as Richard still calls
> it, I instantly felt the unique atmosphere and Richard began
> to visibly relax. It did not smell like a hospital and it had
> rooms like a house. I was overjoyed to be able to talk to
> people who were addressing Richard and really understand-
> ing him as a whole child, instead of just looking at his

hearing loss or his vision or his mobility. I was understood.
I was not the only mother ever to have a child who could
not chew his food at four years old. I was among friends. I
may smile now at my naivity, but the isolation until then
had been very real. The people in the team at the Family
Centre were professional, supportive and genuinely caring.
They taught us how to have confidence in Richard, and
that he would progress and cope. He has certainly proved
everyone right.

As children develop and mature towards adulthood, their parents
have to advance and adjust with them towards a new relationship
with their 'grown up children', taking in their new needs as
adults. For some families this change is the start of another very
difficult journey, for at the end of that journey they will find a
signpost saying: 'This way to letting go'.

When children become teenagers they may begin to acquire
new skills, feelings and perspectives, and parents need to be ready
for this transition so that as those teenagers become adults they
are ready for them to form new relationships and have new
experiences *without their parents*. This should be viewed as an
inevitable part of life, which parents need to think about and plan
for. Sometimes they need help from other parents, in talking
about this major change in their lives, now that the child that
they have cared for has become the person that they always
planned—an independent individual. Sometimes, parents have
invested so much of themselves in working towards this independence that when it arrives their lives become quite empty.

*   *   *

In this chapter a few parents' thoughts have highlighted some of
the experiences and challenges that many parents meet. Norman
has captured the essence of his changing perspective on his adult
son:

My son needs those who know him best to advocate for and
support him. Those people are the ones he lives with now.

As time passes the knowledge increases among them as it decreases with me. That is how it should be.

But it would be a tragedy if I were not a continuing part of his life. The balance shifts because I am becoming 'one of the important people in his life' instead of 'the only one'. And that is good. He needs all of us.

Everything will hinge upon our maturity rather than his, and upon our ability, emotionally as well as cognitively, to join in working for his benefit rather than our own. Then he will be able to play his most adult part along with us and we shall all glory in his successes.

People who work with parents need to have the ability to understand the real meaning behind the stories the parents tell them about their children, and which they tell from the heart.

People need to appreciate that some parents have made a life-long, perhaps traumatic journey with their adult 'child'. This journey may have been all consuming so, whilst working towards the process of letting their grown-up child move on, parents may require as much emotional support as on first diagnosis.

2 The Professional Services

Until 1970, the National Health Service cared for many children with disabilities, and they did not automatically have access to educational services. A major change in provision occurred with the 1970 Education Act, which stated that all children, whatever the severity of their disability, were educable and should be the responsibility of the Department of Education and Science. This was heralded as a breakthrough. At last children with disabilities were acknowledged as deserving the same chance of education and the same treatment as others, as well as all the special facilities previously denied to them. Today children who have disabilities can attend special schools, and many are well provided for in mainstream schools, supported either by special units or by visiting advisory teachers.

There are many services available to families who have children with multisensory impairments. When a child is first diagnosed it is likely that a team of professional people will become involved in her ongoing care and treatment. This team will change as the child's needs change and services available may depend on where the family lives. The child may have medical problems that need to be addressed by a range of specialists both in hospital and in the community. All children's circumstances are different and parents will work with their specialist teams according to their individual child's condition. These are some of the professional services available:

THE PAEDIATRIC COMMUNITY TEAM

This service, attached to a hospital, enables certain children to be nursed at home, either when they are chronically ill or when they need other nursing care. Regular home visits by professionals allow the children to stay at home, rather than having long stays in hospital.

THE CHILD DEVELOPMENT TEAM

If a child's special needs are apparent at birth or soon after, then a member of the Child Development Team is usually designated to explain things to his parents. The Child Development Team can be based in a hospital or in the community—this varies from district to district. Even if the child's needs are not recognised until later in childhood, the team will usually be the first contact for families.

The team liaises with the different types of service that are available in the area, such as those provided by the National Health Service, the social services, education departments and voluntary organisations. Many or all of these services offer children and families practical assistance, but it is often the Child Development Team to which the child regularly returns for developmental checks.

Referrals to the Child Development Team can be made through health professionals such as general practitioners or health visitors. Members of the team can include:

- a consultant community paediatrician
- a specialist health visitor
- a paediatric physiotherapist
- a paediatric occupational therapist
- a paediatric speech and language therapist
- a clinical psychologist
- a community paediatric dietitian
- other regional or area specialists.

The consultant community paediatrician

Consultant community paediatricians are senior children's doctors who specialise in the care of children with developmental or neurological problems. Working mainly in the community, they usually see children at the local clinic.

Consultant community paediatricians receive information

about children's birth details, illnesses and developmental progress, and may make recommendations for further medical treatment or refer them on to various specialists or therapists. The paediatricians will often make sure that the local education authority is aware of individual children's needs at the appropriate time, and may provide relevant medical advice towards a child's Statement of Educational Needs.

The specialist health visitor

Specialist health visitors are trained nurses who have specialised in the care of children with special needs. They may visit families together with the family health visitor. They can take part in the initial assessment of a child's special needs, and may visit to help explain what his or her developmental needs are. Specialist health visitors may discuss with the parents the kinds of help that are available, such as day care, nurseries, respite care and welfare benefits. They may also put families in touch with support groups and voluntary organisations.

The paediatric physiotherapist

Physiotherapists specialise in the treatment of people who have special needs relating to movement. Paediatric physiotherapists assess and treat children and are often based in the local hospital, but they may also work in the community in nurseries, schools and other settings.

Paediatric physiotherapists help children to improve movement and balance. They can use different techniques, or exercises, to minimise stiffness in the joints and to strengthen muscles, and for children who have breathing problems they can advise parents about breathing and coughing techniques. Physiotherapists also help families to understand why their children have difficulties with movement, and explain how movement patterns develop. They often advise and train staff in nurseries or schools so that everyone understands how best to promote individual children's motor development.

Together with other specialists, they may recommend specialist seating and other equipment in order to help to maintain children's posture.

The paediatric occupational therapist

Some occupational therapists specialise in the assessment and treatment of children with special needs. Paediatric occupational therapists, who have taken extra training, may, like paediatric physiotherapists, visit children at home or at nursery or school. Some paediatric occupational therapists help children to gain more independence through coordinated developmental and physical activities, as well as helping them to acquire daily-living skills.

Together with other specialists, they may recommend specialist seating and other equipment in order to further children's independence skills.

The paediatric speech and language therapist

Paediatric speech and language therapists specialise in the assessment and treatment of children's early communication, speech and language. Where appropriate, they will discuss alternative means of communication such as the use of signs, pictures, symbols and technology aids for the child (see p. 77). Many also offer advice and help in exploring ways to assist children who have physical difficulties in developing eating and drinking skills.

The clinical psychologist

Clinical psychologists specialise in the assessment and treatment of children and families with emotional or behavioural difficulties. They aim to help parents come to a better understanding of their children's behaviour, and to find ways of helping to change or manage this behaviour. Sometimes they work individually with children to assess and/or treat their difficulties, but more often they work with children and parents and other key members of the family together. In addition, they may offer group-based therapy and support, sometimes for groups of children with similar difficulties and sometimes for groups of parents whose children have similar needs.

The community paediatric dietitian

Community paediatric dietitians specialise in working with children who have particular dietary needs. They offer advice on many aspects of diet, from allergy to weight gain. Community paediatric dietitians may work with people whose children are tube-fed, or with children who have problems with bowel movements.

A community paediatric dietitian's workload can include training both health professionals and groups of parents and/or carers, working closely with other members of the Child Development Team. Referrals to their service are made through general practitioners or through the hospital doctor.

OTHER REGIONAL OR AREA SPECIALISTS

Health visitors

Health visitors are part of the NHS community health service. They are qualified nurses, with special training and experience in child health, health promotion and health education. Health visitors visit new babies and their families soon after birth. They offer advice and support to parents and may continue to see children at home, at the health centre or at the local doctor's surgery, particularly if the child has developmental or special needs.

Sometimes health visitors assess children's need for nappies and, depending on local authority practice, these may be free for children over the age of two who are not toilet-trained. Eligibility to benefit from this service varies from one part of the country to another, and may depend on age, special need and other circumstances.

The audiologist

Referrals to a children's audiologist are made through health professionals such as GPs and health visitors. A child will be referred to an audiologist if there is any concern about her hearing. If the child is unable to cooperate in tests by responding via action or gesture when she hears a sound, the audiologist will use other methods of testing her hearing. He checks that the ears are healthy by looking into them. He can perform a test that will confirm whether or not the ear-drum is free to move, checking for fluid catarrh behind it. There are also other tests that they can perform, to establish the type of help and aids that the child may need if she has a sensorineural hearing loss.

The ophthalmologist

Ophthalmologists are specialist doctors who treat eye disorders, and usually work in the ophthalmology departments of hospitals. They diagnose and treat eye defects and disease, through surgery and other types of medical care where possible. They may prescribe glasses if they are needed, but it is usually the optician who fits and supplies these. Referrals to an ophthalmology department are made through the GP or the consultant community paediatrician.

Orthoptists, qualified to identify and treat certain eye conditions such as squints and double vision, may work in the same department as the ophthalmologist.

The genetic counsellor

The GP, the Child Development Team paediatrician or any other doctor who regularly sees the child may refer the family for genetic counselling. Sometimes parents are referred for counselling in order to establish whether they are likely to have another child with the same syndrome. Genetic counsellors may spend time explaining in great detail particular syndromes to parents, to give them as much information as possible about their child's potential and future needs.

LOCAL AUTHORITY SERVICES

Depending on local authority practice, buggies and wheelchairs may be provided by Health or Social Services. This service is for children, often from the age of two, who have serious walking difficulties. Special seating needs in buggies and wheelchairs are assessed, and a double buggy may be provided if a parent has another child who is not walking.

SPECIALIST SERVICES

Specialist services, available throughout the country, often include a team of advisory teachers for children who are hearing-, visually or multisensorily impaired. Advisory teachers working with children who have sensory impairments have trained first as teachers and have then undertaken further training to equip them to advise and work with children who have sensory impairment. As well as advisory teachers, the specialist teams often include therapists, rehabilitation workers and other professionals who work together to provide a multidisciplinary approach towards meeting the requirements of children with special needs.

Some teams include 'Portage', a regular home teaching service that supports families by providing advice and activities for children and parents. These activities are jointly agreed upon by the teacher and the parent and, as well as providing useful guidance on the development of the child, the service can act as a regular monitoring agency, referring the child on to specialist educational advisers as and if the need arises.

The educational psychologist
If a child is thought to have extra or special educational needs, he or she may be referred to the educational psychologist. It is the job of educational psychologists to identify, assess, monitor and advise about children's special needs, working closely with parents, schools and other professionals. Educational psychologists are involved in the 'statementing' procedure of children (see page 50) with special educational needs. They always have a teaching qualification and a degree in psychology, together with postgraduate training in educational psychology. Depending on the demands of the service the main focus of their work is usually assessment and consultation.

VOLUNTARY ORGANISATIONS

Some voluntary organisations, such as the Royal National Institute for the Blind, the National Deaf Children's Society and Sense, provide specialist national services.

THE FAMILY EDUCATION AND ADVISORY SERVICE

The Family Education and Advisory Service (FEAS), set up by Sense, offers hands-on help and advice through its four regional teams. In 1983, realising the importance of early intervention,

Sense created the first of these advisory teams, aimed at families whose children were under the age of two. The service gradually expanded to include children up to seven. Although it has recently begun to change its focus, since its inception its basic aim has remained the same: to make the earliest possible contact with the child and her family, and to offer parents teaching and therapeutic advice, guidance and support, during the child's vital early learning years. The FEAS seeks to work in close cooperation with, and to the mutual advantage of, all those who have a responsibility towards the child. In particular, the service strives to ensure that the parents are knowledgeable about their child's condition, and that they feel secure in their understanding and in their abilities, and confident of the best ways to help her achieve her full potential. The services provided by the regional FEAS teams include:

- coordinated individual planning to develop key skills
- observational and development work to meet specific needs
- consultancy to nursery and school staff
- advice in relation to Statements of Educational Needs
- developmental assessments
- INSET (in-service training) and specifically tailored courses for nurseries and schools
- support groups, workshops and activities for families.

Specialist teachers with experience in working with children who are deafblind, or multisensorily impaired, deliver these services. The children who access them have a range of needs:

- moderate to profound auditory and visual impairments
- moderate to profound auditory and visual impairments, plus other significant disabilities
- problems with processing their vision and hearing
- progressive sensory impairments
- visual impairment and possible loss of auditory processing mechanisms which can be associated with other severe disabilities such as severe communication delay.

As well as sensory impairments, the children who use the Sense Family Education and Advisory Services may also have a variety of other difficulties. Some go to schools for children who are hearing- or visually impaired; others attend units for children within other schools or schools for children with severe learning difficulties; some are integrated into mainstream schools. The children's real capabilities may often be extremely difficult to assess. But since the major educational legislation brought about by the landmark Education Act of 1970, as well as changes in attitudes towards children with disabilities, these children have more chance of success and of reaching their full potential through successful school placements.

The educational placement of a child who has multisensory impairment will call for very careful consideration. It will involve assessments by many professionals, as well as taking account of the advice and opinions of the child's parents. When special educational need has been identified, long-term observational assessment procedures will be employed, so as to give as full a picture as possible of the child's achievements. The assessment will then be presented to the local education authority. This procedure follows recommendations outlined in the 1981 Education Act, together with the revised guidelines of the 1993 Act. The next stage is for the child to receive a Statement of Educational Needs. This will be reviewed annually, to ensure that at each stage of her school career her individual needs and appropriate provision are carefully discussed and monitored. In the interests of giving the child the education that best suits her, she may occasionally move from one school to another as she grows and develops.

The FEAS operates by providing a variety of services from its Regional Family Centre bases. It helps parents and co-workers to monitor the child's progress and observe her development, with a view to deciding on appropriate new activities for her. Often the ideal place to meet the child's other teachers and therapists will be her home or local placement. Sometimes parents prefer to visit a Sense Family Centre which, with its informal learning environment, is often found to match the home atmosphere.

Children who are deafblind do not automatically benefit from teaching or therapy designed for children with only one sensory impairment. Children who are deafblind may have communication and mobility needs that children with one sensory impairment do not have.

Formal tests are usually inappropriate to the needs of children with dual sensory impairment. Instead, detailed and systematic developmental observations that record the child's skills are used to determine her needs. Over a period of several years, the FEAS worker assigned to the particular child, along with the parents and the professionals already involved, records her physical and mobility skills, fine motor and manipulative abilities, visual and hearing skills, methods of communication, social and self-help skills, and her ability to play, imitate, interact, follow instructions and manipulate her environment. Once teachers, therapists and parents have discussed these developmental observations, appropriate activities to further the child's skills will be recommended and agreed as she develops and her needs alter.

The individual activities suggested will reflect the child's own particular needs and extend her emerging skills. To this end, all children who receive the FEAS service are the subject of a carefully written report that portrays them in detail as unique individuals. Each is offered a programme of suggested activities that fits *her* specifically—it is never a question of 'the child fitting the programme'. Monitoring the child's progress over time is seen as an important part of the work that parent and FEAS advisory teacher undertake together.

Parents see the FEAS service as particularly important. They often say that their involvement with the FEAS enables them to 'put their child together again'—in other words, they appreciate the fact that he or she is seen as a whole person, as opposed to separate parts needing separate intervention techniques. Holistic child-centred developmental assessments, based on careful observation together with the parents, help to provide a coordinated plan which takes account of the child's vision, hearing and other skills in combination with each other. Feeding, toileting, dressing, washing and other social skills are also addressed, with the help of therapists who work alongside advisory teachers at some of the regional centres.

Early intervention helps to set parents on the right track; the hope is that it will continue to inspire in them useful and practical ideas that will enable their children to attain appropriate and realistic goals. Early intervention also aims to ensure that, as far as possible, the children are offered appropriate age- and stage-related activities in cooperation with their other involved professional workers.

A Family Centre is a place where everyone learns together. It is a place for teaching sessions, and for the interchange of information between parents and professionals; it is a resource centre, a place for the children to try out new toys and equipment, and for parents to get advice on welfare and statutory rights. It is a place characterised, above all, by the giving of mutual support.

Parents appreciate the family atmosphere—bringing brothers and sisters along is important—as well as the fact that time is allowed for everyone to discuss and plan their requirements. Ensuring that everyone is given time to absorb information is an essential part of the visit. FEAS advisory teachers send follow-up reports to parents and to the other professionals involved, and visit the child's home, nursery, school or other placement at the invitation of professionals and parents to give further advice on his or her continuing needs.

Ideally the work done and the advice given by the FEAS are based not only on the individual needs of the child, but also on the requirements of the family as a unit. Whether the child is seen at home by the visiting advisory teacher or at a Family Centre will depend very largely on the parents' and child's needs as well as the staff time available.

FEAS advisory teachers can organise workshops for both parents and professionals. Sometimes these are formal, structured courses, and sometimes they include a social event or a meeting for parents only. Crèche facilities are often provided, so that both parents can attend courses together if they wish. The workshops are designed to give people the opportunity of learning alongside others about the general needs of their children. At all of them there is an emphasis on parents' own particular needs, and making time for group discussion between parents with similar problems helps them to gain from shared

Children enjoy the family atmosphere.

experiences. Many workshops aim to give theoretical as well
as practical assistance. As well as helping parents to establish
in their children mobility and self-help skills such as feeding,
dressing, toileting and washing, the workshops also help them
to evolve techniques for making the best use of their children's
residual vision and hearing, so helping them to acquire essential
communication skills.

However useful they may be, no workshop could ever replace
the individual developmental assessment work that is the vital
core of the Family Education and Advisory Service. Its philos-
ophy reflects the fact that Sense, as an organisation committed
to families, works in complete partnership with parents.

Much of the work done by the FEAS focuses on helping parents
to establish individual communication techniques with their children. Parents understand, probably better than anyone else, that
the primary need for any child is to make relationships and to
communicate with others. Until the child learns to respond
actively to people, until she experiences the pleasures of com-

municating, parents often feel as frustrated as she does, for they are unable to make sense of the world together. The child's first teachers are her parents, and parents need to feel that their child is interacting with them. The more she is able to do so, the greater the incentive, of both child and parents, to increase the communication between them.

The FEAS approach is based on the premise that there are ways of providing the child with experiences that will help her reach, in her own way, those milestones necessary to further her achievement of personal skills. The aim is to help everyone involved to become more effective in their interactions and provisions for the child; to stimulate and motivate the child to use all her abilities in all areas of development, and to encourage her to function at her optimum level. Children may acquire new skills rapidly, or slowly, according to their abilities and the environmental influences that impinge upon them. Parents may need help in understanding how to modify the environment or the activities in which they wish their child to participate. They will probably always need some help in observing and interpreting her progress. In addition, it may be useful for them to observe a teacher or therapist working with their child before they implement the advice given, or they may want the teacher or therapist to see them working at home on certain activities. Demonstrations of the methods and techniques to be employed may occasionally be necessary, particularly when embarking on the teaching of new skills.

SOME AIDS TO ASSESSMENT

Having been helped to structure their child's learning and play environment, and having had their confidence in their role as teachers of their child boosted, parents may still need to be helped to see exactly how much progress is being achieved. This is where a little bit of modern technology comes in: occasionally, by recording a child's progress on *videotape* and then playing it back, parents are able to see in a way not hitherto obvious to them that she is making vital progress in many areas; or, as the case may be, that certain areas need more attention. They can see immediately how she is using her residual vision and hearing, as well as how her communication, mobility and other skills are progressing.

It may be necessary to help parents take a careful look at their child's development, both in detail and as a whole. It is rare for the FEAS to use a formal assessment tool, but guidelines such as those devised by the Callier Center for Communication Disorders at the University of Texas at Dallas may occasionally provide just what is needed. The purpose of the *Callier Azusa Scale* is to supply the information necessary to 'synthesise developmentally appropriate activities for a child and to evaluate [his] developmental progress'. It is composed of eighteen subscales covering five areas:

Motor development
Postural control
Locomotion
Fine motor skills
Visual-motor skills

Daily living skills
Dressing and undressing
Personal hygiene
Feeding skills
Toileting

Social development
Interactions with adults
Interactions with peers
Interactions with the
environment

Perceptual development
Visual
Auditory
Tactile

Cognition, communication and language
Cognitive development
Receptive communication
Expressive communication
Development of speech

Since the skills that can be assessed using the Callier Azusa Scale encompass the sensory, motor, language and social abilities of the child who is deafblind, it can be useful to those wishing to evaluate such a child's global needs. Guidelines such as these can help to remind observers of the whole range of activities that may need to be considered when using less formal, observational,

Feeding. Hand over hand, the adult guides the child to hold the drink and bring it to his mouth.

Washing. Hand over hand, he is helped to learn to reach for the towel to dry himself.

Dressing. Hand over hand, he is shown how to pull up his socks.

Toileting. Hand over hand, he is shown how to pull down his trousers.

Signing. Hand over hand, he is shown how to say, 'Want play'.

Exploration of objects. Hand over hand, the child is shown how to manipulate her toy.

Exploration of the environment. Hand over hand, the child is shown how to 'trail' his route from one place to another.

Visual training. Hand over hand, he is shown how to reach for the torch that attracts him.

Auditory training. Hand over hand, he is shown how to beat the drum that he hears.

Play activities. Hand over hand, he is shown how to start the musical toy.

Swimming. Hand over hand, the child is shown the water before she steps in.

assessment methods. Note that no observational scale attempts to measure cognitive ability. The usefulness of assessment procedures lies in their ability to help parents and professionals to gain a clearer view of a child's skills, so as to formulate effective development programmes. The prime aim of any assessment is always to further the child's developmental skills.

The assessment of any child takes time and skill. When a child has combined sensory impairments, it may present problems for the assessor. For example, when a child is suspected of having a hearing loss, the assessor may have difficulty in gaining the maximum information from the available tests. It is at this stage that she may choose to adapt one or more of the tests that she intends to use. An example of this is given by Jo Franklin, an advisory teacher for the hearing impaired who works at the FEAS Family Centre in Ealing, London. Here she describes the *distraction test*, and how it can be adapted for use with children who are multisensorily impaired:

> The distraction test was developed as a hearing test to be used with all babies at approximately seven months (plus). Developed in 1944 by Ewing and Ewing, it was modified during the 1980s (as described by Barry McCormick in *Screening for Hearing Impairment in Young Children*, Croom Helm, 1988) with the aim of making it simple enough to be widely used. It was never intended to be more than a 'detection test'—that is, to identify the presence of a hearing loss. Remember that fully assessing hearing is a very complex and difficult task, and far more so with children who have additional difficulties. It may take many years to reach a clear understanding of these children's hearing.
>
> For screening purposes, the distraction test should usually be done by trained health visitors. For children with multisensory impairment, however, it is often done in an adapted form by clinical audiologists, and is sometimes referred to as 'behavioural testing of hearing', or 'behavioural observational audiometry'.
>
> The test should be done in a quiet room, preferably soundtreated (with a sound-level meter showing that the room is

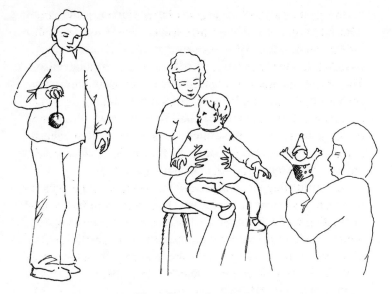

The distraction test.

quieter than 40 decibels). The child should sit on the knee of an adult well known to him, facing the person who is going to 'distract' him. It is this person's job to capture his attention to just the right degree, so that when the sound is presented he is ready to listen—this process is called 'inducing fade'. It is important that, to present the various sounds, the tester (the sound-maker) stands approximately one metre behind the child, on a level with his ear, and that care is taken not to allow the tester into the child's residual peripheral vision.

Practice varies considerably, but the sounds presented can include tapping a cup with a spoon—it's very hard to be specific about exactly how loud that sound is—speech sounds such as 's' or 'mmmmm', frequency-specific rattles, and sounds produced by a free-field audiometer that 'warbles' in middle, high and low frequencies. This tests both ears—if there is a profound loss in one ear only the child will eventually hear it in the other ear and may respond towards that side. The standard response expected is a turn towards the sound source.

It is most important when assessing the hearing of children with additional difficulties to have knowledge of the individual child. Most specialists see very few children who have hearing loss combined with other sensory impairments. The important point is that professionals trying to assess such a child's hearing listen to those who will know whether his reaction is likely to be repeated, and is a reliable indicator of his having heard the sound. It is a very good idea to make a video recording for careful analysis of what might otherwise be very easily missed reactions.

Perhaps the biggest modification to be made to the distraction test concerns the role of the distracter. A purely visual distraction technique is not suitable for most children with multisensory impairment, so some gentle tactile stimulation may seem the best alternative. Unfortunately from this point of view, most of the children I work with are too easy to over-distract with even minimal input to one of their senses. A little touch, for instance, far from ensuring that they will be ready to listen out for a sound presented behind them, engrosses their attention to the extent that they ignore the perhaps less interesting information reaching their ears. The most difficult thing to assess in children with multisensory impairment is when they are ready for the tester to present a sound. Again, it is vital to rely on the parents' or carers' observations. Many of the children I see show a sudden change of body tone and facial expression, when they are ready, that can best be described as a 'listening look'. When they are in this ready state, sounds can be presented and findings recorded, until the moment when they may need to be distracted out of the ready state so that the changes in their reaction can be observed once more and the process started again.

The most audiologically helpful sounds to use in these tests are 'warble tones' of specific frequencies (measured in hertz (Hz)) and known intensity (measured in decibels (dB)). These may not be the most meaningful sounds for any small child, let alone one with multisensory impairment, but for some it is their very strangeness that can, indeed, make them worth reacting to. Other children produce far more obvious reactions to more familiar and relevant sounds such as voices or specific toys. Using a sound-level meter to test the loudness of such sounds can provide invaluable information, even if their frequencies are less easy to measure. In all cases the emphasis should be on being adaptable, and, first and foremost, on using what best suits the child's needs.

The information that we can gain from modified distraction-testing, and from other clinical tests such as brainstem-evoked response audiometry, is bound to be helpful, but equally valuable is the information that can be amassed from observing the child closely. Observation of the way she reacts to sound gives us clues to the way we should work with her, play with her and so on, so that detailed answers to the following questions will provide information as valuable as any clinical tests:

- What types of sounds interest your child?
- How does she react to them?
- How loud does the sound have to be, and how near or far away?
- Does your child react to particular voices?
- Does she attempt to find the sources of sounds?
- Does she have a preferred side?
- Does she like particular sound-makers or types of music?
- Does she make noises herself?

Hopefully, by putting together observations from parents and professionals and the information gained from audiological tests, we can begin the slow process of understanding what the individual child can hear. Then comes the process of amplification selection, such as hearing aids, after which we are ready to start auditory training.

THE IMPORTANCE OF ACCURATE ASSESSMENT

When testing and assessing, any or every part of each test may need to be adapted so that for each individual child the long-term developmental assessment gives as true and accurate a picture as possible of her potential in each skill area.

A good assessment team will be concerned that action be taken as soon as possible to begin to plan for the individual child's activities. As we have seen, assessment teams may consist of parents, paediatricians, therapists, teachers, educational psychologists and health visitors. Sometimes social workers and child psychiatrists are involved too. Assessment teams use as a basis for their findings the developmental sequences that all children are expected to attain. In order to give as accurate an assessment as possible, teams will often consult with specialist sensory advisory services so that a child's global needs in relation to her sensory impairment are taken into account throughout.

Some assessments of children with special educational needs produce the kind of comprehensive information about the child that will direct all involved with her towards positive action and appropriate individual goal-planning. Parents have the right of access to information about their child's assessment for schooling and must, by law, be involved if their child is being assessed under the Education Act (1996). Under part three of that Act, there is a Code of Practice that provides practical guidance to local education authorities and schools on their responsibilities towards all children with special educational needs.

Depending on the child's circumstances, parents may ask the local education authority to make a statutory assessment of their child, or the GP, health visitor or other professional involved with her may recommend it. The LEA then gives the parents the name of one of its staff—referred to as the Named Officer—who will be able to inform them about statutory assessment procedures. If a decision is made to proceed with a statutory assessment, the LEA informs the parents and gathers information about the child's special needs from them and from the professionals involved with her. As always, parents have an important part to play in the assessment procedure—no one knows their child better than they do, and the information they can provide is invaluable. The Named Officer will often be able to supply the addresses of support groups and voluntary organisations, in addition to answering questions about the assessment procedure.

THE STATEMENT OF SPECIAL EDUCATIONAL NEEDS

When the LEA has collected all the advice about the child's skills and educational needs, it will decide whether to make a Statement of Special Educational Needs ('the Statement'). This is a document that sets out the child's needs and the special educational help that the LEA recommends. The LEA then sends the parents a 'proposed Statement', asking them to let it have their views and comments within a specified time. Parents have many rights within the law, and can express a preference for which school they would like their child to attend, but the LEA must agree with their preference in order for her to be placed there. It will base its decision as to whether a school is suitable on the child's age and her educational needs, and on the efficient use of its resources.

The process of issuing a Statement of Special Educational Needs should take twenty-six weeks, and this is how that period breaks down:

Considering whether a statutory assessment is necessary	6 weeks
Gathering information towards making the assessment	10 weeks
Drafting the 'proposed Statement'	2 weeks
Finalising the Statement	8 weeks

Both parents and professionals are always advised to make every effort to keep within the timescale allowed when responding to requests within the statementing process.

Many parents begin to visit a variety of local schools that may be suitable for their child, to see exactly what they can offer. It is at this stage that some parents obtain information and advice from local and national voluntary organisations, in order to make as broad and informed a choice as possible. Some, while looking at local schools, also want to visit schools out of their immediate area, in which case they will be able to get the addresses of specialist schools from the voluntary organisations dealing specifically with their child's condition.

Children with special educational needs can be integrated into mainstream schools, often with the help of advisory teachers and support workers, or the use of special equipment. Other children attend special schools—schools for children with specific educational needs. These provide for children who have, for example, hearing impairment, visual impairment, learning difficulties and physical disabilities. When the needs of a child cannot be met within the LEA—usually, when the child has very specific special educational needs—it will sometimes be recommended that she attend a school outside the local area.

Code of Practice 3:75–3:77 of the 1993 Education Act gives guidelines to be used when assessing the educational needs of children with sensory impairments. It states:

A significant proportion of children has some degree of hearing difficulty. Hearing losses may be temporary or permanent. Temporary hearing losses are usually caused by the condition known as 'glue ear', and occur most often in the early years. Such hearing losses fluctuate and may be mild or moderate in degree. They can seriously compound other learning difficulties. Schools should be alert to such evidence as persistently discharging ears.

Permanent hearing losses are usually sensorineural and vary from mild through moderate, to severe or profound. Children with severe or profound hearing loss may have severe or complex communication difficulties.

Early recognition, diagnosis and treatment, and specialist support for pupils with hearing difficulties, are essential to ensure the child's language acquisition, academic achievement and emotional development do not suffer unnecessarily.

Code of Practice 3:81 states:

Visual difficulties take many forms with widely differing implications for a child's education. They range from relatively minor and remedial conditions to total blindness.

Some children are born blind; others lose their sight, partially
or completely, as a result of accidents or illness. In some
cases, visual impairment is one aspect of multiple disability.
Whatever the cause of the child's visual impairment, the
major issue in identifying and assessing the child's special
educational needs will relate to the degree and nature of
functional vision, partial sight or blindness, and the child's
ability to adapt socially and psychologically as well as to
progress in an educational context.

In addition to guidelines addressing hearing and visual difficulties, there are others within the Code of Practice that relate to
other conditions which may require special educational provision—conditions such as learning difficulty, and emotional,
behavioural and physical disabilities. The Code of Practice gives
guidance to LEAs and has accessible information for parents
about all the procedures (guidelines available from all LEAs).

All schools are required by law to have a special needs' policy
statement. This policy should contain information about a
school's special educational provision, about its procedures for
the identification and assessment of any pupils who may have
special educational needs, and about its staffing policies and any
partnerships it has with bodies outside the school. All children
with special educational needs have a right to a broad and well
balanced education, with appropriate access to the National Curriculum. How a school plans to provide for children's special
educational needs, in terms of funding and personnel, has to be
included within its policy.

The law also provides for a Special Educational Needs Tribunal
that may be resorted to when parents and LEAs cannot agree on
the type of provision for an individual child. This tribunal is an
independent body that has absolutely no connection with the LEA
and that can make impartial decisions about a child's educational
needs. LEAs are obliged to give parents information about Special
Educational Needs Tribunals where agreement cannot be reached
using more informal means.

The provision of some services may depend to a large extent
on the facilities of the particular area, and within each area the

strength of the voices of concerned parents and involved professionals can go a long way towards achieving specialist provision. Professionals can help parents by supporting them in their efforts as a group. Ideally services should provide for the individual and changing needs of each child, and should recognise that children may have different needs as they grow and develop.

Parents' groups may need help in presenting a unified and comprehensive approach to the Local Authority services. The priorities of the parents are usually the priorities of the professionals, and there are many parents' groups and voluntary organisations working together, reviewing current needs and evolving strategies in partnership with LEAs, all giving each other advice, information and support.

Some children supported in mainstream schools may have their individual educational plans and programmes coordinated by a Special Educational Needs Coordinator (a SENCO). Some SENCOs assess children's ongoing needs, draw up individual education plans and teach individual students, while others act in an advisory and coordinating role, depending on the school's organisation and the statemented needs of the students. All schools organise annual reviews for children who have a Statement of Special Educational Needs. This is a requirement under the 1993 Education Act, providing for the Statement to be formally reviewed and, after consultation, it may offer an opportunity to revise the original Statement.

At fourteen-plus a transitional plan for the student will be drawn up, again following guidelines incorporated within the Education Act. At this stage the student may be included in the discussions about her further education options. Other agencies, such as careers officers and social workers, become involved in the transitional plan. A reassessment will be requested, if it is thought that the student's educational needs may have changed over time. The next time she and her family may require in-depth assistance in the planning process will be a year or two before leaving school, when they will be looking more closely at options for further education, as well as at work prospects and at opportunities for long-term future provision.

3 Children Who Are Deafblind

Some functional interpretations of deafblindness are:

- having moderate to profound auditory and visual impairments
- having moderate to profound auditory and visual impairments, and other significant disabilities
- having central-processing problems of vision and hearing
- having combined progressive sensory impairments
- having moderate to profound visual impairment together with loss of auditory processing mechanisms, often associated with severe physical disability and severe communication delay.

Many people who are deafblind have severe communication difficulties that are over and above those associated with people who have a single sensory impairment. Regardless of the 'categories' of deafblindness, many individuals have some useful residual hearing and useful residual vision. The spectrum of people thought to be functionally deafblind covers a wide range of abilities (and disabilities) and a wide range of medical diagnoses.

The meaning and impact of deafblindness, and the experience of being deafblind, are unique for each person. One significant factor is that some people are born deaf and blind, whereas others acquire deafblindness in later life. It is often the degree of difficulty that individuals experience in communicating, and specifically in using language, that defines the particular services they need: those with very significant communication needs often have a high degree of dependence, while those who are able to communicate through sign language, speech or Braille are often able to function independently, albeit with some support.

There is a variety of causes for the sensory impairments of children considered to be functionally deafblind, or multisensorily impaired. Often the causes are not specified, or they may be the result of rare syndromes. In Britain until about the late 1980s, a major cause of multisensory impairment was congenital rubella syndrome. Since the introduction of the MMR (measles, mumps, rubella) vaccination programme, the incidence of children affected by congenital rubella syndrome has decreased. Unless there is a very high take-up of the MMR vaccine, however, rubella outbreaks will continue to occur.

RUBELLA

As is well known, when contracted by the mother in early pregnancy, rubella can be the cause of sensorineural deafness, visual impairment, associated heart conditions and a variety of other physical disorders. The eye can be affected in many ways, including microphthalmos (very small eyes), permanent scarring of the cornea, cataracts, congenital glaucoma and eye movements such as nystagmus. Cardiovascular malformations can occur, including patent ductus arteriosus (a circulatory malfunction), transposition of the great arteries and other ventricular defects. Children affected by rubella are often premature and may in their early years have feeding difficulties. There may be associated physical disabilities and bone disorders, and some observers have noticed late onset of epilepsy and diabetes in a number of adults affected by congenital rubella syndrome.

As a result of the great numbers of children born in the rubella pandemics of the 1960s and 1970s, there have been many comparative studies of people affected. This has been fortunate for the children born later because there is now a heightened awareness of the likelihood of their having combined sensory impairments and disabilities, and so diagnosis and treatment can happen early in their lives. Children affected by rubella who are known to have hearing and sight problems are monitored, and their performance is checked very carefully. Parents are informed of the need for regular eye and ear check-ups, so that any change in their children's condition is noticed immediately.

While the physical effects of congenital rubella syndrome are well documented and indisputable, some of the behaviours that have been traditionally associated with it have needed to be recon-sidered. In the 60s and 70s, children with a combination of dis-abling conditions such as a profound hearing loss and severe visual impairment used to have to wait, sometimes for many years, for hearing aids and glasses to be issued. The effect of this delay could have been that their brains did not 'switch on' to some of the auditory and visual stimuli that they might other-wise have been capable of interpreting. Nowadays, much earlier medical intervention is the norm. Many young children have none of the behavioural characteristics apparent in older people affected by rubella. The conclusion can be drawn that much of this improvement is due to early medical intervention, as well as to the work of teachers for children with hearing impairment and visual impairment at the children's early critical learning stages.

In most of the earlier literature describing children affected by rubella mention is made of behaviour such as light-gazing, eye-poking, head-banging, random hand movements, finger-flicking, tripoding (walking with hands and feet on the floor and never gaining an upright position) and severe feeding difficulties. The fact that rubella-affected children are now identified and treated early, are fitted with hearing aids when they are very young and can wear contact lenses while they are still babies, must have contributed in large measure to the progress made by many children. As well as the early-intervention programmes that teachers for the hearing- and visually impaired can now offer parents and children, the advice available from specialist child development clinics and centres also contributes to the positive behaviour of many young children.

The progress of the children described in the following pages, all of whom have congenital rubella syndrome, illustrates the importance of early intervention.

LEE

Lee, who was five months old at the time of referral, had had cataracts removed from both eyes and contact lenses fitted. He had no complications with the lenses, which his mother removed every night. He was able to look at faces and sometimes make eye contact. A hearing loss was diagnosed and he was issued with post-aural (behind-the-ear) hearing aids at the age of eleven months. Lee has no feeding problems. He explores familiar and unfamiliar environments visually as well as by touch.

He walked freely at fifteen months, although as a young baby he was hypotonic (very floppy). Under the guidance of a physiotherapist, his parents encouraged him to move and change his position as often as possible. It was recommended that he should be put on his front for some activities, so that he could learn to turn his head to look at objects from that position. Early visual activities were started with him, and at the age of eighteen months he could pick up objects as small as jelly sweets. Lee's walking was very sure, and he was able to step over or around objects and up steps without hesitating. He could move from sitting to crawling and kneeling without support; and he preferred to walk—and could do so, with one hand held—up and down stairs. He was able to use a chair in order to reach inaccessible objects.

The *total communication approach* (see page 145) was used with Lee, and he had a few natural gestures of his own as well as ten signs that it was clear he understood. He made a variety of noises and expressed his desire to take part in activities with his parents. After being fitted with hearing aids he 'stilled' to the sound of a voice, and his babbling increased. All his self-help and social skills developed so that at age-appropriate times he could spoon-feed, finger-feed and hold a cup. He enjoyed being bathed, and held out his hands for the towel. He tried to put jumpers on over his head and his arms in the sleeves. He could take off his shoes.

Activities that Lee's parents can do with him

- Use Lee's interest in food to increase his use of visual motor skills, by putting small jelly sweets on a plain white plate slightly out of his reach. Leaning forward to grasp the sweet may help Lee to look at what he is picking up.
- Use Lee's ability to stand to increase his interest in his environment, by putting his chair near the sofa so that from the chair he can stretch towards the adult sitting on the sofa.
- Use Lee's natural gestures and shape these slightly to increase

his use of gestures so that he knows they have meaning. He can move his hands up and down, and if he is shown that when people leave the room *they wave to him* within his range of vision, it is likely that he might wave to them.

RUTH

At the time of referral Ruth was two years old and was known to be severely partially sighted, to have a severe sensorineural hearing loss and feeding problems. She showed some of the behavioural characteristics associated with children affected by congenital rubella syndrome:

—light-gazing and overattention to bright, shiny objects
—lack of interest in eye contact with adults
—feeding difficulties
—frequent hand movements (moving her hands in front of nearby light sources).

Ruth had regular visits from a teacher of the hearing impaired. Her major need was to be helped to use her vision to look at people and objects other than light-reflecting ones, for she appeared to be more interested in things than in people.

As far as her *gross motor skills* were concerned, she appeared to walk with a slightly unsteady gait as well as climbing stairs on her hands and knees (unsupported). In the area of *fine motor skills*, she demonstrated that she could use a thumb–index finger pincer grip to pick up small objects, looking closely at them as she did so.

Ruth can now open the right doors of her shape-sorter—they are each hinged on a different side—using her index finger, and she will attempt to use her index fingernail to prise open the lid of a container. She spontaneously reaches with two hands to pick up a large object, and with one hand to pick up small ones. She can feed herself chopped-up foods, which she scoops up with a spoon or stabs with a fork. She holds a biscuit while she eats it. She can drink from a cup.

Ruth has always mouthed objects, and although this has diminished over the past few months, mouthing continues to provide her with a lot of tactual information. On some occasions, if she is having difficulty opening a container with her hands, she will attempt to do it with her mouth.

Observing Ruth's *visual motor skills* shows that she has an awareness of where certain favourite or needed objects are to be found. She looks for her toy-bag and searches in it to find toys. She will go to the dining-room door to find the key in it, and to the kitchen to look for her cup when she is thirsty. She will go upstairs to rummage in her brother's and sister's toy-boxes. She will search to find an object if she has seen it hidden, and unwrap a loose paper parcel to find an object inside. She will look at and touch a doll's face with interest. Given a container with a lid on, she will often try to ascertain whether or not there is anything inside it before trying to open it—to do this, she looks through clear plastic containers, and shakes opaque ones.

Ruth subjects most objects to close visual scrutiny, usually holding them close to her face and looking at them in different lights and from different angles. She enjoys looking closely at pictures or print, and will tap at pictures as if trying to remove objects from them. She enjoys watching and touching her own shadow, and watches as her hands move and create moving shadows on the wall or floor. She scans the area around her visually, and has a good memory for where nearby objects are; she can reach for an object successfully while looking in another direction. She has often spotted something the size of a pen or a teaspoon, lying on the floor up to twelve or fifteen feet away, and gone to get it. She tracks moving objects in both the horizontal and vertical planes.

Ruth has made some attempts to scribble with a crayon in imitation of someone else doing it, but she prefers to watch an adult scribbling, or to have an adult guide her hand while she holds the crayon.

She prefers playing with objects to playing with people, and all the objects she chooses are the sort that provide a strong visual stimulus—for example, shiny metal or plastic, clear objects containing liquid, things like plastic baskets with an open grid-work pattern, or lines of print on paper.

As far as her *auditory skills* are concerned, Ruth shows little response to sounds, although certain patterns have begun to emerge. She sometimes responds to a loud drum sound within a range of up to a metre—by smiling, by momentarily stopping what she is doing, by suddenly moving away from where she is standing, or by some combination of the three. She shows some recognition of the direction from which a sound has come, which she demonstrates by distinctive body movements, but she does not turn to familiar noises.

She is demonstrating an awareness of familiar routines and is beginning to show displeasure when these routines are broken. Her responses to spoken language are limited. She is beginning to show more response when speech is accompanied by signs presented clearly and near to her face, within her residual visual field. For example, when the words 'Ruth, time for your bath' are said and signed they produce a consistent response—she takes her mother's hand and leads her towards the stairs to go to the bathroom.

Ruth responds appropriately to certain physical cues; for example, when she is being helped to dress she will lift an arm when it is tapped, and she will sometimes sit down on her chair if she sees downward-gesturing movements. Her family are signing *coactively* (see page 107) with her at appropriate times, using signs for the following to accompany spoken words:

up	sit down	play	eat/food	bath/wash
drink	more	walk	car	toilet
sleep	biscuit	jump	dinner	good

In the area of *expressive communication*, it is noticeable that Ruth vocalises during much of the day. She produces a range of sounds, mostly repetitious, including 'a-a-a', 'eh-eh-eh', 'ooo', 'or', 'ma', 'wah-wah', 'eeah', 'mum-mum-mum', 'ungha-ungha'. Over the past two months she has begun to demonstrate a slightly wider range of intonation while producing these sounds, and is particularly inclined to vocalise when playing with an object, during rough physical play with another person, or when leading him by the hand to show him something. She will use a whole-hand point to indicate a desired object that is out of reach, and will vocalise to an adult to give her a favoured toy.

Children with sensory impairments may have residual vision and a profound hearing loss . . .

Ruth will often search for an adult, then take his hand, pull him to another room and place his hand as near as she can manage to the object she desires but cannot reach herself—she will do this, for instance, to have a door opened. If she is particularly enjoying an activity with an adult, she asks in appropriate ways to have it repeated. For example, if her hand has been tickled, she will offer her open palm for more tickling; if she has been bounced up and down on a lap she will move around as if asking for more bouncing. In these repetitive activities Ruth is able to anticipate and wait for short periods, often producing lots of giggles as she waits for the game to restart.

It is clear that Ruth's play is becoming less self-contained. She enjoys a wide range of rough-and-tumble play with others if they initiate it. She is becoming increasingly aware of the usefulness of other people to get things that she cannot reach, and will go to some lengths to get their cooperation in this. Her mother reports

. . . or they may be blind with a severe hearing loss.

that she seeks out familiar people quite deliberately, initiating
contact by touching, holding hands or by climbing on to their
laps. She usually smiles to herself while doing this, and may
make fleeting eye contact with the chosen person.

On a number of occasions, Ruth has knocked objects together,
such as two shiny, bright bricks, in imitation of an adult. She is
beginning to cooperate in dressing and undressing, and as well as
raising an arm when it is tapped to have it put in a sleeve she will
remove a vest or jumper if it is removed as far as the crown of her
head. She is generally very relaxed and happy, even when she is
slightly unwell. She is keen to explore and will scrutinise an object
closely for up to a minute at a time before discarding it to look for
a new one. She is showing signs of becoming interested in other
people; physical play such as jumping and rolling offers a useful
way of helping her to sustain interactions with another person.

It is the combination of hearing and visual impairment that is so important to remember.

Activities that Ruth's parents can do with her

● Use Ruth's interest in objects, and the fact that she will look at them closely, to help to increase her interest in people. We need to think of them, for a short time at least, as objects for her to look at. She needs to be able to look at faces and be more interested in them so that she can increase her personal communication skills. Adults can wear a hat for her to take off, or a pair of silly party glasses or a red nose, so that she becomes intrigued by faces as objects to look at.
● Use Ruth's ability to look closely at pictures to encourage her to look at photographs or line drawings of people, perhaps matching up photographs of people who are in the room with the individuals as they sit, stand or even move around.

- Use Ruth's natural gestures and her ability to accept coactive signing to help her look at people occasionally when they are signing in front of her. It is very important of course not to over-insist on this and not to intrude on her private space, otherwise she might retreat further from people.

PRITI

At the time of referral at the age of four, Priti was known to be totally blind in her right eye, but with useful partial sight in her left eye, and to have a severe sensorineural hearing loss. She manifested some behavioural differences such as tripoding, lying on her back and light-gazing, finger-flicking and making random hand movements.

Priti walks with a slightly unsteady gait, which is probably partly due to her combination of visual and hearing impairments. She is able to run in an unconfined flat space, just occasionally falling over. She climbs on to furniture, walks up and down stairs, and gets up and down a slide unaided; she shows some awareness of danger during these activities, but is still likely to bump herself or fall. She enjoys being lifted, swung through the air and moved up and down by an adult. She likes to play on all kinds of large playground equipment (swings, slides, roundabouts, climbing-frame), and will often do so unaided. She can also turn a somersault unaided.

Priti can kick a large bright-red ball from a standing position towards a target or person a few feet away. She tries to roll the same ball towards an adult when he or she is sitting facing her on the floor about five feet away. She enjoys knocking a shiny helium balloon up into the air and then loves the surprise of finding it as it floats to the ground, sometimes chasing it. She is also able to throw small, soft blocks, in primary colours, into a 36cm (14in) diameter bucket lined with shiny reflective paper, about 76cm (2.5ft) away, always managing to get some of them in. She is becoming increasingly aware, when she retrieves the blocks from the bucket, of their reflection as they pass the reflective paper.

Priti can scoop dry rice with a seaside spade or a spoon and, with some spillage, tip it into a container. She can stack ten

2.5cm (1in) blocks. She enjoys painting and scribbling spontaneously with crayons, both horizontally and vertically, and in zigzags and circles. During painting sessions she often rinses her brush in water before changing colours—which she does frequently—and when using felt-tip pens she removes and replaces the caps without being asked to. She will scribble in imitation of an adult, and is attempting to trace around templates, also in imitation. Priti is very interested in cutting paper with an adult, using training scissors.

Another activity that she enjoys is blowing bubbles with a bubble pipe, but she needs an adult's help to stop her sucking the bubbles back into it. She is able to pop bubbles using a gentle index-finger point. She also enjoys holding large bubbles in her wet hands, and is very amused at being able to stretch and squeeze them. Apart from bubbles, she also enjoys a wide variety of other tactile substances that she feels with great interest—dry rice, dry pasta, water, and washing-up liquid mix. When playing with Play-doh she will knead and roll it, try to cut it with a knife, and poke it with her finger to make holes in it. She spontaneously threads large beads, using a long-stemmed threader. When replacing inset puzzle pieces, she often experiences difficulty in manoeuvring them into their holes; she pays close visual attention, but tries to push the pieces in using her whole hand rather than lifting them by their handles and placing them in.

Priti enjoys symbolic play with dolls, soft animal toys and a tea-set. She prefers to play with these things alone, without adult involvement. Occasionally, however, she brings an adult to sit and play with her. She will spontaneously place dolls on chairs, then bring the tea-set to them and proceed to organise a tea party. Her pretend play with a tea-set is impressive. Unprompted, she will place a cup, saucer and spoon together, and a knife, fork and plate together. She pretends to pour from a teapot into the cup. She picks up the spoon and pretends to take sugar from the sugar bowl to the cup, then stirs. She spoons 'food' from a large bowl on to a plate, and then pretends to eat it using a knife and fork. She includes the dolls and toy animals in all this, and will offer them 'food' and 'drink'.

With pictorial inset puzzles Priti is now recognising a growing

Priti demonstrates her understanding of many objects by her use of them.

number of pieces and demonstrating this in a variety of ways. She pushes a lorry piece along the table, saying 'Bm, bm'. She puts a cup piece to her mouth as if to drink, or touches it and says 'Ot'; she attempts to turn the dial on the telephone piece, or puts it to her ear and says 'Ello'. She uses gestures to identify jigsaw pieces such as the doll, the book and the ball. Priti also enjoys playing with inset boards, and is learning through repetition where the pieces go. She completely mastered a four-piece geometric formboard on her third attempt; with more complex puzzles she usually persists, using a trial-and-error approach, until they are completed.

She enjoys a lot of cause-and-effect toys. She will watch an adult carefully in order to imitate him and then make the toy work herself—for instance, she can turn a key to wind up a clockwork toy, and switch on a variety of battery-operated toys. She demonstrates her understanding of many objects by her use of them. She knows items of clothing, and correctly uses a dustpan and brush, a toothbrush, a handkerchief, the vacuum cleaner, talcum powder and skin cream, a hairbrush and comb, tissues, and items of cutlery and crockery. She is also recognising many objects from photographs and drawings in books, and will spontaneously point at them, sometimes looking around for the object.

Priti has a spontaneous vocabulary of about sixteen words. These are almost always used appropriately, except on occasions when she is clearly deriving pleasure from rehearsing some of them. She will sometimes break off from playing and slowly say a few words to herself, smile broadly, and then carry on where she left off with her play; she does the same with the ten British Sign Language (BSL) signs that she knows. Priti will also use a word or a sign (or both combined) as a communicative device. For example, she will ask for a biscuit using the word and the sign combined, and gets quite upset if this does not produce the desired response from the adult. She can ask an adult to sit down with her by tapping at his hands and then signing 'sit down'. She is often the first to say/sign 'Hello' on meeting an adult, and will wave and say 'Bye' to an adult as he or she is about to leave.

She can respond appropriately to a number of spoken questions or requests, without any contextual clues—for instance, 'Priti, let's take your coat off' (she begins to remove her coat); 'Priti, do you want a drink?' (she sits at the table); 'Priti, give this to Mummy', 'Priti, put the pens in the box', and so on. She understands a larger number of statements if gestures or signs accompany them, but she misses these clues if she is not paying close visual attention to the people around her. Her responses to adult speech are more consistent when she is looking at them. She can appear not to hear at all if she is really absorbed in an activity.

Priti enjoys a wide range of noise-making toys, from rattles to an electric organ. She often holds a musical box or an electronic toy siren up to her ear and rocks in time with the vibration and the sound. On some occasions while doing this, she has also attempted to vocalise in imitation of the sound of the object. She sometimes attempts to repeat a word she has heard, such as 'baby' and 'cat'.

She once 'stilled' in her mid-play to listen to a loud clock ticking nearby, then searched around the table until she found the source of the sound. She will sometimes turn when her father or mother calls her name. When Priti is given a portable cassette-recorder, she vocalises at it and then gives it to an adult to play it back for her. She has listened to recordings of her voice, giggling and smiling as she does so.

Priti can take herself to the toilet, and manages the whole routine unaided. She can wash her hands quite well, but needs to be reminded to use soap; while washing her hands she often gives her face a token wash. She drinks from a cup and eats well, jabbing or scooping with a fork, or scooping with a spoon. If given a knife, she will attempt to cut food with it. She looks for a tissue in the tissue box (which has been highlighted with reflective paper), and wipes her nose with the tissue spontaneously. With adult encouragement she can dress and undress, but needs some help with zips, buttons and sandal straps. If left to her own devices she can usually find her way into her clothes, although they sometimes finish up back to front or inside out.

Other people do not normally receive very close visual attention from Priti, although she recognises a number of familiar ones on sight. She uses other people as tools to help her if she cannot manage a task: she will take an adult's hand to the handle of a door she cannot open, or give him or her a box to open if she cannot manage it. With her parents, she often brings a toy to show them. She will follow an adult's pointing finger and, if she is sufficiently interested in an activity, pay close attention to the adult involved in it to see how it is done. Through this close attention and imitation she has learnt how to do a number of things very quickly—to blow on a kazoo, trace around a stencil, turn on a toy siren.

If Priti gets upset it is usually possible to distract her attention and get her interested in some form of play. She shows signs of anticipating certain routine activities and is beginning to get the idea of putting a toy away before she starts to play with another one, although she often still needs prompting to do this.

Activities that Priti's parents can do with her

- Use Priti's interest in physical movement to help her change her position more often and encourage her to use more gross motor skills on a circuit. Giving her a circuit (see page 116) that will encourage an upright position will develop her ability to use her residual vision from standing or sitting.
- Use Priti's ability to accept coactive signing to help her appreciate that she can manipulate adults by using sounds,

signs or gestures for activities such as 'eat', 'play' and 'jump'. The adults working with her need to be aware of any attempts on her part to babble or sign and should respond positively as soon as she does so.

- Use Priti's ability to play with a variety of age-appropriate toys to create situations in which she is dependent on further interactions with people. Her communication skills need extending. Use adults to help her to obtain toys or activities or to complete something. For example, she often finds out by herself how to do something. In order to increase her communication with adults, sometimes put her favourite tea-set and toys slightly higher up in the cupboard and show her that she can ask an adult to get these down for her. This might help her to increase her use of babble, sign, gesture and eye-contact.

*   *   *

Lee, Ruth and Priti, all of the same age, all affected by congenital rubella syndrome, have sight and hearing impairments in common. But this is where their similarities end. Each of them has a different combination of sensory impairments which, together with their individual life experiences, determines the way in which they are able to master skills. Their vision and hearing impairments range from severe sensorineural loss through profound hearing loss together with blindness in one eye and severely limited sight in the other, to useful residual vision in both eyes. They have all been worked with from an early age by professionals such as doctors, advisory teachers and therapists. One of the children has had heart surgery, one has balance difficulties; one is showing evidence of specific learning difficulties, whereas another appears to be functioning at age-appropriate developmental levels.

All children, whatever the cause of their dual sensory loss, need to be thought of as unique in their skills and abilities. It is very unusual to meet two children with the same dual sensory impairment who can utilise the same programme or the same approach towards achieving their individual developmental goals.

Usher syndrome and CHARGE association

Many children described as deafblind have no known cause of their combined hearing and visual impairments. For their parents, this may mean countless visits to hospitals and treatment centres, trying to track down information that will secure a firm diagnosis and prognosis. Of the known syndromes associated with deafblindness apart from rubella, Usher syndrome and CHARGE association are, in this minority disability field, relatively well known.

Usher syndrome is a genetic condition that causes deafness from birth and sight loss over a number of years. The information leaflet of Sense gives the details:

> This sight loss often begins in late childhood and is caused by an eye condition known as retinitis pigmentosa (RP). This is a major cause of sight loss in people under forty. The early symptoms include difficulty seeing in the dark and in different lighting conditions. Over time, vision gradually deteriorates until tunnel vision develops. Usher syndrome is an inherited condition which is passed through the family. It is possible to be a carrier of Usher syndrome but to be unaffected by the symptoms. Often parents are unaware that they are carriers until their child is diagnosed as having the condition. For the child to be born with Usher syndrome both parents must either be carriers of the faulty genes or have the same type of Usher syndrome themselves.

There are three types of Usher that are known about at present:

Type 1   Children are usually born with profound deafness, then develop a visual impairment in their teens or earlier. The first sign of visual problems is often night blindness. Usually children with Type 1 start walking later, have poor balance, and may have difficulty seeing in the dark or in bright sunlight.

Type 2   Children are usually born with partial deafness and then develop a visual impairment in their teens. Unlike people with

Type 1, there are usually no balance problems noticed in early childhood.

Type 3 Children usually have normal hearing and sight at birth, but then develop a hearing and visual impairment around the age of twenty to thirty. Balance difficulties may also arise.

The characteristics of what came to be known as 'CHARGE association' were first noted in 1979, and the acronym CHARGE was first used two years later. David Brown, head of the FEAS, London and S.E., writes: 'This acronym is the name of a condition that is found in a very varied group of people who exhibit at least four of the features starting with the letters of the acronym, including either choanal atresia and/or coloboma.' The identifying characteristics of CHARGE are:

Coloboma, an eye deformity involving the absence of part of the eye
Heart defects of various kinds
Choanal atresia—a blockage of the passages at the back of the nose
Retarded growth which may become evident as the child matures
Genitalia anomalies: specifically, incomplete development or underdevelopment of the external genitals, common in males who have the syndrome
Ear anomalies that affect the external, middle or internal ear; in people with CHARGE, mixed hearing loss is commonly found: that is, conductive loss combined with a sensorineural loss.

Apart from these critical features, there are many other anomalies found in people with CHARGE association, including cleft lip and cleft palate, facial palsy and kidney abnormalities. The exact cause of the condition is unknown. David Brown writes: 'Evidence from families and involved professionals suggests that people with CHARGE association cover the whole spectrum of intellectual ability, from severe learning disabilities through to normal or even high intelligence.'

OTHER CAUSES AND PREDISPOSITIONS FOR DEAFBLINDNESS

Many children may become deafblind as the result of illnesses such as meningitis and encephalitis. There are many other conditions associated with deafblindness such as Down's syndrome and toxoplasmosis (a parasitical infection). Useful addresses can be found in the Resources at the end of the book (note that CAF and other organisations are constantly updating websites).

If a child has had sight and hearing for a few years and then loses one or the other as a result of accident or illness, he may retain skills that can help him to learn in a different way from those children who are born deafblind. Helen Keller, who lost her sight and hearing when she was less than two years old, was such a child. Through intensive intervention from her teacher, Annie Sullivan, she was enabled to reuse her previous knowledge in a different way. Many children and adults who lose their hearing and vision retain throughout their lives the ability to use their favoured communication mode, such as speech or sign.

Children who are born deafblind follow a different learning path, one that often includes compensating for the visual and auditory skills that they have never had. Children born deafblind, or who become deafblind in the first few months of their lives, may be deprived of the bonding experiences that babies normally have with their parents. They may have been born in a distressed state. If they were premature or very ill, they will immediately have been taken to special care baby units and will have received all the treatment that this usually entails. Special care baby units nowadays make good provision for parents ensuring that as soon as possible they are able to handle their babies—they are often encouraged to use gentle massage to assist in the bonding process. Some older children born deafblind did not benefit from modern knowledge and understanding about the importance of parental bonding and interaction, or the undoubted advantages of being held gently as early as possible. Many of them may manifest some of the behavioural characteristics described in Chapter 8. Hopefully, fewer younger children will be affected by lack of early bonding.

It is important to note that prematurity is often associated with children who are deafblind. From the medical history of many of these children it is clear that they were very ill as newborns or had a recognisable syndrome at birth (or soon after). Children who are born 'early for dates'—that is, from approximately thirty-two weeks' gestation onwards—are as likely or as unlikely to have vision and hearing problems as the rest of the population.

THE IMPORTANCE OF EARLY AND ONGOING ASSESSMENT

A major problem, when a child is born deafblind, is that the parents may have to endure many time-consuming and traumatic hospital visits before a clear picture of his needs and of the treatment he requires emerges. With some children, it may be years before any definite prognosis can be reached. The developing skills of these children will need to be carefully observed by multidisciplinary teams able to assess them by means of a holistic approach. The following example illustrates this.

A child who is blind may develop speech at an age-appropriate time. If a child with a severe visual impairment does *not* develop speech, it may be difficult to assess whether he is hearing normally. Many such children do not turn to sound. They may 'still' to it, or alter their facial expression, but they do not turn as a sighted baby does. The kind of test situation that requires the child to be actively engaged when he hears a sound will not usually work with a child with severe visual impairment. Many ways of adapting observational methods may have to be devised and tried out before a clear picture of the child's ability to hear or use residual hearing can be gained. Sometimes the creative use of sounds can engage the child. Here's an example.

Joseph, who was born totally blind, can speak, but his mother realised that his speech was difficult to understand by people who did not know him well. Joseph and his mother discussed the problem with the audiologist. As Joseph is a teenager, he had no difficulty understanding a test situation which involved him responding to sounds heard through headphones. His response to the sounds that he was presented with gave useful information—he could hear

certain sounds which he described as rats, and others as mosquitoes. From these responses the audiologist was able to gain a
reasonable degree of information about Joseph's hearing. He
stilled to the sounds that he heard, but could not cooperate in
any test situation that involved him in saying 'yes' to a sound.
Any sound that he heard intrigued him, as did the strangeness of
the situation. (To a child who is blind, being requested to listen
for sounds without there being anything to touch is very odd.)
Watching Joseph, and being creative in her interpretation of what
she perceived, allowed the audiologist to give useful information
to his mother. The audiologist had achieved this by:

—watching for Joseph's body language
—observing changes in his facial expression
—using his interest in animals
—engaging his attention in order to intrigue him in the situation
—capturing a particular interest of his, thereby making the situ-
    ation have meaning for him.

The hearing of many children with residual vision can be as
difficult to assess as that of the child with no vision. Those
with some vision may be so visually aware that they ignore
environmental sounds or sounds that have no meaning for them
(note that Joseph's audiologist responded to his way of describing
the sounds, calling them 'squeaky rats and buzzy mosquitoes').
Many children are fascinated by light, and will gaze particularly
at fluorescent lights or at the nearest light source, such as a
window. If a child's hearing is tested in a brightly lit room and
account is not taken of his obsession with light—of how much
of his attention is being absorbed by it—then a true assessment
of his hearing will not usually be obtained. Furthermore, unless
the child with residual vision has speech, test situations can be
very difficult for all concerned. Often, being in a room with
diffuse light will help to give observers a truer reading of what
it is the child is able to achieve. He will be less distracted, and
creativity on the part of the observers as well as a willingness to
use the skills of the child and of the people who know him will
usually help to obtain a reasonably true picture of his abilities.
  But seeing how children function in a quiet, controlled situation

gives only part of the picture—helping them to make the most of the skills they have in the busy classroom or home will often take much skill and many years to achieve.

For children who have physical disabilities as well, assessment situations can be even more difficult. Continuous assessment throughout their school life may be the best option. Long-term observational assessment strategies are more likely to give reliable evidence of the way some children use their vision and hearing in functional situations.

It would be costly, but extremely worthwhile, if every health authority were to set up a systematic referral procedure whereby all children known to be blind or partially sighted could go to an audiologist who had a specialist interest in working with them. The automatic screening of such children could identify, for example, the child with intermittent conductive hearing loss (a *slight* loss can become a serious difficulty if a child has a severe visual impairment). Similarly, if all children in a health authority known to be deaf or partially hearing could attend a specialist ophthalmologist skilled at working with children with a hearing impairment, that health authority would be able to give advice, information and treatment at the earliest possible moment. The automatic, regular vision screening of children who are deaf might result in the early identification of Usher syndrome in teenagers and of others who acquire deafblindness as they grow older. (If the fact that a deaf child needs glasses to correct even a minor refractive error is missed, then he will not be able to function at his optimum capacity, possibly resulting in him under-functioning.)

TREATING THE WHOLE CHILD

Fundamental to a child's ability to learn is that those who care for him should have a thorough knowledge of his individual requirements. This can only be achieved by the global assessment of his needs as a *whole child*. If he is seen by different specialists for different conditions, the fact that each special need compounds and influences the others may be overlooked. Coordination of his treatment, care and therapy is therefore essential. There are some extremely good child development centres that can provide specialist help for children who are deafblind, in which their medical, educational, social and therapy needs are comprehensively dealt with. Where services are coordinated in this way, the professionals see the children and their parents *as individuals*. They ensure that the parents understand the complex needs of their children, and help them to tackle their difficulties as a whole. Parents and professionals share their knowledge and understanding of the child together in these centres.

WHAT KIND OF EXTRA HELP IS AVAILABLE?

Nurseries and schools, too, can provide information in the assessment procedure of children. Some mainstream schools have units attached that can cater for children who have acquired deafblindness. These units tend to be *either* for children who are deaf *or* for those who have severe visual impairment. Some schools for children with sensory impairments or learning difficulties have their own specialist units for children who have multisensory impairments. Many children attend their local schools, but some, as noted earlier, go to day or boarding schools out of their own local authority area. The situation has gradually improved during the last twenty years. At the time of writing, all children have a right to National Curriculum subjects; some have a different route to this access and may learn more slowly. Many are able to go on to further educational opportunities after school leaving age.

Some children in mainstream schools are supported by teachers of the visually impaired, of the hearing impaired and of those with multisensory impairments. Some have access to special needs assistants, or intervenors, working with them in mainstream or special schools. An intervenor assists and supports the children, often acting as an interpreter and enabling them to mix with their peers in social situations. Intervenors often undertake individual work under the guidance of a child's teacher, but their main remit is to interpret actions, activities and situations for the child, helping him to become as independent as possible within the school.

Intervenors are employed for specific children who:

- are experiencing difficulties in developing communication skills and who therefore need to learn how to use adapted or augmented forms of communication;
- are experiencing difficulties in developing movement and mobility skills which call for modifications to the immediate environment and specialised learning programmes;
- are having difficulty integrating the information they receive through their other senses, and therefore require individual activity-based programmes, using a multisensory approach, that encourage the consolidation of sensory input;
- have restricted access to the environment: they have inadequate feedback because of their sensory impairment. This calls for a greater structuring of the environment which will promote exploration and reinforcement of experiences;
- are encountering difficulties in regulating their own actions and drawing generalisations from their experience of objects and situations; this calls for approaches that allow opportunities for activities to be repeated and for fostering the acquisition and transfer of skills.

As already mentioned, the population of children who are called deafblind encompasses a wide range of abilities, disabilities and diagnoses. In the proceedings of the National Symposium on Children and Youth who are Deafblind John McInnes states:

From my experience as a consultant, when working with professionals and administrators whose expertise lies primarily outside the field of deafblindness, I have refined my presentation concerning the identification of those who should be considered deafblind to two questions:

1 Does the individual in question have sufficient vision to permit him to fully function as a hearing-impaired person without any significant problem?
2 Does the individual in question have sufficient hearing

to permit him to function as a visually impaired person without any significant problem?

If he cannot answer 'yes' to both of these questions without reservation, the individual should be considered deafblind.

*   *   *

In summary, children who are deafblind need positive assessments; they need the input of professionals who will work with them with the aim of emphasising their skills and abilities and encouraging them to participate in developmentally vital aspects of their programme. These aspects include important issues associated with the acquisition of communication, such as child–parent bonding and interaction, and environmental strategies such as keeping spaces clutter-free, which enable the child to perform within his abilities. Some children are exposed to so many varied sensory experiences that they are unable to cope with an environment that they find frightening, confusing and alien, and as a result they may underperform. Some of those who experience this difficulty have cortical visual impairment combined with auditory dysfunction, and may need to have very carefully constructed environments, uncluttered both visually and auditorily.

Children who are deafblind range in ability from those who have very severe learning difficulties to those who are extremely able and likely to go on to further education. One such student—Kevin, aged 14 at the time of referral—attends a mainstream school. The way his local authority supports him illustrates how, with planning, students who have dual sensory impairments can function and learn alongside their peers. Kevin receives advice from a mobility officer and a teacher for visually impaired students, as well as having daily support from the Hearing Support Unit attached to his mainstream school. A Sense advisory teacher makes an annual visit in order to give an outside independent opinion about the facilities available, and to make suggestions towards Kevin's individual programme.

It is enlightening and encouraging to see how aware mainstream staff are of Kevin's needs as a student who has combined vision and hearing impairments. All staff who interact with him receive updated information each term, and there is an on-going awareness programme throughout the school. This ensures that teachers use very clear speech and natural gestures, explaining tasks very precisely. Each classroom has a white board and teachers check with Kevin that he can see it and that the lighting in the room is correct. He himself checks that the angle of his desk enables him to see clearly. His work has been enlarged to suit his visual requirements, he always sits at the front of the class, and by using his radio aid he can follow everything that happens during the lesson.

Kevin has personal hearing aids which are tuned to his individual hearing needs and can be switched to receive input from the radio aid setting. They effectively amplify sound for him up to about one metre distance, while the radio aid cuts down 'interference' and amplifies sound from a longer distance—which is particularly useful to him in group lessons or when there is a great deal of ambient sound.

As an integrated student within a mainstream school, Kevin has access to hearing–sighted and hearing impaired peers. It is clear that his peer group is aware of his needs. For example, when he goes swimming he has to remove his hearing aids and glasses, so a 'buddy system' has been set up which alerts him to all essential information whenever the swimming instructor changes the activity. Selected students are there to let Kevin know that something extra is being conveyed, thus minimising any difficulty that he might otherwise have.

In Britain children who are deafblind can go to school as early as two years of age, and they will certainly be in school by the time they are five. The type of school that individual children attend depends on their specific needs and on the recommendations of all those involved with them. Local education authorities can provide for the needs of children who are deafblind by ensuring that they attend suitable schools, backed up by a range of specialist teachers and therapists. Given that all children's educational needs change over time, the annual review is an essential tool for reassessing programmes, strategies and progress.

4 Making Sense of the World

The entire life of a child with multisensory impairments can be affected by the approach that people have to her and her needs. If she is seen as a child who must be protected against all danger and challenge, and if she is nurtured in an overwhelming cocoon of emotion because she has disabilities, these attitudes may well limit her abilities. If, on the other hand, she is seen as a child who is capable of learning, then she is likely to learn more, and grow, mature and function to the best of her ability. People's attitudes and reactions to children have the power to limit or promote their achievements quite considerably.

Parents and teachers of children with disabilities need to view them as children with skills of their own that can be extended. Their disabilities may affect the *way* they learn, but most children can learn if given the opportunity. How much and how fast a child learns can never be forecast, and it really doesn't matter how long it takes her to achieve her own goals, so long as she gets there in the end. Providing her with lots of fun and interest in the process of learning, and setting realistic targets, are the keys to progress.

The difficulties that some children face in making sense of their world are often so great that people may forget the very fact that they are children. A child is not a robot to be programmed with a view to fulfilling adults' set goals—she needs child-centred activities. She is a real child—in this respect, like any other—with a need for love, companionship and enjoyment in everyday situations. For some parents, having to teach their children skills takes over their lives. It can be helpful to remember that children need to experience everyday situations in as natural a context as possible.

The child with multisensory impairment needs many more opportunities to absorb information and to touch, smell and taste

in an exploratory way and for a much longer time, than the child
without sensory impairments. Anything she can sense, experience
for herself or be in charge of will further her progress. Anything
that she can be actively involved with will add to her knowledge
of herself and usually lead to her acquiring further skills. Anything we encourage her to do that gives her control will encourage
her to experiment more. We need to be supersensitive to the
child's individual input, and constantly aware that that input is
one of the keys to her further learning.

As the child's awareness of the environment begins to grow,
she begins to develop a range of responses. If her experiences
have been pleasurable and non-threatening, she may begin to
experiment. For example, a very young child may sit absolutely
still. If she becomes aware of a noise and if she knows that the
environment is non-threatening, she may move her hands, arm
or body slightly towards the noise-maker. Then, she may *discover
for herself* that her bottle, cup or toy (or whatever) is there. She
has learnt, by herself, that movement gains a reward. She has
learnt by making a meaningful movement that the environment
can provide her with pleasurable experiences. (What she does
not know is that the parent or teacher has deliberately ensured
that her favourite sound-maker is close by and available, and that
what has just happened is part of a planned approach.)

People are often concerned that their children do not try to
explore their environment. What we have to remember is that
the child needs to know *why* it would be a good idea to explore
the environment. What is out there for her? What incentive is
there for her to *want* to explore?

The child's environment in the early years should be consistent.
She needs to know that the objects that she encounters, such as
furniture, will always be there; that the toys she is given will
continue to engage her; and that the people she meets will understand her and give her pleasure. The child with these experiences
becomes a child with concrete internal knowledge.

Many children with multisensory impairments remain isolated
from their environment. This may be precisely because they lack
the ability to use the two major 'distance senses' of vision and
hearing, through which the rest of us gain information about the

world. Reduced vision and hearing can deprive children of the means to be aware of anything beyond their own bodies, which, in turn, can mean that they have little chance of understanding people, objects or places. Such children may have no way of anticipating people or objects and so they cannot know that the world contains anything *stable*. Through negative experiences, they may become overcautious about touching, and they may appear to be retreating from activities that other children find stimulating and fun.

If we look at the development of young children without sensory impairments, we see that their early play experiences, consisting of naturally occurring contact with people and objects, provide important learning opportunities. When they move from the 'grasping everything' stage (including their parents' hair!) to throwing everything out of the cot or buggy, then to being able to play all by themselves with toys and people, they are also learning about the world and its stability.

When children who are deafblind are young, and especially if they have additional difficulties, they may experience the world as much too large and complicated for them to *exercise any control*. Their experience may only be of having things done to them, not of *doing things for themselves*. They may have objects put in front of them to look at, but *may not have any choice* in the matter. They may have things put in their hands, but may not be given enough time to explore them *in a meaningful way*. They may be given things to listen to that they cannot switch off, or at a volume that they *cannot control*. They may often want to move towards something, but *the effort of doing so* may be so taxing that they give up.

We must ask ourselves these questions:

- How can we give our children with sensory impairments the chance to make the same vital voyage of self-discovery as children whose senses are intact?
- How can we help them to learn about their bodies in relation to the outside world?
- How can we give them the confidence to experiment with objects?

- How can we give them the knowledge that there is an exciting world out there which they are part of?
- How can we encourage them to know that they are in control?

REACTIVE ENVIRONMENTS

A reactive environment can be thought of as one in which the child becomes aware that her actions can make things happen. It is an environment that has meaning for the child, and that provides objects, within a safe space, that have specific interest for her. The space is carefully planned so that everything is positioned where, if she wants to, she can make contact with chosen objects.

Providing a reactive environment for the child to gradually discover means that she:

- can explore objects by herself, at her own pace and in her own time;
- has the opportunity to look at or listen to objects and toys that she has selected;
- begins to understand that this particular environment is a safe place within which to experiment.

Creating a reactive environment

There are many ways of creating suitable reactive environments. They are basically safe, child-sized areas whose sides the child can reach, and within which she can have her own toys and other objects to explore.

Many parents and teachers devise wonderful, ingenious environments out of all kinds of materials such as large, sturdy cardboard boxes, playpens, or more permanent wooden or per-spex structures. It is important to remember that this is *the child's space*. It is vital not to overload it. There is no right or wrong way to create a reactive environment, and so each one will be different, according to the individual child's needs. Imagination and ingenuity are the keynotes.

A feature of the reactive environment is that there is space enough for the child to interact with one or two objects without

A reactive environment, or 'little room'.

overload. If we think of the space as creating an opportunity for

- *active* use of residual vision
- *active* use of touch and exploration
- *active* use of residual hearing,

we will ensure that we are creating the right environment from the child's perspective.

The child's skills and her ability to look and listen will determine which toys and activities you provide, and her preferences for or dislike of certain textures must be respected. Remember that it is essential to carefully fix all the equipment within the environment, as well as to regularly maintain it. Parents and teachers will have many more ideas for equipment that can be used as a 'starter kit'. It is important to move along with the child and be ready to improve or change her environment, as she increases her skills, by altering the toys that you provide or by changing some of the textures on the sides of the environment.

We need to remember that the child's world probably consists anyway of many other small environments. When she is ready, begin to look around with her at all these other environments, try to imagine how she must experience them from her limited standpoint, and help her to make links between them. To explore these environments, she needs to feel very confident within them. If she has any useful residual vision or hearing, being given the time, space and opportunity to explore and experience each environment for herself should give her more confidence to move on to the next. Providing just enough equipment—not too much clutter, not too little stimulation—is the secret. This will enable you to observe her often fleeting and subtle reactions.

Children are sometimes described as not having useful vision, but then, when they are given the opportunity to experience a *distraction-free* environment, it becomes apparent that they do indeed have useful residual vision. On questioning the adults concerned, it may transpire that the children's opportunities to use vision have been limited because too many overstimulating activities have been introduced, with the result that they have 'switched off', in effect rejecting their visually cluttered environment.

Giving children the time and opportunity to focus their eyes upon one attractive object, that remains in the same place, is part of the routine that needs to be established. Sticking to this principle will ensure the long exposure to a stimulus that is often needed by children with severely impaired vision and additional disabilities. They will probably become aware, gradually, of the visually stimulating object, and will look for it the next time they are in their special environment.

Touching and listening
Knowing that things are *there* and within reach creates a chance for the child to *want* to reach and touch. As she reaches out with her arms and moves her legs, she may come into contact with the sides or back of the reactive environment. She will be making discoveries about spaces and walls that may, later on, help her to explore other, bigger environments. Children who have been described as having tactile or additional difficulties will often learn to touch and trust the toys and textures that they find within this special space.

The softest sounds will be amplified within this small space. Vocalisations made by children in reactive environments produce much greater feedback, and parents and teachers often find that they consequently make many more sounds; sometimes they are seen to be concentrating on listening much more to their toys and to themselves.

Other factors to consider

A small environment provides a place for self-initiated activities, it is a valuable resource where the child has no adult to interact with her, and it is somewhere she can take her own time to explore. It is important to observe the child within the environment extremely carefully at all times, so as not to miss the important milestones that may well be reached there, such as:

—an increase in her babbling
—an increase in her use of visual skills
—an increase in her use of hearing skills
—an increase in her spatial awareness
—an increase in her knowledge of the environment.

It is vital that she feels comfortable and that she is in the best position to benefit from the experiences presented.

It is also very important to consider the child's progress at regular intervals—otherwise, you may miss the opportunity to devise ways of helping her to move on and develop in her play activities. Although she needs to have fun experiences and to be given the time to play, the reactive environment is essentially a place for absorbing, for reaching out and for learning. Learning opportunities are created for the child, and this in turn permits you to learn more about her and her skills.

When designing the interior of a reactive environment for a child who has severe motor problems and very limited movement in addition to multisensory impairment, it is essential to bear her extra difficulties in mind:

- You can securely cover the sides of the environment with different materials such as corrugated cardboard, shiny reflective paper and interesting textured fabrics.
- Suspend from the 'ceiling' toys such as bright, good-quality rattles and silvery jingle-bells or other musical toys, at safely

spaced positions where she has the opportunity to see, hear or touch them.

- If she has a favourite sound-making toy, place it on the floor of the environment—any sound made inside it will be amplified.
- Safely hang a bright, shiny, yellow, red or silvery toy within her visual field, so that gradually she becomes aware of it. She may also get fun out of cardboard tubes that have had silvery paper glued on to them.
- Ensure that the environment is in the best position from the child's point of view. For example, if she needs light to emphasise the presence of a toy, put it in the best place for light to shine on it.

SAFETY POINTS

Obviously, all children's toys need to be safe, non-toxic and too large to be swallowed. In addition, toys that appear to be safe for children with sight and hearing may be extremely dangerous, as well as pointless, for children who are multisensorily impaired.

An adult must be present all the time, not only because some toys and equipment used are potentially dangerous, but also to observe.

Remember that the reactive environment is not a place for the child to be put in and left. When the deafblind child encounters a toy or a piece of equipment for the first time, she will need to explore, move and manipulate it over and over again before she is confident enough to handle it 'correctly'. We should never assume that, without this initial exploratory time, she will be able to manipulate objects for herself in the right way. Watch any child who is given a spoon for the first time, and you will see that she bangs it on the table, turns it over, mouths it, maybe looks at her reflection in the spoon's bowl, then uses it in a variety of ways. Only after considerable experience of being spoon-fed and using a spoon herself will she appreciate that this object, 'spoon', goes into the mouth and is rarely used for anything else. Taking time to observe children with multisensory impairment in their play activities usually provides clues and guidance towards providing them with relevant experiences.

She needs time to be left to explore the toy.

LEARNING THROUGH EXPERIENCE

Depending on the child's individual abilities, it may sometimes be necessary to reach out coactively with her, in order to help her learn to explore for herself. By putting your hand over her wrist and gently guiding her hand towards the object, you will give her the opportunity to reach it. Care must be taken to ensure that she is guided towards the object *in her own time*. Do it in a non-intrusive way—otherwise, she will feel hurried and will not understand the purpose of the movement. She needs to be intrigued by toys and activities, and to be encouraged to manipulate them *for her own pleasure*. At an early stage of development, a ring, a rattle or a string of large beads should delight her, as will any toy that makes a noise when hit or squeezed. Showing her that the toys are there and what they can do ought to be sufficient. She then needs time to be left to explore them whenever she wants to. Although changing them occasionally, introducing toys with different sounds, colours and textures, should keep her interested, it is always important to be able to return to old favourites from time to time.

Examining a toy with your eyes closed will sometimes help you to appreciate its potential, and what it is likely to mean to the child with multisensory impairment. Learning to press a switch that gives visual reward is fun for a child with residual vision, while learning to press a switch that gives a sound as well as visual reward will be more fun for most children with residual hearing as well as residual vision. Be careful about naming a toy until you have discovered the way the child uses it. Often, naming the use to which she can put a toy is helpful when that toy has one specific characteristic or when you need to distinguish it from other, similar, toys. For instance, there are many types of ball: one may produce a squeak, one may bounce and one may wobble. If you name each ball according to its main feature, the child ought to be able to anticipate which ball is part of the present game. Then 'Here is the squeaky ball' or 'Let's play with the bouncy ball' or 'Try to hold the wobbly ball' should have more meaning to her.

The way children play has a direct impact on all other aspects of their daily life. If a child has good experience of different toys, different textures, different environments, she is much more likely to be adventurous. If she has very poor or no experience, she may become 'tactile-defensive' and make little progress in most skill areas. The acquisition of self-feeding skills illustrates this point:

—the child needs to be able to put her hand into a container in order to take something out
—she needs to have awareness of her mouth
—she needs to know that she has fingers and to use them with some dexterity
—she needs to be willing to explore and to play with soft and hard objects
—she needs to have the ability to hold objects using a pincer or tripod grip (thumb and fingers), in order to be able to hold a spoon
—she needs to be able to rotate her wrist
—she needs to have tolerance of different textures
—she needs to have an interest in food.

This list is not exhaustive, but it gives some idea of the observable skills to be considered before embarking on self-feeding skills. If some of these skills are missing, it may be necessary to provide appropriate experiences before we can expect the child to learn how to feed herself.

Sometimes children appear to like only certain foods, actively resisting others. Do this experiment. Blindfold yourself, and ask someone to feed you without warning you what the food is going to be. You will notice that it is very difficult to 'be fed'. You need time to identify most foods unless they are distinctively sweet, sour, spicy, hot or cold. You also need time to take the food off the spoon and to move it around your mouth and chew it. You may need to be persuaded to eat bland foods or those with which you are not familiar. You will discover that the front of your tongue tastes sweet things while awareness of bitterness is at the back, something of which we must be aware when children are depending on us to feed them. Experimenting, too, with different head positions—forward, upright and backwards—will make you realise how difficult it is to swallow in certain positions, and how much trust you need to have in the person who is feeding you from above, behind or below.

In trying to make sense of the child's world we should always be looking at things from her point of view. We need to know why we are asking our children to achieve certain self-help skills, and we must always ensure that they are developmentally ready for whatever skill is being planned for them to acquire. We need to make sure that those children who have additional physical disabilities are given even more time to explore objects with their hands or fingers. If a child is only given the opportunity to touch the nearest surface of an object without being able physically to 'look around' it with her fingers, she may not appreciate the properties of the object and may have no idea of its dimensions. If a child's physical disability is so severe as to prevent her from exploring objects at all, it is our job to look at ways of empowering her—by thinking up additional activities using switches and other equipment, for instance, or by getting more advice from her physiotherapist and occupational therapist.

Always look at the child as a whole child, and provide her with the kind of activities that will help her to increase her understanding of the world. None of our programmes for individual children should incorporate features that isolate their skills.

Children are not made up of separately functioning bits and pieces, and their needs should not be compartmentalised. They are whole children, and their individual educational programme should reflect this. They need to be provided with activities that have meaning to them as individuals, and that will help them to learn from us and from their environment.

An individual child may need to learn to practise her walking skills. Using the principles outlined above, first of all we look at the end goal—that of practising walking—then work out how she may best be able to make sense of the activity. Depending on her interests, there will be various ways of doing this: it could be a question of learning to walk towards a favourite activity, along an interesting tactile or sound-making wall, or in the company of a favourite person. There will be a preferred way for each child, and the means to the end will incorporate our knowledge of her visual, hearing and other skills, and of her particular interests—all with a view to reaching a successful outcome in a way that has been tailor-made for her.

A movement programme might aim at teaching the child about her whole body and how her body parts connect with each other. She needs to appreciate that her head moves in different ways, that she has a back and a front, that she has two hands and two feet. She may need to practise using two hands so as to learn that she can achieve more with two hands than with one. She may need to learn that other people are fun and that it is great fun to move towards them. She will need many opportunities to experience movement in space before making spontaneous movements for herself. Some children have only a very primitive knowledge of themselves and their surroundings and need to be given opportunities to move both inside and outside, and they need to go out in all weathers. Our aim should be to increase their knowledge of themselves in the farther as well as the immediate environment.

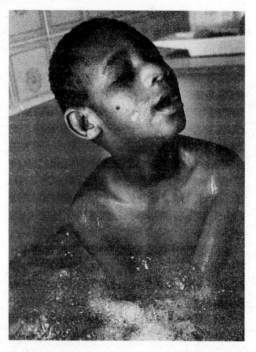

**The child needs to know as much as possible about his body
in different situations . . .**

HELPING TO MAKE MORE SENSE

Sighted–hearing children make sense of their environment and
the objects and people they encounter daily within their world at
a very early stage of development. Children with multisensory
impairment may need to be helped towards compensatory experiences that will give them the same opportunities to make sense
of things:

- Inform the child when she is being taken from one part of
  the room to another.
- Let her know who is speaking to her.
- Let her know if a new person comes into the room.
- Let her know what is about to happen, sometimes using sound
  cues or sound-makers to give more meaning to the event: for

. . . and that other people are different.

instance, a distinctive sound-maker can be attached to the
front door, informing her that someone is coming in or going
out; if she is alerted to the pinging of the microwave she will
soon recognise it as the signal that the food is ready.

- Draw her attention, through textural cues, to ways in which
  she can recognise where she is—hard-weave carpets, pile
  carpets, thick rugs, wooden floors and tiles can all act as
  indicators identifying different areas of a house or other
  building.
- Inform her, by the use of significant objects, that a certain
  activity is about to begin. For instance, decide upon an object
  that will signify the act of swimming to her each time you
  are about to take her swimming. This object should be something that she can touch, and preferably hold, such as her
  costume, towel, swimming bag, swimming cap or armbands.

Take great care to ensure that the object chosen is something that she will willingly hold and that it is absolutely relevant and significant to her within the context of the activity.

● Inform her, by the ritual use of significant objects, that activities follow each other in a structured routine. Using objects that represent favoured or routine activities can give more meaning to the child's day—drink can be represented by a cup, play by a ball, swimming by a towel, and so on for all activities throughout the day or week.

● Alert her to regular events through whole-day activities that are associated with particular festivals or anniversaries.

The prime motive in using objects in this way is to give the child as much information as possible to enable her to understand situations. Choose the objects after careful consideration of her individual skills and abilities and of her particular interest in the activity in question. The objects you choose must have:

Significance to the child
Tactile appeal for her
Activity-based interest for her
Reference points for her

STAR objects, or *referents*, need to be chosen very carefully so that it is always the child's *use* of the object which governs their choice. When adults choose things as referents they have to remember that objects that are significant for them are not necessarily significant for the child. For example, giving a child *car keys* to indicate that she is going out has no relevance for her, whereas giving her *her coat* is much more likely to convey the message.

It is most important that each child's STAR object for each activity is his or hers alone and clearly relevant to that activity. Here is an example of good practice concerning the use of objects as referents. There are four children in a certain class at a unit for children who are deafblind. All four go regularly to the physiotherapy room, and all four have different relevant objects that indicate to each of them that he or she is going there:

- One child has a soft red ball that she puts in a basket in front of her rollator (walking frame).
- One has a piece of blue plastic material exactly like the physiotherapy mat, which he puts in a bag on his rollator.
- Another has a large cube covered in green material that he carries on a tray.
- The fourth has a clear line drawing of the physiotherapy room in her pocket.

All four children are able to walk with knowledge and confidence towards their destination. When they arrive at the physiotherapy room the school's multidisciplinary approach is immediately evident. The physiotherapist uses each object of reference in her greeting routine with each child, placing the object where he or she can collect it again before starting the return journey to the classroom—at which point will be added for each child another different object, this time one symbolising 'classroom'.

Individual children need to have their lives structured in an individual way, and to help them understand and anticipate the daily, weekly and annual routines, all their activities need to be planned. Clues or reference objects may need to be used for a considerable time so as to build up the significant memories for each event or each day—they will help the children to move forward, investigate or participate with more understanding.

The individual child needs referents because he may have difficulty in remembering what comes next in a series of events, or because he has not yet acquired a way of indicating his understanding of situations through speech or sign. He may need referents to alert him to his personal significant events, or as reminders of past and future group activities. Incorporating such referents into his life, and using them regularly over time, can help to build a pattern that gives those significant occurrences more meaning. As the child matures and moves on in his appreciation of significant events, the referent objects can sometimes be phased out or used in other ways. For instance, a 'tactile timetable', which consists of a series of objects used throughout the day as indicators, may be introduced. Making a long box or tray with compartments for each object or picture, that the child moves as each activity takes place, is an extension of this idea.

A STAR object can be likened to an overture. When the overture is played, we know that it will lead us into another piece of music. We also know that within the music there are likely to be recurrent themes that we will hear enough times for us to be able to remember them. When we hear the overture music again, we will anticipate the theme. So it is with the child's reference object: when he encounters it, he knows that it will usher in a specific life experience, minor or major. We may have a variety of reasons for our choice of reference object for any particular activity for any particular child. Most important is our commitment to helping the child in a significant way: *this child* needs to receive and understand *this message*, just as we understand that a certain overture heralds a certain theme.

LINKING

All rooms and buildings are linked by spaces that we understand. We know that a kitchen is a kitchen, a bathroom is a bathroom—through using them. In order to understand how places are linked, a child who has multisensory impairment will need to be given the opportunity to understand for example, that:

—his bedroom has a bed which is *next to the wall*
—the same bed is *opposite the play cupboard*
—the same bed is *by the window*
—the same bed is *near the door*
—the same bed is *on the floor*
—the same bed is *for sleeping in.*

and that all other pieces of furniture that he finds in the bedroom, such as the chair, have constancy. Bear in mind that once he has orientated and discovered the furniture for himself, it needs to stay in place and should not be moved without him being there to supervise where it goes.

LEARNING THROUGH TOUCH

Many children stay longer than others at an early stage of skill development because they have not yet made sense of the things that they touch. Sometimes they will immediately pull their hands away from new textures or new toys. If they are very defensive about touching unfamiliar things, they need lots of opportunities to experience a range of different materials and activities before they are able to become courageous enough to explore.

One way of encouraging children who are defensive in this way is to provide them with water play. Start off with tepid water in a large bowl, gradually adding texture to it so that the mixture gets thicker over a period of weeks. Adding flour or cornflour—or, if there are no contraindications, soap or aromatherapy bubble bath—can help individual children to begin to enjoy the sensation of water. Many nurseries and schools now have access to Jacuzzis or hydrotherapy pools. If they have the whole-body experience of learning to relax in water with trusted adults, the sensitivity of defensive children to a range of materials will often begin to decrease.

To encourage a child to explore new substances, you can start with dry materials such as rice, pasta and pulses. At first, put them into a favourite fabric bag so that the child feels the rice and so on through it. Then—providing you are confident that he is safe with them—put them on a tray for him to explore and move around, or into an upturned tambourine, thereby adding a sound factor to the activity. Also, you can try putting different soft materials on top of favourite objects, then encourage the child to uncover them. In this way, in order to retrieve a toy, for instance, he will begin to move his fingers over a variety of different textures.

There are many materials that children can learn to touch by grasping or by moving their hands over them—for instance, corrugated cardboard or ribbed paper, string, chains, scarves and towelling. Well sealed bags with marbles inside and lavender bags, and bags that incorporate textures such as Velcro, velvet and silky material with sound-makers or scrunchy paper inside may all prove to be positive experiences. A favourite activity with some small children involves the adult putting different types of material into each leg of a pair of tights, then making a soft cushion out of the top of the tights for the child to rest his head on. He may enjoy lying back and playing with the legs of the filled tights on each side of him.

For some children their first conscious experience of temperature may be that of warm and cold food. Showing the child that cold food comes from the refrigerator or that his hair can be dried with a warm hairdryer provides him with more experience as he matures. Massaging their hands and feet occasionally, perhaps using a small amount of grape-seed oil, may be a pleasurable experience for some children, helping them to learn to relax their hands and feet. When they are more relaxed, it is likely that they will be more ready to touch different materials.

There are many ways in which you can help the child who is defending himself against new activities and experiences. Give him lots of opportunities to practise and consolidate his skills, and move very gently and slowly, and in his time-scale, towards the acquisition of new ones.

SAFETY POINTS

School and nursery personnel don't often massage any part of a child, not even hands and feet, unless there is clear written permission from parents and supervision by a therapist. Nor do they use any creams or lotions on a child without express consent, because some children have skin that is very sensitive or allergic. Note also that for some children massage is contraindicated for health or medical reasons.

Remember never to put the palms of tactile-defensive children directly on to materials or surfaces that they might find offensive, such as glue, sandpaper and any sticky substances that they can't 'get away' from.

LEARNING THROUGH LISTENING

All children need to be aware of the meaning of environmental sounds. Some children, in particular, need their parents or a significant adult to feed back all their spontaneous sounds as soon as they are made so that they know that those sounds are being received. If a child is blind or very severely visually impaired he may not be aware that his sounds have been heard by anyone else. If this happens, he may lose the desire to make more sounds, thus becoming less likely to communicate via the two-way turn-taking process involved in all such interactions.

Children need to be aware of a sequence, or pattern, to their sound-making:

1   Mary babbles and makes a sound.
2   Her parents repeat the sound to Mary.
3   Mary makes the sound again.
4   Her parents repeat the sound to Mary again.

and so on. Consolidation and turn-taking games such as this will help Mary to make more sense of her playful sounds.

After a while, Mary begins to realise that, just as her parents can imitate her, she can imitate them. Although she is not conscious of it, this is the beginning of her knowledge that communication is a two-way process. If Mary is encouraged to realise that her parents and other involved adults respond to her when she 'speaks', then she is much more likely to repeat the activity in other environments. Familiar adults will continue to interact with her in this two-way activity, and her skill will be extended when they play two-way games involving sound and sound-makers. Mary will soon begin to learn that she can share interesting sound-making activities, for instance, by using switches that she can press or turn or by listening to and taking turns on a musical instrument such as a drum.

She will by then be ready to become more receptive to environmental sounds. She will gradually appreciate that everyday sounds such as a door opening, a bell ringing, a car passing by in the street can all be interpreted—that sounds have meaning. Even laughter may have absolutely no meaning to a child such as Mary unless she hears it over and over again or until she has matured enough to be able to show that she appreciates that people laugh, cry, sing and make a variety of other sounds too. Interpreting environmental sounds will be something that Mary may continue to do throughout her life, whenever she is in new and unfamiliar environments, such as a railway station, a farm, an airport and so on.

Mary may need to learn to search for sound makers. Some children, when they drop something, feel that the object has gone completely. If Mary is encouraged to listen out for the toy that she has dropped, she can be helped, *coactively* (see page 107), to practise searching and scanning with her hands or feet until she finds it again. Using our knowledge of individual children is always important: we need to be aware that some will use their feet and legs to search, in the same way that a sighted child will use his hands. For a given individual, at a particular stage, this may be a valid and useful skill. Later, he may use more sophisticated searching techniques.

Cause-and-effect toys such as musical boxes, Jack-in-the-boxes, switch-operated toys and many battery-operated sound-making ones are very useful when it comes to showing a child that he can make sounds happen. Some toys have an inbuilt vibration that gives him an extra incentive to learn to manipulate. Remember that those children who, as well as having a severe visual impairment, also have a severe hearing loss, will enjoy toys that have the additional quality of vibration.

EXPRESSING AND RECEIVING—A TWO-WAY PROCESS

If we want to ensure that the child's world continues to make sense to him, we have to bear in mind that his means of communication may change as he grows and develops. The adults involved with him need to work together to make sure that, in all circumstances, he is in his most favourable 'communicating environment'.

When Frances was young, words were spoken and signed with her because she needed additional information. She was blind and had glue ear, and so she functioned like a child with a dual sensory impairment. Words were spoken on to her hand, so that she could get the idea of where the sounds that she could only hear indistinctly were coming from. Had she been sighted, she would have been able to follow some conversation by lip-reading.

Frances is now a teenager, and she can hear well because her intermittent conductive hearing loss, caused by the glue ear, has been successfully treated. But she has learning difficulties, which means that even though she is now able to hear, she still needs to be given extra explanation as well as more time to assimilate information.

Frances' mother has developed alongside her daughter, and so their communication methods have developed and altered too, in an interactive partnership. She knows that she must share Frances' real-life experiences with her. 'Just talking' about activities does not necessarily communicate anything to Frances. Listening and being receptive to the child's needs, interpreting her body language, are all vital. She knows that Frances' state of health, her environment, whether or not her hearing is affected by a cold or by background noise, whether or not her attention is caught by the moment, will affect the way Frances speaks to her and the way she speaks to Frances. Her mother will mirror and match her needs. When she says 'Good morning, Frances. How are you?', she will *listen*, watch and be aware. When Frances replies 'Fine', or 'Tired', or 'Happy', or 'Excited', or 'Feeling much better'—in other words when she responds appropriately—she does so because she has been *heard*, accepted and understood enough times by a responsive adult.

When deciding how they are going to plan for a child's communication needs, people sometimes forget that receiving signals, words and gestures is only part of the story. The variety of ways the child may have of expressing himself also has to be considered. Equally important, but also often forgotten, is the fact that language demands a natural setting, spontaneity and interest on both sides. The child needs to know that the adult is really interacting with him, is really interested in him, and that the communication between them is a natural part of their life together.

THE IMPORTANCE OF ROUTINE

Frances' mother has worked out a very useful strategy with her, which enables Frances to plan real choices for herself and build them into her day.

Structuring routines that are right for the child and for the family enables choices to be made. Frances' day always starts the night before! Every night when bedtime approaches, she is happy to follow certain planned routines that include getting ready for bed, going into the sitting-room for a chat, a record, a story or even a snooze, then finally going to her bedroom. Before going to sleep she always decides what she is going to have for breakfast the next morning—the range is wide, and her choice is always respected. It is interesting to note that she has evolved this routine together with her mother from a small incident that happened a couple of years ago. One morning she went into the kitchen for breakfast and asked for an egg sandwich. Her mother, who is a working, single person with very little time in the morning, explained that it takes time to boil an egg and prepare a sandwich, and that if she wanted an egg sandwich in the morning she must remember to say so the night before. Ever since then, perhaps as a private insurance policy, Frances has always ensured that her mother knows what is to be on the menu the following day!

REAL-LIFE EXPERIENCES

Frances knows that at the weekends, when they are together as a family, there will be different types of meal experiences: hot dishes, sandwiches, take-aways, meals with and without starters, puddings—an exciting and varied selection of food—as well, perhaps, as different places to eat in such as restaurants and cafés. Frances is able to go anywhere for a meal because she understands that there is a range of options open to her. She is able to differentiate and anticipate what will be on the menu in different restaurants. She knows that an Italian restaurant is likely to mean pasta and all the exciting pasta sauces, and that at an Indian restaurant she can have spicy hot food, if she wants to. Why is this so important? The answer is to do with choice-making, participation and ensuring that Frances has a reality base for her life.

Everyone who is not disabled participates on his or her own terms and in his or her own way, throughout life. Sometimes children with disabilities, especially children such as Frances who are totally blind and who have learning difficulties, cannot make choices, cannot understand the options open to everyone else, because they themselves have not been able to do things in a real hands-on way. The less a child does, the less she is able to participate in the process of choice-making and communicating her decisions. As a result of her rich, varied and concrete experiences, Frances is not in this predicament.

In summary, these are the important points:

- By looking at real-life experiences and structuring some approaches towards further learning, we can introduce into our children's everyday activities, in a natural way, opportunities for real choice.
- Whether or not they have disabilities, all children have the same social, emotional and developmental needs.
- All children function at their best when they have the opportunity to learn through their own experiences within an ordered, realistic and meaningful environment.
- Our children share our lives, and we need to respect their needs so that they can make sense not only of their world but of the world at large.
- Children's communication strategies may change—the adults involved with them need to adapt as they move from one stage of development to another.
- Encourage your child to make choices, to adapt, and to work towards independence. When it happens, be ready—for anything and everything!

5 Movement

Children differ radically from one another—each is unique. When a child's sight and hearing disabilities are further compounded by physical disabilities, the role of parents and professionals alike is especially challenging. They need to work together to devise appropriate individual programmes, with realistic goals, with a view to helping the child to reach his appropriate developmental milestones.

Judith Peters, paediatric physiotherapist, writes:

Helping a young child to learn to move and to want to explore his environment because it seems a good and exciting place must be an enjoyable experience for both child and parent. This cannot be overemphasised. As parents, teachers and physiotherapists, united under the umbrella title of 'developmental therapists', our aim is to work as a team through the medium of structured play, in cooperation and with mutual exchange of ideas, in order to help the child achieve his potential.

It is as well to remind ourselves that, in our children with sensory impairment, movement occurs in response to sensory input to the body. Sensory messages are received via the muscle–joint receptors, and this is an area often overlooked; if you close your eyes, then lift your arm up to shoulder level and bend your elbow to a right angle, you are able to do it accurately because every tiniest tension within your muscles and tendons is relayed to your brain. A child must experience movement and the feel of varying positions to learn about his body and how to move with smooth coordination.

It is vital to assess accurately a child's stage of development. The equivalent stages may not be attained simultaneously in areas of motor, language and social achievement, and it can be confusing to know a child's chronological age while observing motor development that may be only at the level of a tiny baby. However, if this is the level at which the child functions, he must build from this stage, for to miss out the foundation stones of development would only lead to insecure body control.

At birth, babies exhibit reflex asymmetrical, jerky movements. As the nervous system matures the movements become smoother, symmetrical and purposeful. Head balance and a degree of trunk control precede the ability to sit. Being able to put arms out to save oneself from falling must develop before standing or walking can be achieved. At the earliest stage, symmetry and experience of a variety of positions are encouraged. Prone (tummy) lying is of particular importance for stimulating head control and stability of the shoulder girdle. Side lying is vital to help the hands come together, where they are able to explore in midline. Head-turning leads on to the beginnings of rolling, which is the great trunk-strengthening activity.

As the trunk and neck muscles come under control and strengthen, the scene is set for gaining sitting balance. This may need to be helped by the support of a suitable chair— frequently required by children with hearing and visual impairment. The very experience of the upright posture stimulates increased muscle power and places eyes and ears in an optimum position for receiving signals. Learning to support the body continues, needing much practice and encouragement until, as the rising-to-stand reactions appear, the child is able to explore the standing posture.

As with the problems to do with sitting, the child with visual impairment may be unmotivated to pull himself to a standing position. I often use the fun experience of being stood up (with support) as a stimulus for the child himself to want to 'have a go'. The pressures occurring within muscles and joints, and on the soles of the feet when we stand, are quite different from those we experience while

lying down. These stretches and pressures—or propriocep-
tive sensations—are in themselves a stimulus to maintain
standing. For this reason I frequently place a child in a
standing-frame and ask teacher colleagues to think up a
really enjoyable activity for him while the standing session
is in progress. The standing experience, like every other part
of therapy, must be a happy one.

Many of the children I see have either muscles that are
too tense (hypertonic, or spastic) or muscles that are lacking
normal tension (hypotonic, or floppy). It is important for all
members of the developmental therapy team to understand
the reason for these variations in tone, and the special ways
of handling the children. Special footwear may be needed
and, certainly, watching for correct foot and leg positioning
during play, sleep, carrying, feeding and dressing is
essential.

Finally, physical development takes time and maturity.
The ladder towards full motor control is similar for all children, but for some the speed at which the rungs are climbed
may be slower. Progress will be faster at some times than
others, and the plateau periods can seem long. If on some
days you have less time to work at therapy, or there are
moments when you, or your child, feel less inclined to work,
remember that an off day may well be a pause in preparation
for a spurt forwards at another time.

Movement skills for a child who has multisensory impairments
may be built on touch. He may often need whole-body cues—
involving things that impinge on his body—in order to participate
fully in, to make full use of, the things we offer him to play with.
Few young children with visual impairments are motivated to
move forwards. They may have little or no knowledge of what
their bodies can do in space. Some children more readily achieve
positive movement and mobility if they are encouraged to use
whole-body movements, which help them to become aware of
their own bodies in space. Where this seems appropriate, it will be
part of their individual programme. Sometimes, using equipment,
such as a large physiotherapy ball—with a therapist's advice—to

encourage a child to move and to 'lose balance' may help. Holding him safely and firmly, place him in a comfortable position on top of a large physiotherapy ball. Then move him gently forward over the ball, so that he begins to move towards the floor, still on the ball. Using a fun activity like this, he can begin to gather information about himself and about his ability to move and balance.

Before engaging in many gross motor activities, it is important to establish trust and a good relationship with the child. He needs to know that the adult will not let him down, that she is 'safe' and is going to share with him activities that they will both enjoy. This approach invariably encourages the child to explore more. He trusts the adult, and knows that his environment is stable. Some children often learn best when they are in close physical contact with an adult, and for these children it may, for some time, be the only way they can learn effectively.

Sharing movement with an adult, coactively, may be a vital step towards developing trusting relationships. *Coactive movement*, as it is sometimes called, is an invaluable teaching technique that can add an extra dimension of meaning to potentially confusing activities. For some children, progress in movement and mobility depends on just this kind of close physical contact. The child whose difficulties are compounded by reduced sight and hearing may need the additional information provided by the adult's body moving closely alongside his. Thus a stable relationship plus coactive movement may make all the difference to the child's progress in this field. Movement and mobility, in turn, can lead to exploratory behaviour.

In all of this, trust, touch and shared whole-body movements are the vital ingredients. Once he realises that the world is stable, that adults are useful, reliable and fun to be with, the child can allow himself to be drawn into enjoying other experiences.

Young children with visual impairment are unable to model themselves on adults or copy other children, and those who do not automatically reach out to the environment may need to be physically directed towards the most effective ways of gathering information. It is important to take time to show such children how to do things, using coactive, hand-on-wrist movements. From behind or from the side, you can guide the child to use both his hands in a purposeful way while maintaining close physical contact. As he begins to master a skill, you can gradually reduce the amount of physical direction you give him.

If a child dislikes the experience of touching new things, he is likely to be reluctant to explore all the objects that he discovers within his environment. He may be less likely to feel motivated to move towards them. New tactile experiences can be made gradually more acceptable to him if you start by introducing him to things in small spaces. If you can get him interested in exploring one particular small space, you may have achieved the first step towards interesting him in objects and activities within that space. From the exploration of one small space, as described in Chapter 4, he can be encouraged to move on to the next small space and beyond. All children need to be motivated to explore their environment. Many children with multisensory impairments need adults to help them move out into space, and will often use an adult's presence and touch, over long periods, to increase their knowledge of safe, familiar areas.

Exploring is fun!
All children need to know that every journey has a purpose and that it is fun to achieve an end goal.

The child who is deafblind can use different body parts in order to gather information about a new room and build up a picture of it. So as to encourage further exploration, tactile cues can be provided. Tactile cues may act as indicators for certain activities in the room, and above all they should be fun for the child to explore. For example, you can put chime bells on a door handle, so that when the child reaches it and encounters the bells he receives an interesting 'touch reward' as well as—if he has some residual hearing—a sound reward. Like any kind of indicator, tactile cues need to be very carefully thought out, otherwise they may be of more meaning to you than to your child. Is it a good idea, for instance, to stick towelling on to the bathroom door if he doesn't like being dried after his bath? This raises another important point, mentioned earlier: the cue must have pleasurable—or at least acceptable—associations for him. Will

Learning to explore his own environment.

he actually get information from the cue, such as the chime bells, that will help him to move on past the door?

Consider everything from the child's point of view, so that he gains as much information as possible from the cues you devise. In this way you will help him to master his surroundings.

As children gain confidence in mastering the skill of exploration, support of this sort can gradually be withdrawn. Many have useful residual vision, but they may still need to use touch or sound cues to reinforce the information they are receiving. They will need to explore the objects they discover in the room, to pick them up and mouth them or finger them or move their hands over them, just as the sighted child would explore them visually.

When a sighted child enters a strange room he may glance, look, search. When a child with visual impairment encounters objects within his environment he may move his hands slightly (the equivalent of glancing), finger or mouth (look) or slowly scan with his hands (search). These actions constitute skills that need to be encouraged and given time to develop. As well as using their fingers and mouths, some children use their heads or other body parts to explore the objects they find in a room. Usually this exploratory style is valid, but we have to guard against it developing into an activity that distracts them from exploring further. All children who are deafblind need time to gather the information that will permit them to discover the whole of the room as well as parts of it. Without an interest in touch, a child may be hindered in his ability to move about in all environments. So foster his interest in touch whenever you can.

INTENSIVE INTERACTION

Intensive interaction is often used to help a child form a warm, trusting relationship with an adult. One of its aims is to enable him to learn that the adult will join in his activity, reproducing it with him, responding to the pattern that he establishes. In this partnership activity, the adult carefully watches the child's movements before joining in with them. It may involve swinging, swaying, singing and movements of hands and body—whatever happens to be the child's preferred activity at that moment. *Mirroring and matching* his movements gives him an opportunity to understand that they have meaning—not just for himself but for the adult involved. This is a tried and tested good-parenting technique: by observing which movements the child prefers to make, then doing them with him, the adult encourages him to practise and extend his skills further.

No child learns in isolation. One of the important aspects of helping him to learn through intensive interaction is to give him the confidence to be adventurous in his movements, to recognise that the environment is a safe place to explore. Having been encouraged to move in unison with an adult with whom he feels secure, he may well be willing to do so again, at a later date.

Before you embark on intensive interaction, check that:

1 *you know the child*, and which skills you want him to achieve
2 *you have identified his abilities*, in order to help him to master more skills
3 *you have looked at his needs*, with a view to meeting them within the intensive-interaction activities
4 *you have observed him*, with a view to ascertaining what special features he will enjoy within an intensive-interaction situation. For instance, if he is a very quiet child he will probably not enjoy loud sounds; if he is extremely active, he may respond to strong rhythms and songs.

Through intensive interaction, he will increase both his bodily awareness of himself and his awareness of those committed adults who are prepared to replicate his body movements; he will be drawn towards those adults, and will be willing to imitate and eventually to initiate activities himself.

Many children who are deafblind have a very poor body image. One of the aims of an intensive session could be to promote an awareness of where, say, the child's hands, head, feet, arms and legs are, and of the different ways he can move them. When he has shared this activity with you, he will probably be willing to imitate other movements. It cannot be overemphasised that this kind of imitation will be much more likely to happen if the child has a useful, trusting relationship with you. Intensive interaction is an ideal way of achieving this.

It is often possible to devise activities that will help children to manoeuvre their heads and bodies into different positions, giving them a feeling of freedom within movement. As well as strong rhythms, songs that echo and match their natural movements will be of help in this respect. Songs about rocking, smiling, shaking, moving backwards and forwards can all be incorporated into the intensive session. When he has learnt to trust an adult, a child will allow himself to be moved up or down in space, and will be ready to reach out and to move his hands and body into different positions. When he realises that movement is an enjoyable experience, he can begin to learn about how his body moves through the environment.

Intensive interaction with an adult is one means of helping a child to gain the confidence to move his body, limbs and hands, and to learn that the objects and places he locates have meaning. When he has gained that confidence, he may continue to need to be motivated to move his body forward, sideways, backwards and so on. He may need extra help in order to absorb environmental information, to recognise clues and to explore further.

GROSS MOTOR SKILLS

Without movement a child will be unable to take individual steps, to explore the world; and he may not move unless he is given an incentive to do so. It is quite usual for a young child with severe visual impairment to prefer to lie passively, often on his back. If he has additional disabilities, then his incentive to move will be further reduced. It is extremely important to ensure that he is encouraged to experience being in different positions as soon as he is physically able. With the advice of a physiotherapist or occupational therapist, and obtaining a chair that will give him support so that he can experience the upright position, can encourage enjoyment of sitting.

Many children who are blind do not crawl. They may progress instead by rolling, squirming or bottom-shuffling. Once a child has learnt to stand and walk forward, he may feel safe enough and have a good enough mental map of his environment to crawl. When he crawls, he is in danger of banging his head on the furniture, which may be one reason why children with severe visual impairment sometimes prefer to sit and shuffle. Another reason for children remaining in a sitting position is that some have floppy muscles (hypotonia), and may not feel safe when they slightly lose their balance in a forward motion. (Many children who are hypotonic bottom-shuffle.) Another reason for sitting may be, subconsciously, to maintain a safe, wide base.

Our incentive to move is often dictated by visually attractive objects or people that we see and want to get nearer to. By placing a child who can perceive light quite near a light source, such as a garden door, you can help him to grasp, for instance, that if he moves towards the light source—the door—it will lead him towards his swing.

Gathering information about the children in their care who have multisensory impairment enables parents and professionals alike to provide for their movement and mobility plans, taking account of each skill area. Before a child's individual programme can be planned, you need answers to questions such as:

—does he have light perception?
—does he prefer certain colours?
—is he aware of certain sounds?
—is he able to locate sound?
—does he have people preferences?
—does he have activity preferences?
—does he have tactile interest?
—does he have movement interest?
—does he have muscle differences (floppiness or stiffness)?
—does he appear to be alert and aware?

This information will help you to help him to achieve maximum benefit from the movement and mobility plan that you devise for him. Some children with a visual impairment, particularly if they are totally blind, occasionally walk backwards rather than forwards. The checklist above may provide a basis from which to help such children to move around.

Some deafblind children stand and hold on to furniture, or cruise around holding on, for much longer periods than their sighted hearing peers. This is within their normal range of behaviour and should not be hurried through. Sometimes adults are anxious for a child to cross open spaces, without having stopped to consider whether, if they could not see, they would be willing to do so themselves. The best way to appreciate the child's situation is to try crossing the space yourself, wearing a blindfold. Then, if it is clear that the gap between the furniture, or from the swing to the slide, is too great, you can think up ways of adapting the route. For example, will a non-slip rug between the furniture help? Will a wind chime help the child to recognise the fact that he is approaching the swing?

Some children when learning to go upstairs, need to be allowed to make their way up on all fours for a longer time than those without disabilities. The visually impaired child needs plenty of time to feel and appreciate the depth and height of the stairs before being encouraged to stand and hold the banister rail. When coming down the stairs, he may need adult assistance for a very long time before he feels, and is, completely safe. Some children are able to walk down the last step but take quite a long time before they can descend the whole flight of stairs independently. (Always check that the banister rail goes completely to the bottom of the stairs, otherwise the child may 'launch into space'.)

Some are able to explore a familiar room with no difficulties, but those who have additional physical disabilities will be unable to do so unless they are helped, coactively. Children affected by cerebral palsy, of which there are different forms, fall into this category. The child with spasticity, for instance, has disordered control of movement and tends to be stiff, often needing physiotherapy to help to relax and move his limbs in the best way for him. Another kind of cerebral palsy, athetosis, causes frequent involuntary movements that interfere with the normal movements of the whole body. Ataxia, a third type, causes the child to have an unsteady gait and/or difficulty with balance. Some children with cerebral palsy also have perception difficulties, and their problems may be compounded by a distorted sense of touch, rendering them unable to distinguish the important tactile features of objects with any clarity. If a child with cerebral palsy has a visual problem such as cortical visual impairment, his ability to move around and explore his environment will be further limited unless he is given consistent, coordinated, careful help.

Many children with cerebral palsy receive advice and therapy from a paediatric physiotherapist or occupational therapist. Parents, teachers, therapists and advisers need to coordinate plans so as to ensure that the child has the same opportunities for exploration as his more mobile peers. His environment will need to be structured, so as to give him every opportunity to understand where he is at all times. If he uses a wheelchair, it needs to be explained to him every time he is moved from one part of the room to another, or to places outside the room—to the cloakroom, the toilet, the playground, or any other part of the school or home.

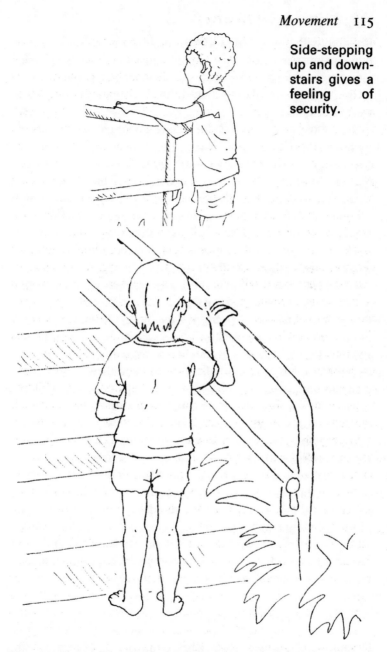

Side-stepping up and down-stairs gives a feeling of security.

The child with visual impairment needs plenty of time before being encouraged to stand when going upstairs.

Children with physical disabilities combined with severe sensory impairments need more time, more explanation, and more opportunity to explore for themselves if they are to get the most out of life, and to play their part fully in the life of their school as well as at home.

Trying to govern the way we behave to our children by always 'putting ourselves in their place' gives us as good a chance as any of getting it right. If we were them, we would ensure that people always spoke to us clearly, that they always explained where we were and what we were about to do. We would certainly try to ensure that we knew in which room we were sitting. We would prefer our chairs to be the right size, neither too small nor too large, and that our feet were in the right, comfortable, position when we were sitting on them.

In the classroom and at home, some children who are visually impaired should be able to take their shoes and socks off, unless this is contraindicated, because they can gain valuable tactual information through their feet. They can get clues about textures and temperature changes as they move from one part of the floor to another, thereby adding a little bit more to their knowledge of their environment.

The child with physical disabilities should have his position changed as often as his more mobile peers whenever possible. When playing, he should sometimes stand, sometimes sit and sometimes lie on the floor. Unless his physical need demands it, he should not sit in a wheelchair all day. With children who do have to use wheelchairs all day, always consult the physiotherapist and occupational therapist about opportunities for changing their position. The child in a wheelchair will need help to explore a room, and if he feels safe and secure, he will do so with confidence—but remember that if he has an additional, visual impairment he may need to be supervised and protected from danger.

CIRCUIT WORK

Circuit work can best be described as an enjoyable way of using movements to achieve a goal, and it helps many children towards greater mobility. It consists of a series of movements or activities that start with a signal, or marker, and stop with another signal or marker. It is important that the child realise that there is always the same start and the same finish to the chosen activity or activities, and always a movement reward at the end. The marker might be a certain chair, bench or stool on which he sits to start the activity, and to which he returns at the end of it, sitting there with the adult for a few moments before starting something else. Movement activities such as lying on a large physiotherapy ball and using a series of planned movements while on it, climbing over frames, using rockers or trampolines—and any other equipment that the particular child enjoys—are all part of circuit work. Circuits use a variety of skills and activities, and are structured so as to give scope for the maximum amount of movement and exercise, accompanied by fun and a sense of achievement when the circuit is completed. Here are two different circuits, each tailored to the needs and preferences of the individual child:

1   This child starts with a coactive activity on the exercise mat, and is then helped to move from the mat to a physiotherapy ball, and from there to the final destination, a vibrating cushion—his reward for having accomplished the first two activities. (This activity has been planned to help him to appreciate the 'feeling' of movement.)

2   The other child starts by sitting on a chair, then moves slowly along a bench, stepping from there through the rungs of a ladder, which is strategically placed so as to lead him to the trampoline—his favoured activity, and his ultimate goal and reward combined. This particular circuit has been designed to help him to move carefully from one place to another.

FINE MOTOR SKILLS

Just as practising gross motor activities helps the child by giving him more mobility and movement, so practising fine motor activities helps him to become as independent as possible in performing everyday tasks. Fine motor skills are essential if he is going to manage to feed and dress himself, for instance, with any degree of competence. In order to assess what he should be concentrating

Reaching for an object.

on next, you need to observe his hands and the actions he is able to perform with them. For example:

—what movements does he make with his hands?
—how does he hold objects?
—how does he transfer objects?
—is he aware that he can hold and pull?
—is he able to hold and turn an object?
—can he move forwards or sideways to retrieve objects?
—does he have equal strength in both hands, or is one hand stronger than the other?
—how does he use his vision and hearing?

MOTOR COORDINATION AND SELF-FEEDING

As well as fine motor skills, self-feeding calls for other skills such as postural and motor control, touch, vision and hearing. The child's posture is important, because he needs to feel comfortable throughout the meal. He should have his feet supported, and his ankles, knees and hips should be in the most comfortable position—usually, bent at right angles. If he is sitting comfortably and confidently, he will be able to give his full attention to feeding. The dish needs to be well within his reach and, of course, within his field of residual vision.

How does he hold objects?

How does he transfer objects?

Once he is sitting with his trunk well supported, with his arms free and his hands in the best position, he can be guided. The sequence of skills involved in self-feeding is common to all children, but those with a dual sensory impairment will develop at a different pace, and the steps that come naturally to some children usually need to be taught. Probably, a child's first experience of spoon-feeding will be having the food put into his mouth. Usually he will participate in the process by opening his mouth, although this can be delayed for a variety of reasons. For instance, he may not have had a 'good' experience of feeding. This is particularly the case with children who have physical disabilities. You may find that if you stand behind or beside the child, you will be in a position to hold his hand over the spoon, guiding it from his plate to his mouth. You may also need to help him to load the spoon. As soon as it is obvious that he is able to manage without physical prompting, withdraw your help—but gradually, proceeding from hand over hand, to hand over wrist, to hand over elbow, until it is not needed at all.

As already noted, the child's ability to self-feed is closely related to tactile experiences in general and to motor skills. If he is unable to pick up small objects from a container and transfer them to another, it is unlikely that he will become completely independent in feeding until this skill has been achieved. Analysing the skills necessary for self-feeding will help you to decide what route the child needs to take in order to be able to do it. You can then incorporate the relevant skills into his other activities. Picking up objects from a container, for instance, leads to picking up food from a dish; lifting and holding a drumstick can give him the ability to gasp; grasping a spoon to convey food to the mouth is part of the continuum of necessary skills.

Note that children who are severely visually impaired particularly need the opportunity to finger-feed, and for longer than usual, before learning to use a spoon and fork.

Note also that it is essential to ask for guidance from a speech and language therapist skilled in the acquisition of feeding techniques if the child has chewing or swallowing difficulties.

MOTOR COORDINATION AND COMMUNICATION

No skill should be considered in isolation. Fine motor skills, as we have seen, are linked with other skill areas—no activity takes place without movement. For example, when considering a child's ability to communicate using sign, we have to take account of his hand function and motor coordination, as well as his postural control, vision and hearing and his understanding of situations. He will be more able, for instance, to use sign successfully if he is able to make fine motor movements. Any vision he has will affect the way he uses his fine motor skills. If you look carefully at those skills in particular, checking and noting how he uses his hands and fingers, and record it all in an objective way, you will be able to draw on that knowledge to help him to develop his skills further. Then, once you know what he can do, you can plan appropriate activities that will help him to achieve the next goal.

Zoe, Colin, Robert, Gillian and Joseph are children who need different types of activity to help them achieve fine motor and gross motor skills.

ZOË

Zoë is a young child who is deafblind. She has light perception, but she is profoundly deaf and unable to hear anything other than an extremely loud noise when she is wearing hearing aids. She has a chromosomal condition resulting in hypotonia, and is unable to stand alone unsupported. She enjoys using her hands to explore things, and is tactually aware of her surroundings.

Motor activities that adults can do with Zoë

Zoë's tactile awareness is well developed. Her tactual memory and her use of her hands to explore any object she is given show a very good degree of coordination. Her deafblindness impedes her independent movement skills more than would a single sensory impairment. She is keenly interested in texture, so this interest and her tactile activities determine the plans that are made for her acquisition of more motor skills:

1 Put Zoë on a large bouncy ball and, having let her explore it with her hands, encourage her to move from side to side and then drop forwards, to give her the feeling of moving, balancing and saving herself with her hands.

2 Her parents can put her over their legs, on her front, with her arms in front of her on the floor, so that she will learn to use both arms and legs as a possible means of movement. While she is on her front, she can be helped (coactively) to stretch forward in order to reach a vibrating toy.

3 Move her arms and legs rhythmically, then roll her vigorously from side to side, back to side and front to side. The adult should wait for her body signals before restarting the movement.

4 Zoë can be helped to become aware of her feet and legs, in the same way that she is aware of her hands and arms, by having her feet and legs gently moved across different surfaces.

5 Put Zoë's feet flat on the floor in front of her table, and then gradually move her upwards from the floor so that she gets the feeling of rising in order to stand and play at the table. When she is secure in this position, she can be helped to work towards moving down from standing to sitting.

6 Zoë needs to be helped towards an awareness of her extremities in space. She knows that she has hands, but does not appear to know that she can use her feet to explore. She needs to spend some time each day learning that she can move her feet as well as her hands, both up and down and side to side, and that her feet can receive tactile information.

7 Help Zoë to reach for favoured toys on the floor and to learn to search for them, so that she gradually begins to realise that her toys exist when she is not touching them.

8 Give her a bag with an unusual texture, to be used only for a searching activity. One or two favourite toys can be put inside it, and she can be helped coactively to feel in the bag and retrieve the toys. She should soon learn to search for them by herself.

9 Help Zoe to place things in a deliberate way, in a place that she will be able to remember. At the moment, as she does not have the distance senses of vision and hearing, when

things are out of reach she probably feels that they have disappeared. She can neither see nor hear that they still exist. She should be encouraged to put things down and then pick them up from the same place—she can have a distinctive box or other container for this activity. Discriminating between when an object is there and accessible, and when it is there but out of reach, and when it has gone, will gradually follow. If she is encouraged to put things down deliberately making the table or box vibrate slightly, she is likely to become more aware of their position. When her favourite toy or cup is removed completely, she should always be encouraged to feel it go and then coactively sign 'Gone'.

10 To encourage her to recognise that different toys can be handled in different ways, they should be brought very slowly towards her. As she begins to realise that objects come into her touching range, she should then internalise the fact that they are constant. When she has achieved the skill of using and playing with toys that are in front of her, and reaching for her cup and spoon in front of her, she can be led towards expecting objects to 'arrive' from different angles—from the right, from the left, and so on.

COLIN

Colin has cortical visual impairment—which means that he has very limited use of his vision—and a severe hearing loss. He has hypotonic muscles, and he will not tolerate having his body moved in any position. He is only happy when he is lying on his back on the floor, and he resists all new experiences. Colin needs to experience a variety of enjoyable positions so that he can learn to participate in many more activities involving movement. His limited movement experience determines the approach to his individual programme.

Motor activities that adults can do with Colin

Everyday activities such as dressing and bathing offer opportunities for gradually introducing him to the idea that he can lie safely across an adult's knee, face down, as part of the dressing process:

1   Stimulating Colin's head and leg extension can become fun if the action of holding him under his tummy is accompanied by rhythmic singing games.

2   Encourage him to move his hands slightly by putting one of his favourite soft musical blocks just at the limit of his reach. Taking advantage of the fact that he is engrossed in listening out for the sound, his parent (or whoever is with him) can encourage him to push the block without Colin being fearful of the slight change of position that this will entail.

3   Stimulate him to push with his feet by introducing him to many bouncing games on an adult's knee.

4   Give him the experience of being tilted and then saved from falling by supporting him at the hips and moving him very slightly on the adult's knee, slowly at first and then more adventurously.

5   Give him experience of sitting by encouraging him to sit up in a warm bath with the water up to his hips. The adult gives him maximum support so that he is not frightened by a sudden splash.

6   Using fun activities, work towards helping Colin to move his hands up and down in the water—but only when he is ready.

As Colin has demonstrated that he is very fearful of movement, only activities that he will quietly enjoy should be offered him, and he should not be hurried through any of them. The keynote of his whole programme should be fun.

ROBERT

Robert is totally blind and hard of hearing. He has good mobility skills. He loves movements and revels in rough-and-tumble play. His confidence is expressed in his gait, which is smooth and well balanced. He shows few of the walking adaptations sometimes thought of as characteristic of children with severe visual impairment: a wide-based gait, hands up in the air, rocking movements when moving forwards and when stationary, or feet kept close together with a guarded shuffling movement, hands outstretched.

Robert enjoys exploring. He avoids colliding with head-high obstacles probably by using some echolocation as well as skilled sweeping hand movements. He enjoys free movement, and trampolining, swings and slides in particular. He has good use of his fine motor skills, and is happy to investigate new objects, using touch. He coordinates his hands in constructive exploration of both objects and the environment. He is beginning to recognise the distinctive tactile characteristics of objects.

Robert is using his residual hearing for mobility purposes. He listens out for quiet sound-making objects, in either high or low frequencies, and locates them accurately, using either hand. He is alert to sound in the environment, and 'stills' to concentrate when any new sound is present. He quite obviously hears the rustle of a crisp packet, even when engrossed in something he enjoys! He recognises many words, including his name and the names of family members, and the voices of other familiar adults. Robert's active curiosity coupled with his interest in sounds makes him ready to associate words with objects. He is able to rediscover distinctive locations in a room by means of sound clues.

Motor activities that adults can do with Robert

Robert is keen to discover and explore the possibilities of known environments. In a room where furniture and landmarks remain *constant* he has learnt how to orientate. He listens out for constant sound clues such as the ticking clock in the sitting-room and the humming of the refrigerator in the kitchen. Robert's interest and his use of movement and mobility skills can be extended in numerous ways:

1   Help him to learn directional concepts such as up/down, in/ out by introducing them through action games. While playing these games, he can also learn the names for the different parts of his body, and then be encouraged, for example, to put his hand up, then down, and so on.
2   Assist Robert to understand that every object he comes across and every sound he hears has a name by ensuring that an adult gives him this kind of information whenever it is appropriate to do so (but without being overintrusive—everyone needs time to themselves and a little consolidation space).

3   Give Robert names for all the things he does, in clear and concrete terms, so that he recognises action words such as 'walking', 'jumping' and 'climbing'.

4   Give him even more opportunity to explore the range of his body movements. He loves jumping and bouncing—the kind of interests that can lead on to learning to roll, climb and swim. The more movement he experiences now, the more confidently he will move in the future.

5   Extend Robert's interest in movement further by using his auditory skills—for example, encourage him to move towards a well positioned sound-maker. This will stimulate his interest in exploring his environment even more.

6   Increase his understanding of how different rooms link up with each other. Listening with him for sounds in rooms other than the kitchen and sitting-room should be fun: the flush of the toilet, the sound of the water flowing into the bath, the ring of the front door bell are all sounds that he will enjoy identifying.

GILLIAN

Gillian has a profound hearing loss, and she is totally blind in the right eye and has tunnel vision in her left. Her motor development is delayed; she sometimes walks on tiptoe and often shows that she does not enjoy activities where she is liable to go slightly off balance, such as when she is turning.

Motor activities that adults can do with Gillian

Gillian can be encouraged to improve her motor development by use of a circuit (see page 116), in which she will learn to complete a series of essential physical skills in a fun way:

1   Help Gillian to learn that movement is rewarding. Start her circuit by sitting her on a chair and encouraging her to hold a hoop with an adult. The adult will move the hoop in a side-to-side motion, and a tape of Gillian's favourite, loud, pop music can be played to accompany the movement of the hoop.

2   Help Gillian to learn to right herself when she is off balance

Gillian's circuit.

by placing her safely on a rocking-horse, slowly moving it backwards and forwards in a regular rhythm. Ensure that Gillian feels safe at all times; because of her limited use of vision and hearing she must never feel that she has been left in an insecure position on the horse.

3   To show Gillian that she can safely move forward, introduce her to a play barrel. At first she will hold on to it, but when she gains confidence she can be shown coactively how to gradually and carefully move the barrel forward, sometimes going forwards on tiptoe and then gradually putting her feet flat on the floor as she moves back.

4   To give Gillian fun in free movement, the last part of her circuit is for free play. After being assisted on to the trampoline, give her at least three to five minutes when she can use different movements of her own choice on the trampoline.

5   To increase her confidence in all the movement activities that make up the circuit, present these at the same time in the same order at least three times a week, so that she begins to anticipate—and to look forward to—the end activity, the trampoline.

Doing things is fun

Children are more likely to achieve motor skills successfully if we do all we can to ensure that their muscle tone is as good as it can be. They will be helped to achieve this by coordinated programmes devised by physiotherapists in conjunction with teachers and parents. They need to understand that movement is for a purpose, and that most of the movement they are encouraged to learn will help them to achieve skills. Some self-help skills that are 'adult led', such as eating, washing, toileting and dressing, may be of less or more interest to a child than play activities. The skill to be learnt and the method by which it is learnt should be governed by his interests, whatever they may be.

If a child is interested in eating he is likely to learn early on how to finger-feed and hold a spoon. If he is interested in outdoor activities, he is likely to learn how to put on his coat, socks and shoes. If he likes having a bath, he is likely to be happy to learn how to walk upstairs to the bathroom. If he likes playing with

Coactive movement to achieve a goal.

particular toys, those toys can be used as an extra incentive to move towards favourite activities. And if he is sociable, people he likes can be recruited to give him lots of fun by participating with him coactively in movement activities.

The fun element usually does the trick for most children—injecting fun into difficult tasks is certainly one of the best ways of encouraging them to learn and perform everyday skills. Fun is especially relevant for children with impaired hearing and vision when it comes to the question of acquiring self-help skills. Taking as individual an approach as possible—one that encompasses the child's particular needs—is equally important: his programme should be designed to fit him, to take account of all his skill areas, as well as his past experience and the scope he has for participation.

DOING THINGS INDEPENDENTLY

Joseph is a totally blind teenager, who has learning disabilities. When he is based at home, he can get on to buses with a sighted guide and use the underground and trains, and can tell a taxi driver where he wants to go. But when he is living at his residential school he is taken everywhere by minibus! How can he gain some sense of the larger environment if he is led everywhere? Joseph needs to participate regularly in everyday activities that include shopping expeditions, exciting concerts, coping with crowded buses and trains, getting wet and cold on a stormy day—so that real experiences impinge on him and so that he really understands situations that everyone else is familiar with. Not being able 'just' to glance down the street to see whether his bus is on its way, not having access to information through television, videos, books, films and computers, teenagers such as Joseph need much more hands-on experience. In fact, they need compensatory experiences that will help them to continue to access the environment.

Second-hand information is not acceptable—and neither are spurious choices which dictate to the individual and limit his options. If we ever hear ourselves asking a young person 'Do you want orange juice or blackcurrant juice?' we should stop in our tracks. Joseph's parents would first say: 'Joseph, *do you want a drink*?' They know, as does Joseph, that real choices are available from a range of drinks, and one choice open to him is not having a drink at all. Joseph needs to know that if his choice is not available on the spot, then there are shops that sell a wide variety of drinks. He needs to know, too, that a lot of drinks can be bought during the weekly trip to the supermarket—a hands-on experience that he will not get to grips with unless he regularly does it himself. Being whisked everywhere in a minibus, often without even being told where he is going, does not help students like Joseph to gain an understanding of their environment.

Joseph finds shopping with his parents enjoyable and fun. Expeditions may include going to record shops to buy CDs or cassettes, going to pay bills, or going to the furniture store to buy a new bed. Shopping with the family is a shared learning experience for Joseph. It is not easy taking a teenager who is totally blind out shopping on a Saturday afternoon just before Christmas. It is not easy taking anyone out shopping. It is not easy—but it can be done.

When Joseph was first taken shopping, the only word to describe the experience, for everyone, was 'nightmare'. At the entrance to all shops, but particularly any shop selling meat, he would scream. Noticing and avoiding the butcher's shop became an art in itself. Spotting when their child is *likely to cry* in the toyshop is a skill that many parents will know all about! Planning the expedition *step by step, little by little*, and knowing exactly what you are going for and where, can go a long way towards solving this type of problem. And always remember to do things at the individual child's pace, whatever the situation—this way, success is much more likely.

One strategy that proved successful with Joseph was to select one shop that he could go into with a parent, for one item—perhaps a vest for Joseph, or a CD. The next part of the plan was to go to two shops, one shop for Joseph and one for his parent. Gradually getting to know different shops, such as chemists, sweet shops and bookshops, allowed him to absorb their different atmospheres, smells and activities. After a while, he understood that shops are constant entities, that they have their routines just as houses and schools do, that they offer things to buy that are useful and that can be taken home. Joseph then began to understand that shops are there for everyone, and this knowledge contributed to his greater enjoyment and experience. He knows what to expect in particular shops and he can look forward to going to them.

His experience of shops has led Joseph into other areas—restaurants and cafés, theatres, concert halls, airports, parks—which all have a life and an atmosphere of their own and which, through his first-hand experience of them, he can understand and explore, within the limits of his own interest.

The range of skills and abilities of children who are deafblind, their mobility and access to their surrounding environment depend not only on physical skills and opportunity, but also on the age of onset of their impairments. Their level of vision and hearing plays as large a role in their ability to receive and follow instructions as does their cognitive ability to understand and remember routes to different places.

Some children will certainly progress to full independence, whereas those whose additional physical disabilities necessitate the use of a wheelchair may remain completely reliant on others. Some, with minimal support from classroom or learning assistants, will be able to participate fully in mainstream life; others will need almost constant one-to-one support from an adult to assist them in every aspect of their daily lives. Five children who illustrate this diversity are described below:

GEORGE

Now in his late teens, George is studying for his GCSEs in a mainstream comprehensive school, with support from an attached unit for students with hearing impairment. He has Usher syndrome and is profoundly deaf, but until the onset of retinitis pigmentosa, causing gradual loss of sight, his mobility around the whole school and the surrounding neighbourhood was excellent. Now, however, he has difficulty in adjusting to changes in light level and is having problems in moving from room to room and from the corridor into the hall. George knows that his vision is likely to deteriorate further, meaning that he will have to adapt to different levels of mobility skills He receives regular advice from a rehabilitation officer and a teacher for the visually impaired. Since he has excellent communication skills he is able to discuss his needs with the rehabilitation officer who is teaching him some strategies for coping with these personal changes.

LUKE

As a young child Luke could both see and hear. Now, however, at the age of ten, he has experienced almost total loss of vision and has a severe hearing loss. At his mainstream primary school he attends an attached unit for students with visual impairment and also receives ongoing advice from a teacher for the hearing impaired. Luke used to see and hear, and he retains sufficient memory of the school layout to enable him to find his way safely about the classrooms and grounds, but new places have to be learnt and new routes memorised with the help of a mobility officer. In order to travel in safety outside the school grounds he will have to learn to use a long cane, and he will need considerable support when he moves to his new comprehensive school where every classroom and the entire geography of the building will be new to him. Wherever he goes, he will not only have to learn the way there, but the way back. It will take the combined efforts of Luke, staff and other students to help him acquire all the knowledge he will need in his new, larger surroundings.

JENNIFER

Jennifer has CHARGE association with a consequent severe visual impairment and moderate hearing loss. In the classroom her mobility is good, and all the children in her mainstream junior school know that they must keep school bags and other obstacles off the floor as Jennifer cannot see them. They also know that when they leave the classroom they must all push their chairs under the tables and never leave the door half open, but either fully ajar or closed, so that Jennifer can find her way in and out. Outside, corners and steps are highlighted with yellow markers so that Jennifer can recognise these landmarks and negotiate them safely. Her problems arise in the gymnasium, where she has difficulty running around with other children racing past her, and in the swimming pool where, without the aid of glasses or her radio aid, she cannot see or hear the swimming instructor. It is at these times that she needs one-to-one support from a learning support assistant to ensure that she continues to be fully able to join in lessons using movement.

CLARE

Visually impaired from birth, Clare does have perception of light, but although she can hear, she is unable to fully process sounds and words. This auditory dysfunction is compounded by the fact that she has hypotonic muscles, a curving spine, lack of spatial awareness and very little interest in her surroundings. She has always preferred to sit and she lacks the motivation to move that would help her to understand more about its possibilities. She needs to make more effort and learn for herself more about what she and her body can do, which is why her parents and teachers are using a Resonance Board with her every day (see p. 263 for instructions on how to make and use one).

These boards are amazingly versatile: they can help children learn the principles of cause and effect, about movement and exploration. Most of all, they can give the child a feeling of control as she lies on the board with objects placed nearby, within hearing, touching or visual range. When she touches an object or toy it will make a louder than normal noise as it resonates on the raised board, which will often encourage and motivate her to repeat her actions. This will give her the sense of excitement, anticipation and control that she would not feel if she were making the same movement on the floor. Having gained a sense of mastery of movement, she may go on repeating her actions on the board, which can promote feelings of *intention* to move, *intention* to explore, *intention* to interact with her surroundings. Further uses for the Resonance Board will be found on p. 164.

ANGUS

Like Clare, Angus has been blind from birth, but unlike her he lacks the advantage of light perception, being totally blind. He has a mild hearing loss which, combined with his blindness, makes it difficult for him to understand and explore his environment. He can only move around the house and school quite slowly, but he is much quicker outside as he has learnt to walk and run with a sighted guide. The guide gives him much-needed exercise and fun, and he can enjoy his surroundings in a way that would be impossible without this essential assistance. He grips the guide's elbow, or occasionally links arms with her, and although this puts her slightly in front of him, he feels that he is in control. The guide has to remember to tell Angus when they are approaching obstacles or hazards such as steps. She must also indicate any fixed landmarks along the way, not only to make the walk more interesting, but to help him remember them for himself the next time they go that way. Sighted guides are, of course, essential for children who use wheelchairs. It is their responsibility to help the children do and understand things for themselves, just as Angus's guide helps him to move about safely and confidently.

STEPS TO INDEPENDENCE

Going out on expeditions together may involve working with some of the following guidelines:

- Establish the person's preferred method of communication with you beforehand.
- Take account of balance, ensuring that the person is comfortably linked with you using their preferred method—gripping your elbow, arm or completely linked arm-in-arm—whatever suits the person best.
- Walk at the preferred speed and on the preferred side of the person.
- Decide together how you will cope with doors opening outwards or inwards, going up and downstairs, walking in small or crowded spaces—safety is paramount.
- Consult the person and a rehabilitation officer (sometimes called a mobility officer), for expert guidance if in doubt. Boarding buses, trains, underground trains, escalators and moving walkways can be hazardous—know *how* to do these before undertaking them.

6 Communication

From everyday experiences the child soon learns that he can manipulate his environment. By smiling at his mother and father and making eager welcoming movements as they come near him, he learns that he is giving them pleasure. He enjoys babbling, and they are delighted when he manages an approximation to sounds that *they* want to hear—'mum-mum', 'dad-dad', 'gan-gan'. His parents interpret his babbling sounds to him, and those sounds are reinforced by their obvious pleasure at hearing them, and they soon become recognisable as 'speech'. The more sounds he makes and the more they are reinforced back to him, the more he babbles and 'speaks'. It is clear that by the age of twelve months a lot of children understand some words, and by eighteen months they are often able to recognise and use more than twenty. The means whereby they have learnt to speak has been that of reinforcement; what they have done at first in a reflex way has been received and rewarded by the adult or adults with whom they interact. It has usually been a one-to-one situation, in which they have practised and reinforced the two-way turn-taking process over and over again in a pleasurable way.

A TWO-WAY ACTIVITY

The same learning processes apply to the child who is deafblind as to sighted–hearing children. When he makes his first movements or sounds, these need to be reinforced and interpreted—for instance, the parent reinforces the sounds 'mum-mum' and 'dad-dad' through sound, and if possible through an identifying movement, gesture or other clue. Whenever the child makes attempts to communicate, people need to notice, interact and reinforce. It is when he experiences individual interaction with an understanding adult that he will begin to expect things to happen. He will be more interactive himself, more demanding, and will make efforts to get the adult to understand him; he will feel that people are aware of him and his needs.

The absence or presence of what people call 'language' can completely alter their perception of a child's abilities. Children who have severe visual and hearing impairments often have their first attempts at trying to communicate misunderstood or misinterpreted. When their individual, idiosyncratic attempts to communicate are not understood, they are sometimes described as non-communicating! What may then happen is that the 'non-communicating' child is taught standard signs for everyday things such as 'eat', 'drink', 'toilet', 'sit down', 'stand up'. But since, apart from eating and drinking, these signs do not convey anything that he finds fun or meaningful, he may well resist rather than interact. He cannot understand why people are manipulating his hands and arms so as to make him produce—to him— meaningless movements, and he becomes very defensive about being touched.

When his attempts to communicate are not taken up or reinforced, the child may well, and often does, lose interest in anyone other than himself. One difficulty is that he has not learnt that he can make things happen—he doesn't know that he can manipulate the environment, that he can tell people that he needs to eat, to drink and to play. Adults need to be constantly alert to the child's attempts at communication; if they do not help him to order his world, everything will remain chaotic for him, and he may never learn to do anything other than commune with himself.

Communication touches on all aspects of development and cannot be separated from them. No two children develop in the same way or at the same speed; but generally speaking, children whose sight and hearing are intact follow the same sequence of development. The child who is deafblind, on the other hand, is unable to use his distance sense of vision and hearing to receive information, and so it cannot be assumed that he is integrating sensory input and extending the use of his other senses at the usual developmental stages. Everything possible has to be done to ensure that he uses his residual vision and hearing to his best advantage and at his best rate, and that his information-gathering keeps pace with them. His particular abilities and the limitations imposed by his sensory impairments have to be taken account of at all times. No one particular 'programme approach' is going to be suitable for any group of children. They all vary in their ability to use their residual hearing, vision and other senses.

CHILDREN WITH LATER ONSET OF DEAFBLINDNESS (ACQUIRED)

- Children who are born blind or whose sight deteriorates in early childhood may subsequently experience a significant hearing loss. But since these children have heard well in their early years, they may continue to communicate by means of speech—they may be more able to interpret sounds, to give them meaning, than children born deafblind. They may also have skills in writing Braille or Moon (see page 158) that they can continue to use as a means of communication.

- Children who are profoundly deaf from birth or early child-hood may, as with those who have Usher syndrome, begin to lose vision from their late teenage years. As these children have already acquired the use of language (signed or spoken), it is likely that they will continue to use their preferred mode when their vision deteriorates. They may be expected to have a visual memory even after their visual ability has dimin-ished—which is bound to affect the way they assimilate knowledge about the environment and their relationships with people.

- Children who acquire both a serious vision and a serious hearing impairment through accident or illness may learn to use sign or may continue to use speech. Their accident or illness may have caused other physical traumas, but if they can still write and read even though their strategies for using these abilities have had to be modified, they may be able to use augmentative communication (see page 139) and com-puter-assisted technology.

CHILDREN WITH EARLY ONSET OF DEAFBLINDNESS (CONGENITAL)

- Children who are born deafblind may be less able to use their residual vision and hearing because of their inability to interpret some of the sights and sounds that they are receiving. It may take longer for them to achieve the same goals as children who become deafblind after they have acquired language, whether spoken or signed.
- Children who are multisensorily impaired may need different approaches as regards their acquisition and use of communicative strategies, which may depend on their physical skills and their ability to make relationships.

*   *   *

Whatever the methods used to help them to communicate, the children's individual capacity to learn will be modified according to their perceptual skills and the age of onset of their dual sensory impairment as well as their physical abilities. Some methods of working will call for the provision of hearing aids and glasses, while others, as already mentioned, will require adapted switches, augmentative communication strategies and computer-assisted devices. Adapted switches such as a joystick can enable a child with significant physical difficulties to activate equipment like a tape-recorder using a very light touch. Augmentative communication strategies will always include looking at the child's best position, his use of vision, hearing and movement, and using pictures, symbols, sounds, tactile clues or objects which are most accessible to him. Computer-assisted technology will include the use of adapted programmes which can be accessed using touch, vision or sound. In all the strategies used the child's sense of security within a structured situation with known adults will be *the* paramount consideration.

The young sighted–hearing child quickly builds up a basic feeling of security. He soon understands that his near senses of smell, touch and taste have meaning. He welcomes kissing, cuddling and rocking and the smell and taste of different food. He is constantly curious about what the world is going to present next.

These experiences are often denied the child who is deafblind because he has limited means of receiving information. He often experiences the stimuli that impinge upon him as extremely frightening, for he has none of the usual warnings that things are about to happen and so is unable to formulate a relationship between himself, other people and his surroundings. Moreover, the child whose distance senses are seriously impaired has little on which to build his own image or that of other people. Because he is unable to organise the various sense impressions that he receives, he fails to discover any structure to them. Often this means that his near senses, too—taste, smell and touch—are subject to distortion for, because he becomes fearful of the lack of warning, he may guard his body against being approached. Unable to understand any of the messages that his parents or other adults have been trying to send him, he may retreat from new experiences. The focus of his behaviour may then centre on his own body, thus limiting his experiences even further.

Amongst the strategies that are often successful with children born deafblind, or who have a single sensory impairment and other significant disabilities, are intensive play (intensive interaction), coactive movement, and the total communication approach. Some children need, in particular, to learn about relationships, and these strategies can help them towards this goal.

INTENSIVE PLAY/INTERACTION

Early child–adult relationships depend to a large extent on interactions. They are the basis for a great deal of learning. If a child has hitherto lacked interaction with an adult, intensive-play activities may go a long way towards compensating for this lack. The child needs to be given another, more expansive and more positive, message about his body, about his actions and about his place within the world. The normally developing child has a natural predisposition towards wanting to understand how his actions will affect the world and the people that he meets; the adult, instinctively, capitalises on these interests. Our knowledge about interactions and communications tell us that the needs of children with multisensory impairments are the same as those of sighted–hearing children.

We join the child in his movements. We help him to understand that through his actions we accept him. We want the child to know that we accept him, and that we acknowledge his movements. We want him to know that he can be joined in his movement patterns. We want to help him to understand that we have time and space to build up our knowledge of him within the play situation. This is sometimes called intensive play or intensive interaction—it uses movements that are familiar to the child, that are *his* movements. These movements are often comforting to him. They can be rocking, swaying, waving—anything that is within his repertoire.

We use the child's movements to help him to realise that *it is he who is in control*. He needs to initiate movement. We follow him. After many regular sessions within the intensive-play situation, many opportunities will evolve for him to come to the realisation that the actions that he does can be copied. When that moment of realisation happens, we follow up the opportunity to

—copy the child
—pause
—copy him
—pause.

—to see if he can also copy us. Does he realise that he needs to do something such as copy or make a body movement in order to restart the game?

In the first six months of life, a child experiences extremely close interaction with one person for most of the time. Finding opportunities at this stage for one-to-one interaction with our deafblind children, and following their developmental sequences, give them, too, the opportunity to learn through close physical contact. Parents of sighted–hearing children gain pleasure in rocking, holding and interacting with them. Similarly, when you are working with a young child who is deafblind you need to convey to him that interaction—intensive play—is pleasurable.

Rocking can lead to side swaying.

You must be as open and as full of fun as *any* parent is with her child. By participating in his movements, you are helping him to understand that you accept him, that he has a reference point for his activities, that it is much more fun to join someone else in an activity than to do it alone. For instance, within the intensive play session, rocking can lead to side-swaying, to being moved backwards, to reaching upwards and outwards. The goal is to help the self-stimulating, self-absorbed, self-occupied child to become a child who is able to interact with others in a meaningful way.

Through intensive-play activities, you are aiming to establish with the child that you are receiving his messages and movements, which should be modified or extended according to his interests and his learning rate. The child gradually becomes involved in the interaction and begins to anticipate restarting a movement after a pause. He may give some minute body indications during the session, which can be interpreted as signals to restart. He may indicate in a variety of ways that he has enjoyed what he has been doing—perhaps by moving his limbs, bouncing on his bottom, pushing you or taking your hands. It is important that this stage is recognised and that the child is encouraged through your response to use interactive movement to effect change in the activity. Within this intensive play, you must be alert and ready for any attempts on his part to signal a desire for such a change, and to treat this signal as communication. Pause sometimes to provide an opportunity for him to communicate his feelings and needs, and watch for any indication that he wishes to continue or stop an activity. Continue if he shows through his actions that he enjoys the activity, but never continue if he shows distress. You need to be aware that it is you who are the provider of information as far as he is concerned. Be prepared to receive his messages about his feelings. Adapt and adjust according to his interest and his emotional level.

Here is a checklist that should be of help when you use intensive-play methods:

- Have I carefully observed the child's behaviour?
- Have I responded to *his* responses?
- Have I looked at him as a source of information?
- Have I given him a constant picture, or a distorted, incomplete picture, about myself?
- Have I provided him with a basis for security, so that he knows what is about to happen next within the intensive-play situation?
- Have I given an order to the intensive play?
- Have I been consistent within the intensive-play situation?
- Have I given a pattern to the actions we engage in that he can always anticipate?
- Have I established routines that he can understand and messages that I know he is willing to receive?
- Have I aimed to help him understand that I am willing to receive his messages?

A child cannot be expected just to 'receive messages' in the form of sign, just to receive signed commands that he is supposed to follow. Establishing a trusting one-to-one relationship with him, helping him to understand that he has an identity that is respected, is the way forward in establishing a communicative environment.

Each child needs to be helped to know that he has a particular quality that makes him unique, different from other people. Each child does have something special, of real meaning, that is his alone. He has many activities or routines that he enjoys. Within the intensive play he expects you to communicate with him through his body movements, which may gradually become modifications of his original ones. The main aspect of intensive play is the fact that the child is interacting with an adult who is alert to his signals and his body messages and responsive to him and his rhythms.

COACTIVE MOVEMENT AND IMITATION

When the child has shown that he understands that you are capable of receiving his messages you should lead him towards imitation, and this can be done through the use of coactive movements (see page 107). As mentioned earlier, coactive movement occurs when the child is willing to have physical contact with the adult: he follows her movements, using his hands to touch and monitor her action. Intensive play activities set the stage for these interactions to occur.

The child needs to know that it is worthwhile imitating the adult's movements. He will have every incentive to reproduce movements, including gestures and signs, which allow him to manipulate and order his environment. Child-centred activity words such as 'play', 'eat', 'drink', 'jump' represent activities that he wants to participate in. His ability to focus on signs that represent actions which are fun for him will be far greater than his ability to focus on commands such as 'sit down', 'wait', 'toilet'. Learning signs such as these, that are essentially for the adult's needs, not his, is an activity that is far less likely to achieve its aim because it contains little incentive for him.

Intensive play leads the child towards being able to form personal relationships with a caring adult. The coactive method of working helps him to interact with people and to imitate them, and it may later on help him to begin to copy sounds that adult and child make in a two-way game.

THE TOTAL COMMUNICATION APPROACH

Sometimes, where it is the policy of a school or further education institution to use a variety of communication modes, the total communication approach may be adopted. This method can include the use of speech, writing, finger-spelling, manual signs, natural gestures, pictures, reference objects (STAR objects, see page 94), models, symbols and line drawings. Some children may use several different means of communication in the course of a single conversation—speaking, signing, gestures, all within the same sentence. It's worth remembering that when a sighted–hearing child speaks it is rare for him or her not to include some natural gestures to aid understanding or to emphasise a point.

When the child's preferred methods have been established, account must be taken of environmental factors such as lighting, background noise and the time of day, so that as far as possible all interactions take place in the child's optimum conditions.

Optimum conditions include the provision of a structure for his learning environment. This helps to generate anticipation in the child, the first crucial stage in creating a situation in which two-way communication can happen. This can be achieved, for instance, by repeating a series of movements, before the planned activity happens, that are significant to him. Children are able to understand situations well before they are able to express clearly that they have understood. A system of anticipatory motor, tactile or other signals can be started at an early age.

Before introducing a tactile information system, we need to look at the whole child and his ability to participate in certain activities. For example, if we would like him to know that it is time for swimming, we can:

—say 'John, it's time to go swimming'
  and/or
—sign 'Swimming now, John'
  and/or
—show him an object, such as a swimming-costume
  and/or

—show him a picture, such as the swimming-pool
   and/or
—give the child a written word card saying 'swimming'.

Which of these we choose depends on our knowledge of the child's needs, with particular emphasis on any residual vision and/or hearing, and his abilities in all skill areas.

BUILDING RELATIONSHIPS

Building up a warm and trusting emotional bond through intensive play activities and coactive participation is the goal. Such a bond does not develop accidentally or immediately, and needs to be planned for by parents and co-workers. If it does not develop, everyone involved may become discouraged and find it difficult to make the effort to continue. The cycle of interaction with the child requires time, effort and sensitivity, and he will need to be carefully observed before it can be decided where his starting-point should be. There are three main areas of observation:

1   observation of general child developmental skills
2   observation of the child's individual skills
3   observation of the adult who is undertaking the interaction.

   Observing the child within his developmental sequence and seeing what he is already achieving leads to an awareness of the areas where he needs help in interpreting and in communicating his needs, as well as an awareness of *how* you can help him. Once you have done this, you are in a position to decide what activities or communication modes might best suit him. Situations must be set up that will stimulate him to interact with the adults he meets, to help him solve his problems and establish relationships.
   For any child, if communication is to be meaningful it needs to be a part of all his waking hours. It is pointless for the school *or* the home to use any 'system' without the awareness and cooperation of the other people in the child's life. If we look at

the developing child, we see that communication does not stem from his parents or his teachers exclusively. Communication is happening at different levels, all the time, with all the people he encounters. Everyone, formally or informally gives him experiences of communication. Only very slow progress will be made if he experiences some communication modes from a restricted number of people, at certain times only. Everyone involved in his life must be prepared to learn his means of communication, so that he can understand, absorb information and respond meaningfully at all times. Above all, he must understand that the adults around him are capable of understanding his messages.

It is vital never to lose sight of the fact that all children are unique as individuals, with their unique place in society, to which they bring their own talents and abilities. However few responses some children may appear to be capable of—perhaps no more than body language—those responses must be seen and celebrated as their own individual communication modes, capable of being identified and used in a positive way.

BODY LANGUAGE

Some children have no clear communication method. But observing a child carefully over time, looking for subtle movements of his face or body, may indicate that he has an awareness of activity. These face and body movements are sometimes called the pre-intentional stage of communication. It is possible to interpret quite subtle body-language movements. Setting up a way of interpreting them helps adults to help the child understand what activities he is being offered.

Sometimes, in order to be quite clear about the meaning of a child's body language, the adults involved compile a *communication book*, in which they record all his face and body movements and their careful interpretations of them. The communication book belongs to the child. It is his way of showing adults how he communicates, it contains important information about him, including photographs of him doing things, and it is written as though it is he who is speaking, thus:

Page 1

Hello, my name is Steven. This book is about me. It will
help you to get to know me.

Page 2

I am six years old. I have an older sister called Maisie. My
mum is called Felicity. My dad is called John. My dog is
called Patch and he barks a lot, which makes me laugh.

Page 3

Facts about me—I can see the difference between light and
dark. I can hear some loud sounds when I am wearing my
hearing aids. I need to wear my hearing aids but I often pull
them out. When you are not looking I hide them in my
mouth or on the floor close by. Sometimes I have fits, which
make my limbs twitch for a few minutes.

Page 4

Things I like—You will be amazed to see how many things
I like. I like lots of things to touch. These things can be
soft, furry, rough or smooth. I like to chew my fingers and
mouth my toys. I like to listen to musical tapes, especially
those with lots of percussion instruments. I like to relax in
the hydro pool. I like to play in the 'white room' and 'soft
room' and roll around on the big white cushions. I like short
sessions in the dark room. I put my head up when the
overhead lights go on. I can track the lights up and down
and side to side. I like going into the garden. I like to feel
the wind and breeze in my face. I open my mouth and smile.
Sometimes the wind takes my breath away. When I am
happy I smile, laugh, giggle, hum, vocalise, bob up and
down in my chair. When I am out of my chair I explore my
surroundings using my hands, and I kneel up and move
around a lot across my space.

Page 5

Things I do not like—I hate it when people do things to me
without warning me first. Please sign with me, then give
me as many tactile clues as you can. My body signs [the
signs used with me] and STAR objects [see page 94] are in

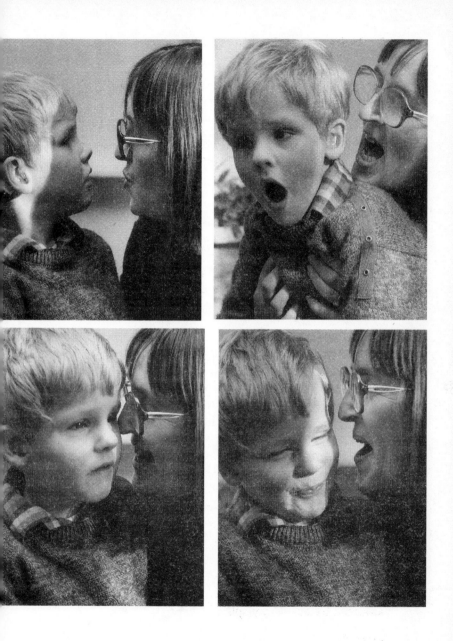

The child and adult need to establish a warm bond
between them . . .

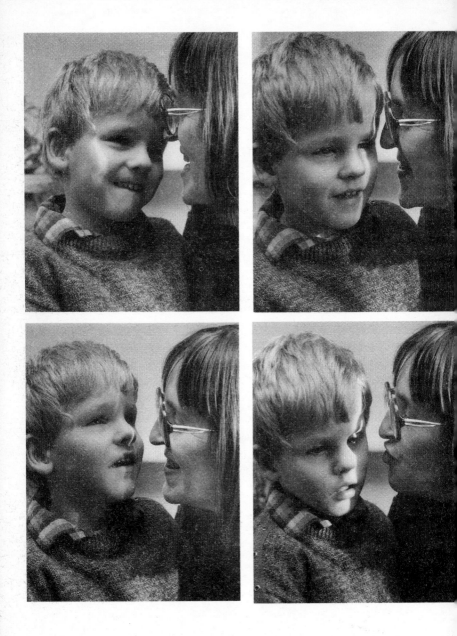

At first the adult will respond to the child's attempts to communicate informally . . .

... and then the child can be expected to start to respond to the adult communication formally.

this book. I do not like having my face washed after dinner. I do not like having my hands messy with glue, paint and cornflour-type activities. My hands touch lots of things to help me to see them, so I don't like having them covered in messy stuff. I do not like having my hearing aids put in. Please warn me first by stroking the aid down the side of my ear, and then pop it in quickly without too much fuss. When I am unhappy I look upset and pout. I grumble and cry. I throw my head and arms back. When I am unsure of people or objects, I hold my elbow up and hide my face.

Page 6
If I am upset, sometimes giving me a change of activity and some space helps. Talk to me, stroke my hands and give me a towelling cloth or a soft piece of material, as sometimes I find this comforting. Take me away from activities for a short time and leave me alone for a minute or two, then I am often ready to start activities again. Sometimes I like you to talk and sing to me into my ear, or you can pat and stroke my back and shoulders.

Page 7
Food and drink—I drink from a cup which is held for me, but occasionally I will hold it, depending on how thirsty I am. Please don't put too much drink in my cup. I would rather have two small drinks than one large one. I like to drink hot milk. I like mango juice at room temperature. I love dinner time and enjoy all savoury dishes. I can eat food that is cut up into small pieces. I like to taste individual flavours so *do not* mix my food together. I like gravy if my food is dry. Give me time to chew and swallow my food (I'm like you—I do not like to have more food in my mouth until I have finished the mouthful). I do not eat cheese, eggs or bananas.

Page 8
Other things that you might like to know about me—My chair is called a Leckey chair. My stander is called a prone stander. My hearing aids need to be checked before you put them on to make sure they are clean and the batteries are

working. My favourite toys are always in my bag. There is a picture book in my bag of all the toys that I enjoy playing with. Many of my favourite toys include those with sound and vibration but I also love exploring different materials, so give me lots of time to explore these.

My book is all about me. I hope that you have enjoyed reading it. My intervenor, Helen, has written it. We both hope it has helped you to get to know me better.

Communication books need to be made with a ring binder, because they will change and be updated as the child's skills change. Usually at the end of each term, the book should be reviewed. Parents and co-workers need to add any significant changes straight away, by removing old pages and inserting new ones. It is best to date the pages so that it can be seen at a glance when the child achieved a certain skill, and to save the old pages in another ring binder. Some people record information such as facts about the child's medical condition, with particular reference to essential medication, and others record more details about self-help skills such as dressing and toileting. Whatever is written, everything is recorded in the first person, from the child's point of view.

WHICH COMMUNICATION SYSTEMS?

Before decisions can be made about the communication modes or systems to be adopted for a specific deafblind child, we need to know which children benefit from particular methods. For any child unable to participate in two-way oral communication, signs may help to consolidate the spoken word. In this way we can help him interpret the information he is being given in a more meaningful and pleasurable way. There is no evidence that the use of sign restricts a child's use of speech. On the contrary, there is evidence that many children understand more speech if it is accompanied by gesture, sign or other means of explanation and reinforcement—such as, for a child with residual vision, the use of pictures, objects or photographs.

Helping the child who is born deafblind towards a recognisable communication system is important if he is to be as independent and fully functioning as possible. Our efforts should be concentrated on understanding the structured environment that needs to be put in place in order for that to happen. The child may use or be encouraged to use different communication methods throughout his life, or at different stages of his development. Some children will always use more than one method. If a child is not speaking, or if he cannot use sign for physical reasons, STAR objects may be used, as we have seen, to give him an indication that certain activities are about to occur. The important thing is that whatever means of communication is used is the child's preferred mode and accessible to him.

A system that everyone can use
Whatever the communication mode we introduce, we do not necessarily restrict our 'language' to that which the child understands. We may sometimes simplify, and place emphasis on important words. But we recognise the need to provide a communicating environment from which the child can draw information not only about individual objects or activities, but about the whole process of social interaction. If we were to use a restricted system where a more universal one might be possible, we would be treating deafblind children totally differently from the way we treat children in other situations. We should expect them to follow the standard stages of development as far as they are able, and we should expect to help them to learn to communicate in recognisable ways, as far as they can. Establishing two-way interactive communication is the province of everyone wishing to be with the child, and its key must be a system to which everyone has easy access.

'BABBLING'

Before children learn to speak, they invariably babble. Sometimes the same sort of babbling behaviour can be expected from the child who is deafblind. If he has been learning signs, he may indeed appear to 'babble', using more hand movements than might usually be expected. It could be that he is beginning to be more aware of his hands and fingers—an interesting development that the alert adult should be watchful for. Accept any approximation to signing that he may produce, and reinforce it by repeating his 'babble' back to him. Welcome all his attempts to make himself understood.

Sometimes people search hard and long for the 'right' signs to use with a child. There are no child development principles I know that would tell the parents of a seeing and hearing child what *words* to say to him. Why should the same not apply in the case of the child who is deafblind? The first words or signs for any child must be those that the parents and the child use in everyday situations. Remember that, as noted earlier, no child can be expected to want to learn command signs—he will have to *understand* what such signs mean, but he will not be expected to *use* them until much later. In this context it is amusing to note the words/signs listed in a particular school as 'appropriate' for a young child who is deafblind to learn: 'please, thank you, toilet, hearing aid, glasses, good morning, stop, sit down, school, wait'. The words/signs which the child would prefer and should be encouraged to use are more likely to be: 'play, eat, more, ball, walk, jump, I want, yes, put on, take off, Mummy, Daddy, love, good, up'. The first words/signs introduced to the child must have meaning for him.

When adults begin to sign with a child, they may often prefer to use whole phrases, because we speak in whole phrases and not in isolated words. 'I want to play', 'Take off my coat', 'Love Mummy', 'Put on my coat and go out', 'Daddy swing me'—are all phrases that a young child can be expected to enjoy using. It follows that the young child who is deafblind might well use much the same phrases in everyday situations. One variation on the way some children are taught is that, whereas signing is always additional to speech, sometimes coactive movements may be added to the procedure. Even with children who can see signs as long as we use their specific visual frame, it may on occasion be appropriate to physically show them a sign as well. If a child is unable to utilise lip-reading and uses signing as his main means of expressive communication, coactive movements will give him the *feeling* of how signs are formed.

If the child is very young, he can sit on an adult's knee and have his hands moved through signing positions while he sits there. As he grows older the parent or teacher can position herself at his side when he is seated on his chair and sign coactively with him. Coactive signing is another means towards independence for the young child, and a means of helping him to manipulate his environment through independent communication. We have to be aware of the paramount importance of hand function and of his need to interact with other people before employing coactive signing methods. He should encounter natural opportunities for communicating through signs throughout his day. These are some of the British Sign Language signs that have been successfully introduced coactively:

eat	pat one hand onto mouth
drink	put imaginary cup to mouth
ball	make two-handed outline of a ball
walk	walk two fingers along outstretched palm
jump	jump two fingers up and down on outstretched palm
I	point index finger onto chest
bath/wash	make washing movement onto body
put on	pull imaginary coat onto the shoulders, using two hands
take off	take off imaginary coat from the shoulders, using two hands
Mummy	tap first three fingers twice on outstretched opposite palm
Daddy	tap first two fingers on top of first two fingers
love	make hugging movement
good	thumb up
stop	two outstretched hands palm down in a quick downward movement
want	open right hand stroked downwards onto left side of chest

It may be necessary to sign with the child coactively until he demonstrates by his behaviour that he can use a particular sign in context or that he can initiate an activity through his own use of the sign. Once he has demonstrated that he knows how to form a sign and that he is willing to sign, he will no longer need to be shown that particular sign's movement pattern. You have to be watchful in your use of coactive signing so as to guard against over-helping the child or over-anticipating what it is he is trying to convey.

Some standard systems

In some schools, different children use a number of communication modes, including:

British Sign Language (BSL) The natural language of the Deaf community, with its own grammar and structure. It has no ties with spoken English, no simultaneity of delivery.

signed English More of a teaching tool than a sign 'language'. It takes a BSL sign for each spoken word and is delivered simultaneously.

sign-supported English Uses a BSL sign for each of the significant elements of each English sentence spoken.

Makaton Has a restricted vocabulary taken from British Sign Language. No grammar is included within this system.

finger-spelling The alphabet is represented by the positions of the fingers, using both hands; this system is used to complement a signing system—for names and places, or to supplement understanding if there is confusion about a sign. It is not a signing system in itself.

deafblind manual alphabet A tactile communication method that 'writes' the finger-spelling alphabet on to the receiver's hand.

clear speech and lip-reading Can be used by children who are hearing-aid users if they are able to see the speaker. This method is often dependent on having a quiet environment and good lighting.

large print Uses large print on good-quality white or yellow paper and thick felt-tip pens with good contrast. Some students can read large print using CCTV systems. Some children can write using thick pens, while others are unable to write but may be able to read large print.

Braille and Moon   These two are tactile means of writing, dependent on the child having good enough sensitivity in his fingers to be able to read back his work. Some children can use Braille and Moon to write, while others read it only.

Tadoma   A method that involves feeling the lip shapes and vibrations of the speaker's throat as he speaks.

USING NAMES

Many children do not have a clear sense of their own name and may need to have it reinforced. Some parents and teachers finger-spell, or use an initial letter to identify themselves and the child. With children who are deafblind, every opportunity should be taken to identify the other people within their environment. It is essential for their understanding of the people, objects, places and activities with which they come into contact that they are encouraged to enquire about names. A curiosity about everything and everyone needs to be fostered, which will stand them in good stead throughout their lives.

Knowing the names of almost everything we see and hear is something that we take for granted. The child needs to be given knowledge all the time about where he is, who is with him, what he is holding, what he is doing, why he is expected to do it, and so on. Naming and identifying for the child's sake is a responsibility that must never be forgotten. The child who is deafblind has to be given far more time to listen, look and feel, more time to absorb information, more time to process that information, more time to practise the skills he is using and more time to consolidate. If this is true of the able child, it is even truer of the child who also has severe learning difficulties. These children need even more input, and may require one-to-one attention throughout the day if they are to maximise their potential.

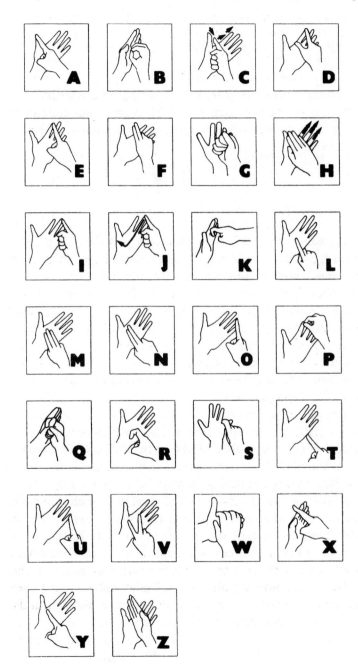

Fingerspelling chart.

Ensure that you:

—name yourself, when meeting a child; do not presume that he
  knows you unless he can speak or sign your name immediately
  he sees, hears, or meets you
—then say hello, and spend time in greeting each other
—then, if you are visiting him for a specific purpose, do the
  activity with him, using his preferred communication method
  all the time
—then always remember to say goodbye
—finally, remind the child when you expect to see him again.

Keep to a *routine* which you know he understands and from
which he will learn. Routines need not be rigid, in fact they are
always better if they have an element of spontaneity or fun. You
will help the child to identify you, and what is going on, if you
always adhere to these guidelines:

  —say your name
  —say hello
  —say where you are
  —say why you are there
  —give good, constant clues, so that the child is kept informed.

Assessing his progress
His general behaviour and his response to your introduction of the
particular communication mode or modes will demonstrate
whether or not you are using the right strategies with him. Check
his communicating abilities regularly, so that you can modify and
adapt as he progresses. There are many useful checklists available
that will help you to assess his progress, such as the one contained in
the Midwest Regional Centre for Services to Deaf-blind Children's
*Manual for the Assessment of a Deaf-blind Multiply Handicapped
Child* which, on the subject of *spontaneous nonverbal communication*, for instance, lists the following pointers:

1 Cries and/or smiles
2 Smiles, vocalises, moves in anticipation or other display of
   expectation of familiar or pleasurable activity

3   Ceases activity in response to introduction of new activity
4   Pushes adult's hand away when wants to retain object, or as reaction to unpleasant thing
5   Places adult hand on object and pushes
6   Hands object to adult and waits expectantly
7   Leads adult to what child wants when it is in close proximity
8   Anticipates on basis of physical situation; definite participating action (example: at juice time child will go to table without being sent)
9   Child leads adult to what child wants in another room.

The *Manual* also lists for checking such areas as *imitation, limb movements, fine hand or finger movements, tactile communication* and *gesturing*.

Obviously, a checklist is only a checklist—a tool for teachers and parents to use to assist them in working towards the further development of the child. Most checklists give types of expressive communication such as non-intentional, intentional, symbolic and formal, and give examples of vocal, gestural, visual (both person-based and externally based) and tactual means of communication. Person-based expressive communication may depend on the child being near a favoured or known adult, whereas externally based expression can happen anywhere in the environment without an adult necessarily being there. Most also give specific examples of the type of expressive communication used by children, as well as guidelines on how to interpret their communicative skills.

One aspect, which is very rarely part of any checklist is *the adult's ability to interact with the child.* We need to be aware all the time, and certainly when using any checklist, that our attitudes to the child, and our involvement and interest in him, will influence his communicative behaviour towards us. It is self-evident that if we are interested in his individual expressiveness, he, in his turn, will be receptive towards our attempts to communicate with him. If all he receives from us is one-word commands—'Sit', 'Wait', 'Stop'—then we should expect to receive the same type of staccato message from him. The aim should be to create fluid exchanges between the two participants—communication, in other words. It is important to bear in mind that the exchange itself can take different forms. For instance, a command may be answered by a statement: 'You are going to sleep now'—'No, I am not'; a question may be answered by a statement: 'Where is my biscuit?'—'In the cupboard'. Any communication between two people should be clear enough for both to be able to identify and recognise the subject and to comprehend the interchange; and it should be of interest to both parties.

Communicational competence takes many years for the child without disabilities to attain, so it is not surprising that it almost inevitably takes even longer if the child has disabilities, and longer still for a child who has severe sensory impairments. Most children have an inbuilt incentive to communicate, and a range of activities and subjects on which to communicate; but in the case of the sensorily impaired child his receptivity may above all depend on the willingness of the adult to respond to his attempts to communicate. Encouragement, reinforcement, paying the closest possible attention, showing a delight in the exchange and a keenness to receive messages—all these things will promote communication. To ensure that we are doing everything possible to build up his language, we should at all times apply what we know about child development—that is that children acquire skills when they are actively engaged.

MESSAGES: GETTING IT RIGHT

When we are communicating with the child, we have to be quite sure that we know what our message is and that as far as possible we give a *full* and non-distorted message to the child. Joseph's mother tells the following story.

Joseph, the teenager we met earlier, who is totally blind, was invited to go on a sailing holiday. A great deal of preparation and discussion went into the holiday, so that he would have a clear idea of what sailing meant. For weeks beforehand he and his mother talked about the sea, which he had visited on several occasions, and they discussed the fact that the boat would sail on the water, over the sea. Joseph spent his first ten minutes on the boat exploring it with his mother, and when he came across a large rope coiled on the deck he felt it and said, 'Can I get up now?' 'Up where?' asked his mother. 'Up on the swing,' he replied. He had been so well prepared for his sailing holiday, but no one had thought to tell him that you find ropes on swings in parks or gardens but also on board boats, and that ropes have many uses.

As Joseph can now speak he is able to convey his needs, but many children who are profoundly deaf with minimal partial sight need even more time to get their messages across. These children, unlike Joseph, may be unable to convey to the adults with whom they come into contact that they are not being given the whole message, or that what they are being told is extremely confusing for them.

Sometimes, we adults manage to get it *completely* wrong:

- When trying to explain to a child that he was wearing pyjamas, the teacher working with him patted his middle and said, 'Pyjamas', expecting him to understand and repeat the word 'pyjamas'. 'What is this?' she then asked, patting his middle again. The child, of course, replied, 'My tummy'.

- At mealtimes, a mother continually cleaned her child's fingers and face while at the same time saying and signing, 'Good food, food is good, eat your food.' If you look at it from the child's viewpoint, you won't be surprised that what he was obviously taking the message to mean was: 'Don't touch, food is bad, food is sticky, food needs clearing up.'

Asking ourselves exactly what message we are conveying and what information the child is receiving, then standing back to observe not only him as the *receiver* of our message but also ourselves as the *conveyor*, will help make us as clear as possible in our exchanges with him.

Is the information we are giving him distorted or incomplete? Have we provided him with a consistent picture? Has he been given enough opportunities for reinforcement? If he doesn't understand what we are saying, what other means are there to help him? Have we looked at our responsibilities as conveyors of messages? Does he trust us enough to know that we will respond to his attempts at communication? Does he know that the situation he is in is controlled and will not suddenly change?

Have we given him time to respond? Have we created a communicative environment that is actively enjoyable and fun?

By observing his behaviour, by responding to his responses, by perceiving the child as the source of our information, we can see what he is understanding, what he is missing and what else he needs—the child is our teacher.

Some very young children, or those with severe physical disabilities, may need extra opportunities to learn that they are in control and that their body movements convey messages. A very useful piece of equipment for some children is the Resonance Board, more details of which are given on p. 263. Observing how a child uses and plays on the board can help to assess how he uses different skills and whether these skills are purposeful and intentional. A way of looking at the Resonance Board is to follow the child's lead and observe his activities:

Use of vision
awareness
searching
fixation
attention
focus

Use of hearing
awareness
location
attention
cause and effect
anticipation

opportunities for intentional activities

Communication
interaction
rhythm
cause and effect
anticipation

**Use of touch,
movement and proprioception**
body awareness
interaction with the environment
cause and effect
anticipation

Careful observation of these skills will indicate his emerging needs.

7 A Structured, Integrated Approach

Children start learning from the moment they are born. Attitudes and opportunities may modify their learning processes, and their conceptual ability will affect their rate of learning. Even so, most parents expect their child to achieve certain goals and will optimise her opportunities to learn, quite naturally and unconsciously, by the things they provide for her to play with and the activities they enjoy together. Parents' perception of their child's learning is largely governed by their own experiences as children and by their views of the child-rearing process, as conveyed to them by their parents, relatives and friends. Some parents attend child development classes and read books about play activities, others carry on as if nothing has changed; but most feel more or less confident of their abilities to provide for their child's needs.

The child with disabilities has the same developmental needs as other children, but the parents' perception of these needs may be affected by the importance that other people attach to her difficulties. They may have been advised that their child must have physiotherapy, and auditory and visual training—terms that they are unfamiliar with or may never have expected to be applied to any child of theirs. The extra information that they may feel they are being suddenly bombarded with may cause them considerable concern. The specialist help their child requires may appear to compartmentalise her, labelling her and her needs. Programmes for the child should take account of the whole child, in the several settings that make up her daily life, and bear in mind that she may find it difficult to transfer her skills from one setting to another.

The whole-child concept embraces the social, emotional and developmental needs of the child. The plans for her future will take account not only of her disabilities, but of her abilities too. Looking at her within child-development guidelines will help her to reach the developmental stages as naturally as possible. She may need different experiences from other children, to help her progress from one milestone to the next. Sometimes her route may diverge slightly, but she will follow the same general path. Parents, the people who usually know most about their child, will play a major role in all the plans for her future, contributing to them and helping to coordinate them with the professionals involved. The child can usually be helped to achieve her own individual developmental goals if all concerned adopt a unified approach to her needs.

LEARNING BY DOING

All children *learn by doing*.

The newborn baby moves his hands in a random fashion and then, as the months pass, he develops the ability to grasp consciously and deliberately for an object. A child with visual impairment can achieve this too, but he needs different rewards and incentives from those of the sighted child. When you watch even a very tiny sighted baby, one of the things that may most strike you about his behaviour will be his determination to achieve a desired object or movement. The child with visual impairment, as well as not being able to see things clearly, if at all, may be further hampered by additional physical conditions and by limited response to other sensory input.

Most children are usually given boundless opportunities for activity, whereas the child with multisensory impairment may be constrained not only by his disabilities, but by outside influences including the ways in which people behave towards him. For example, a mother recently described how her son is being 'taught to sign' in the 'communication room' at his school. Here he is shown an apple and taught to sign 'apple' (note that he is not offered the apple to eat!). That 'instruction' in signing lasts fifteen minutes and is given to him once a week. This is the total communication/language/signing input that he receives—so no wonder that this 'strategy' does not give him any concepts, nor address his need for reality-based learning. He should learn the word 'apple' in context: in the dining-room, in the supermarket, at the greengrocer's, in the orchard, when cooking—anywhere but in a 'communication room'.

THE UNIFIED APPROACH

All children need practice in doing things and the opportunity to learn for themselves, in as everyday setting as possible. In order to make this achievable, it may be necessary to structure the child's day, so as to give it order, realistic content and meaning. By formulating a structure to his daily activities, the unified approach sets up the expectation that in all areas of the National Curriculum his individual needs can be accommodated.

The child's daily activities incorporate his individual plan, and a unified approach is adopted in everything he does. All his needs including those relating to his developing skills such as motor, mobility, auditory, visual, tactile and communication skills, are taken into account. His daily living skills such as feeding, washing, toileting and dressing form part of his individual skills programme. In order to plan his programme, a base-line for his skills in all developmental areas are assessed. Ongoing assessment of his present skills helps to plan for activities that will build on them. If there are gaps in his development that need to be attended to, steps can be taken to provide appropriate activities.

Looking at the way one child's unified programme was planned can give a good idea of how integrated plans may be formulated.

AARON
Aaron is five. He is hypotonic, and at the moment he is unable to move independently. He is totally blind (that is, with no light perception) and partially hearing. He is able to hear some sounds in all frequencies at approximately 40 dB. He lives at home with his mother, father and two sisters, all of whom interact with him at some point after school.

Aaron attends a local school for children with a variety of disabilities. There are no other totally blind children in the school, although there are some who have cortical visual impairment.

When Aaron's daily plan is being formulated, the difference between him and his peers has to be taken into account *all the time*. Everything he needs to learn must be presented to him *differently* from the way things are presented to the sighted children in the class as well as those with cortical visual impairment. Everything Aaron meets, he perceives in a different way from his peers. Good communication between home and school is necessary, in order to help everyone involved to understand more about what Aaron needs. The essential information about him is constantly and regularly updated. This should always be a feature of any child's plan, and in Aaron's case is particularly directed at enabling him to achieve maximum independence both at home and at school. For Aaron's sake, all of the adults involved in his education and care need to maintain an open and trusting dialogue between each other in order to maximise his learning potential. In other words, if everyone works together Aaron should be able to develop lasting, concrete skills in the following areas:

MOTOR DEVELOPMENT

Aaron's postural control and his use of his physical skills call for a structured approach. Realistic motor-development target-setting will take account of his abilities in other skill areas, as well as the fact that he does not have vision to give him an incentive to move. With any child who has very severe visual impairment the incentive to sit unsupported is reduced, and the incentive to pull from sitting to standing, and to stand alone in order to move forward, is similarly affected. The presence of a hearing impairment, however mild, will reduce the stimuli he is able to receive even further. He has hypotonia, so Aaron has even less incentive to sit and stand unsupported. Some of the sounds he hears will have little or no meaning for him and may even seem quite threatening. This may compound his problems and cause negative reaction, leading to him becoming fearful and unwilling to move at all.

Aaron's poor muscle tone needs careful consideration. He can sit alone when placed, but he cannot maintain this posture for very long. He needs assistance and encouragement to sit for longer periods unsupported. He has a suitable chair in which he can sit upright with his hands free to play with toys in front of him on the tray. So that he voluntarily maintains a sitting position, it is necessary to find activities that have meaning for him. Some activities involve playing with cause-and-effect toys, perhaps with the additional input of vibration to increase the time that Aaron will want to sit up to play. Other activities that involve being seated upright can be great fun to engage in at home—for example, sitting on his father's knee with his father acting as his 'chair' so that Aaron can play face-on with one of his sisters at a hand-clapping or favourite singing game. Aaron should gradually learn that he can sit upright in many situations, that it is fun to have time to play with toys in front of him while he is seated, and that it is rewarding to sit upright so as to play with his sisters.

He cannot stand unsupported and uses a standing-frame. Toys and people are the motivating factors to help Aaron achieve independent standing. His low muscle tone means that it can be frightening for him if he feels unsupported. He will be able to learn that in front of his standing-frame, fastened to the edge of the tray, there is a range of sound-makers. This could give him the incentive to move and to sweep his hands forwards and sideways. Toys that move completely *away* from him are ineffective, so ensuring that all toys are anchored firmly is important. Toys that he activates himself are of more value, as well as toys with immediate reward such as vibration or music. (See the equipment list in Chapter 10 for useful additions that could be made to his toys and equipment.)

Aaron needs as many opportunities as any other child to sit and stand, throughout the day. Bear in mind that no movement is undertaken by any child without meaning, purpose and, usually, the prospect of fun. Babies do not sit to please their parents. They sit because they have the muscle power to enable them to do so, together with visual and environmental incentives. There are ways of overcoming many of Aaron's difficulties, but they will take more ingenuity and planning, and they will need to provide him with more opportunities to practise vital skills.

Anything that works for Aaron at home should work for him at school, and vice versa. His teachers, his therapists and his parents need to collaborate over how to achieve his postural goals; consistency and continuity of approach will ensure that many fun practical ways are provided for Aaron in both settings.

It is also important to bear in mind that Aaron, like other children, needs the experience of being on his tummy (*prone*), so that he gets the chance to use different muscles and to move his body in different ways. As well as learning to sit unsupported and to stand, he also needs opportunities for free movement in fun situations. Playing with his sister on the grass is not only interactive and communicative, but it also provides him with the chance to practise being in the prone position. Most importantly, whatever activity they engage in should be fun for them both.

Aaron can roll and twist, and sometimes he propels himself along the floor. He does not crawl forward. As mentioned earlier, some children who are blind prefer to remain still, but they can be encouraged gently, to achieve independent locomotion. The reasons why they may not move around are manifold, and include:

- the fact that they feel much safer with as much of their bodies on the floor as possible: bottom, legs, feet and hands all in contact with the floor may give a greater feeling of security
- poor muscle tone, which may limit their incentive to move
- the fact that when children who are visually impaired move they are much more likely to bump themselves, so some children who *can* move a little may lose confidence.

Aaron needs enjoyable activities that will give him more movement experience. Some games involve placing him over an adult's outstretched legs, in the prone position, and playing rhythmic singing games with him. Games like these can be used to emphasise the fact that he is going to move in different positions, particularly if the songs include essential concepts. Songs like the ones that follow can provide incidental opportunities for demonstrating to Aaron the meaning of activity words such as *up*, *down*, *out*, *brush*, *back and forth*, as well as familiarising him

with the names of everyday objects and the people around him
(by changing the names, as the situation suggests).

Incy Wincy Spider
Climbing *up* the spout,
Down came the rain
And washed the spider *out*.
Out came the sun
And dried *up* all the rain.
Incy Wincy Spider
Climbed *up* the spout *again*.

The grand old Duke of York,
He had ten thousand men,
He marched them *up to the top* of the hill
And he marched them *down again*.
And when they were *up* they were *up*,
And when they were *down* they were *down*,
And when they were only halfway up
They were neither *up* nor *down*.

Aaron, Aaron here you are
Sitting on my *knee*.
Aaron, Aaron, here you are
Sitting on my *knee*
(*sung to the tune of 'See-saw Marjorie Daw'*)

Here we show Aaron what to do,
What to do, what to do.
Here we show Aaron what to do,
Now we're at *school/home* today.

This is the way we *brush* Aaron's *teeth*
Brush Aaron's *teeth*, *brush* Aaron's *teeth*.
This is the way we *brush* Aaron's *teeth*,
Now we're at *school/home* today.
(*sung to the tune of 'Here We Go Round the Mulberry Bush'*)

> Aaron is rocking *back* and *forth*,
> Aaron is rocking *back* and *forth*,
> Aaron is rocking *back* and *forth*,
> Playing here today.
> (*sung to the tune of 'Skip to My Lou'*)

The more Aaron's activities can be accompanied by songs, together with familiar phrases, the better, for this could help him to 'internalise' some words/rhythms.

Fine motor skills
Aaron can hold an object in his hands and will attempt to move it, but when it falls from his grasp he does not attempt to retrieve it. Many children like Aaron need to be in contact with an object just to know that it exists. The sighted child quickly learns that when he releases an object from his grasp it hasn't gone for ever; the child with a visual impairment may take much longer to reach this stage. The sighted child soon appreciates that a dropped object can be glanced at, and if it is not there it can be searched for, retrieved and played with again. A child with severe visual impairment may need to be helped to 'listen out' for the toy he has dropped. An adult can easily make the mistake of silently picking it up and putting it straight back into his hands, thereby preventing him from learning either where the toy went or how it got back into his hands. To him, it apparently just 'flew through the air' and arrived back.

Many blind children scan with their hands to look out for toys and people. Just as the sighted child is encouraged to scan with his eyes—to glance—so the child with visual impairment should be encouraged to scan with his hands in order to find things close by. He needs ultimately to learn to reach out beyond his grasp.

A child often learns to put objects into a container such as a large box. If he finds an object again without any help, his incentive to release more objects and put them into containers, then take them out again, increases. Finding and retrieving for a child with a severe visual impairment is a skill that, with a little thought, can be given much more meaning. Here are two ways of providing children like Aaron with opportunities for practising the same skills as their peers:

—dropping objects—a child's plastic bucket with a silver-foil food container in the bottom makes a fascinating receptacle for children with some residual vision such as those with cortical visual impairment. Although Aaron is known to be totally blind, this activity will still be a great deal of fun for him because the act of dropping different objects on to the food container will make different sounds

—posting objects—if a container which in itself gives a reward, such as an upturned tambourine, is used, when Aaron drops even quite light objects into it they will make a very satisfying clatter.

Some young children may not use their fingers separately, or realise that they have two hands that can be used together. It may be necessary to show Aaron how to transfer objects from one hand to the other. Ways of teaching him that he can use both hands to achieve a goal include holding a drum with one hand and beating on it with a stick with the other, and holding a musical toy in one hand while using the other to pull on a string to activate it. Pressing buzzers and bells with different fingers will help him to use fine finger and different hand movements. When Aaron has learnt that both his hands can work together to manipulate an object, he can be encouraged to hold tactile books or books with sound-makers attached to help him learn how to turn pages.

The child needs to be carefully observed, not only so that realistic goals can be achieved but also so that, as his skills increase, you are ready to alter his activities accordingly.

In the sighted child, both vision and touch regulate the coordination of hand movements. For children such as Aaron, the development of tactile awareness is an integral part of the acquisition of fine motor skills. In fact, the development of all those skills will depend on his use of touch. A high level of reward and some assistance will ensure that he becomes familiar with many fine motor movements. Once he has developed a range of such skills, he will be able to combine them in order to tackle more complex activities and manipulate more objects skilfully. The level of his interest will increase as he becomes more skilful, and he may persist with activities for increasingly long stretches of time. He should gradually be able to transfer objects from hand to hand, hold two objects in one hand, and then use different movements with either hand so as to activate cause-and-effect toys, computer programmes, switch toys and other rewarding activities.

Aaron will always have to be given more time than a sighted child needs to explore, and plenty of time to practise his acquired skills. As he progresses, he will continue to need help from an adult. His interactions with adults will provide some of the motivation that will help to maintain his interest in whatever activity he is engaged in. He may supplement the information he receives about objects by using his mouth, hands and head. If he does use mouthing to supplement his knowledge, he will eventually have enough experience of objects to drop this particular behaviour without any intervention by an adult. Once he has developed the skills of reaching and grasping objects and is coordinating hand movements, the adult's role will be to give him opportunities to practise and extend these skills by himself.

With a lot of individual help and attention, Aaron should master necessary fine motor skills. The degree of control and accuracy he has to manipulate objects, and his fine motor ability, will facilitate the development of his perceptual skills. As he moves on to more complex use of materials, he will practise his fine motor-perceptual skills through his play activities. The enjoyment of those activities will then be its own reward, and he will continue to play in the absence of adults. The high level of interaction that he experiences with adults at an early stage will enhance his skills in achieving independence later on.

The development of fine motor skills in the child who is blind can be encouraged by the rewards and incentives chosen to replace those usually provided by vision. The motivation for each child will be different, and careful choices will need to be made on an individual basis. It is important to take into account the physical abilities of each child, so that expectations are realistic and can be achieved within the child's own time-scale. Often, learning may be fragmented or disjointed so that the adult will have to carefully plan how the child is going to progress from

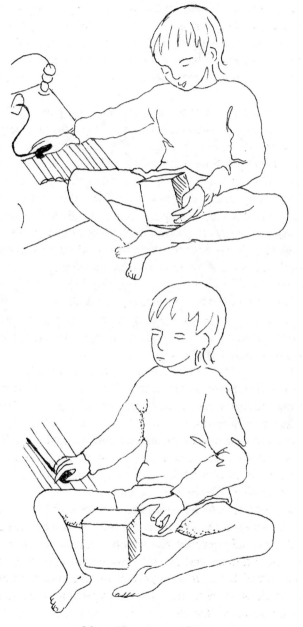

More time to explore.

The adult will need to demonstrate where the child is in space, so that he can gain as complete a picture of himself and his environment as possible.

one step to the next, and incidental learning may be minimal. Plenty of time and the opportunity to practise each developmental stage should be allowed for, so that the child participates fully in activities giving time for consolidation.

AUDITORY DEVELOPMENT

Aaron is beginning to be communicative, using his voice as a means of engaging the attention of adults. An important factor in the development of his auditory skills is his attaching meaning to the sounds he hears. He is aware of sounds, and the questions to be asked at this stage are:

- Can he identify them?
- Can he comprehend them?
- Can he immediately remember what they are?

- When he hears the sound later does he show that he still understands what the sound-maker is?
- Can he relate sounds or sound-makers to past experiences?
- Can he relate them to his present activities?

Awareness of sound is knowing that it exists. The next stage for Aaron is helping him to *recognise* sounds—otherwise, they will have no meaning for him and he may gradually stop listening to them.

In order to assist him, those around him need to be asked to become aware of environmental, everyday sounds and to give him some indication in a conversational way when new sounds occur. Helping him to continue to recognise familiar sounds and to incorporate the new sounds into his repertoire will help him to internalise and comprehend them. It is easier for any child to recognise sounds if he is in a reasonably quiet room with no extraneous sounds, whether at home or in a distraction-free area of the classroom.

Unless Aaron can be given a quiet corner or quiet times, it will be confusing for him to hear constant 'busy' noises. It is so important that all the people working with him should constantly bear in mind that children with multisensory impairment have different needs from their sighted and hearing peers. An adult must be on hand to identify noises for him—otherwise, he will never pick up clues about his environment. Attention to sounds involves concentration, and unless Aaron's attention is drawn to sounds by someone saying, 'Aaron, listen, do you hear the ?', he will quickly become bored and may ignore the sound that he hears. Once his attention has been caught, he will begin to listen more actively and on his own initiative. It will be apparent that he is interested, because his demeanour or behaviour will show that he is alerting to the sounds around him. When he begins to do this it will be fun to say, 'Aaron, what is that noise?', giving him time to listen, and then reply as though he were speaking—'Oh, Aaron, it's the washing machine. We both heard the machine.'

This alert listening stage will lead him on to imitation. At first, he may imitate the banging of a drum, initially joining in coactively. Later, he will be able to listen to rhythms that the adult plays for him, then learn to beat the drum in response, ultimately beating in imitation. He can be encouraged to search for sound-makers, such as a tin with dried peas in it, a carton with rice in it, and other sorts of home-made sound-maker in lower frequencies. Once he has learnt to enjoy sound-makers, he will feel encouraged to discriminate between them—for example, between the ringing of a bell and the banging of a drum. This could lead on to his indicating by movements of his arms, head or hands, or other parts of the body, where he believes the sound is coming from, resulting in a further interest in sound.

Awareness through listening should become part of Aaron's everyday programme. Any little event will serve: for instance, when someone knocks at the door, the adult can signal to him or her to keep knocking. Then Aaron can be taken to the door and the adult will say, 'Aaron, can you hear that knocking? Someone is knocking at our door. Let's open the door. Oh, it's George—he was knocking at our door!'

Part of Aaron's individual plan is to encourage everyone who meets him to help him realise that all sounds are real and that they have meaning. He should be encouraged to listen to all the sounds that come within his physical sphere and to discover their source. At first the adults involved with him may find this difficult to remember, but eventually it will be a perfectly natural adjunct to the daily routine. All the sounds that the sighted–hearing child understands quite casually, such as a bell, a buzzer, a telephone, a refrigerator, a washing machine, will have to be repeatedly identified until the adults are *sure* he knows what they are. Like any other child, Aaron needs to know and feel that his environment has reality and meaning.

We must always try to imagine how it feels to be *him*. Giving him as many clues as possible will help him to process the information that his sighted peers gain incidentally.

We expect a young child, at a certain point in his development, to start to use the phrase 'What's that?' Very often, children go through an intense phase when they are constantly asking questions about the things that they see and eagerly anticipating answers from the adults around them. This phase can often last for months—indeed, the weary parent sometimes feels that it will last for ever. In children who are blind, this stage may be very delayed or distorted. A child may have no curiosity because he does not know that there are objects 'out there'. The adults who are involved with him and whom he encounters casually, who *should* be naming the objects and people that come in and out of his range, may be omitting to do so. People often forget the need to introduce themselves to the child, presuming that somehow he knows who they are; the effect is to cause him unnecessary confusion. People very often do precisely this with Aaron, not realising that they *must identify* themselves.

Sometimes Aaron must wish he wore a badge saying, 'You know who *I* am, but I don't know *you* you are. Tell me first, before you expect me to respond.' Things suddenly happening to him, people suddenly appearing, then disappearing with very little warning, must make the world a very strange place, and may cause not only confusion but distress and a wish to retreat.

For example, Aaron might be about to go out for a walk. His coat is put on, and then suddenly the adult with him remembers that she hasn't turned off the tap, so she leaves him abruptly for a few minutes. She then reappears and takes his hand again, but now realises that it's too hot for him to wear a coat and so takes it off. All of this, although straightforward for the sighted child, must seem a very odd series of events to Aaron. Always remembering to give clear explanations may be difficult for the adult involved, but it is her responsibility to ensure that the child knows exactly what is happening, all the time.

There will be times when it will be fun for Aaron to join in games with other children. He will probably get a great deal of pleasure out of sharing musical activities in a small group. The first thing to do will be to identify the children and the musical instruments they are playing. (It could be a good idea always to introduce them in the same way and in the same order, so that Aaron has a chance to retain some identifying feature of each child and his instrument.) They can then all take it in turns to play with the teacher, who can introduce them thus: 'Mark is playing the bell', at which point Mark rings the bell; 'Tom is playing the drum'—Tom bangs on the drum; 'Fred is playing the kazoo'—Fred blows the kazoo; 'James is playing the piano'—James plays the piano; and 'Aaron is playing the tambourine'—Aaron plays the tambourine.

Aaron must learn everything in ways that are usually *completely* different from those of sighted children.

Once he is showing awareness and understanding of a variety of sounds, all kinds of activities are possible. Within his daily plan, he can be given an individual sound-making session with an adult, learning to make different noises in different ways. The adult will pause sometimes so that Aaron, listening out for different sounds, rhythms and songs, has lots of chances to respond in his own best way: by body movements, hand-clapping and vocalisation. Good rhythmic records or tapes can be played. Aaron can be helped coactively to clap, to move to the music and to put his hands on the speaker of the audio system to feel the music's vibration. He may start to associate sounds or words with certain actions, and gestures such as those for 'more', 'finished' and 'again' can be introduced.

Note that signs and gestures do not *replace* speech for children with useful residual hearing. Aaron will be helped to understand more about what is being presented within the situation if speech, sign and gesture are used together. Sometimes a sign will give meaning to a spoken word which he might otherwise have difficulty in understanding.

TACTILE DEVELOPMENT

Aaron responds to being warm. He permits soft, smooth textures to be rubbed on his hands, feet or body, and moves his hands, feet or body over soft, smooth textures. He reacts to tactile stimulation by body movement, and will explore unfamiliar as well as familiar soft and rough-textured surfaces. He explores objects with his fingers.

If he is provided with more experiences with water and a variety of textured materials, and encouraged to move to music or over different surfaces, he is likely to become even more tactually aware. This kind of activity should also increase his communication level, thereby extending his development in other areas. The more aware he is of himself in space and of his relationship to it, and the more aware he is of his limbs as part of himself, the more able he will be to use his body with understanding in different situations.

Aaron likes to go swimming. It is clear how many opportunities there are for him to develop his tactile sense in the swimming-pool, but while he is there he also gets a chance to understand situations specific to the swimming-pool, to communicate in new ways, to make relationships, to listen for new sounds and to further his gross motor skills—all within one enjoyable situation.

During swimming Aaron can learn about the dimensions of the pool, about mobility in water, and about trust in a different environment. For example:

- He is walked gently by his helper to the side of the pool; he stands at the top of the steps, sitting down on the next step. This experience gives him the opportunity to walk, to socialise, to internalise environmental information, to listen and to make relationships.
- He sits at the edge of the pool, splashing his feet in the water. This experience gives him the opportunity to move his body in space, to find out what his feet can do with water, to appreciate temperature, to smell the chlorine and to begin to relax.
- He puts his hand up towards the steps and moves down them holding on to the banister rail. This experience gives him mobility practice, a feeling of buoyancy as he enters the water, and a sense of independence and exploration.

In other words, the *whole-body experience* of going swimming can be viewed as a chance to incorporate all of Aaron's skills in a structured and integrated way. During a swimming session he will also practise skills such as jumping up and down, moving backwards and floating forwards. In addition, the swimming-pool offers many opportunities for spontaneous speech, sign and gesture. At the end of his swimming session Aaron goes up the steps with his helper, holding the banister, then sits on the top step. With his accompanying adult he shares a moment of hand-clapping because they have enjoyed themselves so much, and phrases such as 'good swimming', 'time to go', 'swimming is finished' are all part of the experience.

COMMUNICATION

The swimming session described above reminds us that communication is taking place at some level throughout Aaron's day. As we have seen, communication is not a skill taught in isolation. The *trusting relationships* and the two-way interaction that have been built up form the bedrock on which communication develops for Aaron. These can be extended and modified to the point at which he can influence and control his world by his own means of communication, whether spoken or signed. Knowing Aaron very well enables all the adults involved with him to interpret his signals and body movements—such as his wriggle that shows his enjoyment.

Speech accompanied by signing is particularly appropriate for children whose sensory impairments combine with other disabilities to cause their own speech to be severely delayed. Signs should be used with Aaron throughout the day in situations that have meaning for him. When he becomes more familiar with the spoken word or sign he will show that he is ready to use them himself as a means of expression. Since he is totally blind, when signing with him it must always be remembered that signs are a tactile experience: sitting or standing behind him, the adult demonstrates each sign's movement, coactively. Occasionally he may like to put his hands on a speaker's mouth or neck to feel the vibration of her speech (using the Tadoma method, see page 158). In this way, within a communicative situation, physical contact can convey the maximum amount of tactile information.

Building up secure relationships will encourage Aaron to communicate more. Adults will need to observe him closely for body signals that indicate he is enjoying interactions with them. All communication skills, including physical and vocal imitation, can be encouraged informally in situations such as that described in the swimming-pool. Many other everyday situations—walking in

Opportunities for close one-to-one interaction and communication are provided within the child's normal range of abilities
and interests . . . learning to use the sign *jump* in play.

the park, going to the shops, trampolining, horse-riding, visiting friends—offer opportunities for spontaneous communication within this structured, integrated approach.

Giving Aaron access to language that he can receive, interpret and understand is the purpose, and could be the key to all his further learning.

ROSEMARY

Rosemary is nine, and is one of Aaron's classmates.

Rosemary is a child with cortical visual impairment and a severe hearing loss, and because of her visual needs she is best helped by being provided with a clutter-free environment. The integrated and unified approach that caters for the needs of one particular child can often create a suitable environment for another. This is the case with Aaron and Rosemary. For example, Aaron needs order, structure and time to learn and consolidate skills, as does Rosemary. Rosemary's visual abilities give her some advantages, as she is able to perceive the presence of certain objects—as long as they are presented in a clutter-free environment. Applied to Rosemary as to Aaron, the integrated approach looks for every opportunity to maximise her ability to understand and perform all tasks as independently as possible, building on her present skills.

For example, at snack time Rosemary sits at the table on a chair that holds her in an upright position and with her feet comfortably on the floor. A clue to the start of each snack time is that the lights are turned on. This light clue alerts Rosemary to the next stage of the activity: she is given a bright blue table-mat, and offered drinks and biscuits on a reflective silver tray from which she can select. (All the objects that she is likely to be able to see will be presented, as far as possible, so that there is good bold contrast.)

As in so many good school situations, choice is built into the snacks activity. Rosemary appears to prefer blackcurrant juice. She has a yellow straw in a green cup. She can sign 'biscuit', and when she signs she is immediately responded to, and given the biscuit after she finishes her drink. She points to her open mouth for more, and then is responded to coactively with a hand-over-hand signing of 'more' by her classroom assistant. In this everyday activity Rosemary is given the opportunity to choose, to use communicative strategies, and to be responded to. As she has a severe hearing loss, her classroom assistant and her teachers speak and sign with her, making sure that within the routine she accesses her residual visual skills. Using a whole-child approach to all activities ensures that even an everyday event such as drinking and eating is experienced in context. Rosemary does nothing in isolation. She tastes and smells the biscuit while at the same time feeling its texture. She tastes and smells her drink, and over time will learn to select and pour more drinks.

The unified approach is applied to everything the child does and experiences. Every achievement is a personal achievement, and everything has meaning within the context of individual need. Every aspect of the curriculum is chosen for its appropriateness to the child as an individual. It will take some children a very large number of very small steps to achieve some of the things in their personal curriculum, but they will get there in the end, and they will have done it in their own way.

Play time
Although playtime is a time of relaxation for Rosemary, it is also an opportunity for the adults to ensure that she can access her own toys and activities independently. Each floor area in the classroom has a distinctive colour. This means that children with partial sight, or cortical visual impairment, can learn first to be aware of one part of the room and then to distinguish it from the others (Aaron can find some of the floor areas because of the large textured carpeted surfaces). The adults make certain that Rosemary's toys are on a distinctive blue mat, which means that she can find her own things to play with. Within this blue-carpeted area is a red chair, which is next to a brown-carpeted area.

Rosemary can find the red chair, which helps her to orientate towards the toy cupboard opposite. Each toy cupboard in each of the carpeted areas has distinctive toys and games on top, so that all the children know what is inside their own. Ensuring that the environment is accessible for Aaron has given Rosemary the opportunity to play there as well because everything is so easily identified.

Self-help skills

If the principles outlined here are followed, every event can be an opportunity for learning. All activities can involve the use of:

- communication skills
- play and interaction skills
- visual skills
- motor skills
- auditory skills

Dressing, eating, washing and toileting all offer opportunities for extending every skill within the child's repertoire, as the following example shows.

Rosemary eats her lunch in the dining-room. Her one-to-one helper, John, with whom she has a good relationship, assists her throughout the meal. He cuts her food up into bite-size pieces. Rosemary then needs gentle guidance from John to put it into her mouth, using a small fork. John is aware that she likes certain food textures more than others, so she is given the opportunity to search carefully with her fingers to locate the crunchy food before she starts to eat. John uses speech, signals and signs for her to continue to eat. Rosemary needs lots of time to eat at her own pace, and John needs to keep her focused and in contact with the task at hand. The excellent interaction between the two of them gives Rosemary many chances for understanding.

She now moves her finger towards her mouth to indicate that she would like more. Sometimes she opens her mouth for more, and if she does not like the food on her plate or is not ready for it, she closes her mouth. John's responses to Rosemary's small signals are important, so as to maintain the two-way communication Rosemary needs during lunchtime. He uses the whole of his time with her during lunchtime to get to know her at all levels, within the natural context of the lunch situation.

So as to ensure that Rosemary has maximum opportunity to understand all situations, every member of staff in her class is

She needs lots of time to eat at her own pace.

aware of her hearing and visual needs and of the impact these have on the strategies required throughout her school day. All her co-workers—parents, teachers, therapists, special needs assistants and support persons—work together, discussing and giving thought to suitable approaches for Rosemary's individual programme. These include:

- Looking at all activities and ensuring that everything is at her optimum visual distance (particularly important when using computer programmes).
- Ensuring that there is suitable contrast on symbol cards for Rosemary to be able to match and choose certain favoured activities.
- Looking at books as a means of information suitable for Rosemary and modifying them so that they have one line of text per page with one clear picture.
- Planning auditory training possibilities in a controlled, distraction-free environment which will give her the opportunity for further use of her listening skills.

- Considering the walls of the classroom as potential visual indicators and ensuring that some areas have plain-coloured backgrounds so that she can move about without being distracted by visual clutter.
- Assessing Rosemary's posture while she is sitting on all the chairs and at the tables provided, so that she is always in her optimum position from a visual and postural point of view.
- Making sure that her tactile equipment includes objects that she can match to an object book, to be retrieved from a separate bag. Rosemary will learn to hold whole objects, matching them to the same type of object in the book. This will lead on to matching pictures to pictures, and then pictures to words.
- Incorporating music and song to help her to internalise the rhythm of some routine activities.
- Looking at each activity as an opportunity to use communication skills, listing the aims of each activity, and always having communication as the first goal.
- Looking at Rosemary's opportunities for participating in the school curriculum, using a variety of visual, tactile and auditory means.
- Ensuring that, in her literacy hour activities, Rosemary has access to the experiences of her sighted classmates. She can have long thin books, short fat books, textured books, matching textured books, 'about me' books, self-help books (including, for instance, toothbrush and comb inserts), and tape books.
- Continuing to give Rosemary STAR objects at the end of the school day, so as to give particular meaning to her home time. Rosemary has a home/school bag into which she puts, each day, an object that has direct relevance to that day's school activity. Before she leaves for home there is a symbolic 'putting of an object' into the bag which her parents then take out when she gets home.

PREPARING THE INDIVIDUAL EDUCATIONAL PLAN

This chapter has described in some detail the approach to plans for two children to achieve their individual goals.

The child without disabilities, who has intact senses, achieves developmental goals and milestones with almost no planning at all. As he grows older, information derived from external factors continues to influence his development. Television, brothers and sisters, his peer group, books and comics, radios and computers— all give him much incidental information about the world beyond his immediate environment. Adults make plans for his work and his play, but they do not have to structure their thinking about his needs to the extent required by parents and teachers of children with multisensory impairments.

Children with severe sensory impairments may be unable to learn anything incidentally from their environment. They need to be introduced to everything that happens in a completely different but natural way. Their individual developmental experiences will determine the approaches used, and their incentive to continue to learn skills may depend to a large extent on having complete trust in a known adult. A strong motivating factor in achieving self-help skills, for example, may be that adult's approval at each stage until the skills are mastered. It may be some time before the child reaches the satisfaction in mastery of a task that children without disabilities usually gain with such ease.

Structuring the child's environment should never mean making it so 'safe' that it becomes boring. Structure should give reassurance. The provision of structured routine should enable the child to gain in confidence. Having gained that confidence, he will be able to learn through his own independence that he can interact with other people and explore fresh environments.

8 Behavioural Differences

The ability to form and maintain strong relationships may account for the fact that many children who are deafblind behave in the same way as their sighted hearing peers. They do not need to self-stimulate because they have good personal communication skills built on firm foundations. The busy child who is engaged and motivated, working at age- or stage-related activities, is not likely to show behavioural problems.

Some children's behaviour, however, causes a great deal of concern to their parents and co-workers.

Referring to the sighted–hearing child is helpful when considering behavioural differences. It is quite usual for a young baby to rock and bounce, to wave her hands in the air in front of her, to giggle and croon to herself and to find pleasure and amusement in her own body. She plays with her toes, tries to bite them, and discovers her feet through playing with them. Many babies rock themselves to sleep, banging their heads on the pillow for comfort. Many children suck their fingers, bite their nails, twiddle their hair, take a comfort blanket to bed, suck dummies, have tantrums, reject new experiences and play to the gallery.

None of these behaviours, if related to age and stage, is inappropriate in children without disabilities. At the age of two or three, it is age- and stage-related to have a tantrum in the supermarket because you think you should be given sweets immediately. It is not so normal if you are still doing this at the age of seven or eight. Some behaviour becomes a problem when it is inappropriate to the situation, harmful to the child or to others, not age- or stage-related, or when it stops the child from taking part in other, more appropriate, activities. Behavioural differences all must have a reason—they do not start, or stop, for nothing.

Unfortunately, negative behaviour becomes a part of some children's lives. If we know why it occurs, sometimes steps can be taken to prevent it starting in a young child, or change it in an older one.

Lack of sensory input is one reason why some children behave differently from their peers.

Crying and screaming
Young children cry because they are hungry or thirsty, because they are wet, in pain or in need of company. All these are normal reasons for crying in the very young child. If the child with disabilities does not have a recognisable means of communication, as she gets older crying may become her only recourse, and it may get more and more angry, loud, distressed and confused. When a child continues to cry and scream for a long while, it is obviously important to find out why she is behaving in this way, what is causing the screaming. As well as this we have to investigate how we can help her to react to her stress in a way that will be quickly understood and satisfactorily dealt with from her point of view, and result in her reacting to distress without screaming.

One idea when trying to help children who scream is to look at their communication skills and to ensure that we have many ways of letting her know that we understand her.

Attention-seeking
If a child is attention-seeking, she may manifest this in several ways—for instance, by throwing, by calling out, or by moving up to and staying very close to the adult she is with. Sometimes, in order to gain attention, children deliberately put themselves or another child in danger. We have to provide for a child's emotional needs and ensure that she is *given* attention so that she does not need to work at getting it.

One idea is to provide a one-to-one adult-to-child ratio at *set* points during the day, when she is given close attention and physical contact. Some children are able to learn to make relationships with a limited number of adults with whom they can learn other skills.

Throwing

Object-throwing can be difficult to deal with because the object may be of value or, worse, when the child throws it it may hurt another person. It is always important to carefully consider the situation before attempting to eliminate the behaviour. Has the child or the object received so much attention through throwing that her negative behaviour has been inadvertently reinforced? Many people follow the 'ignore negative behaviour' maxim, but this may not work if the child has multisensory impairment. Sometimes she will need to know the consequence of her actions—she may need to be given information about the results of throwing before she can learn *not* to throw. If the throwing appears to be random, it may be due to the fact that the child does not see the purpose of the object that she has thrown. As we have already established, children who are visually impaired do not have the same concept of toys and other objects as sighted children. What to us is a pretty flower may be a soft, perhaps prickly, even rather unpleasant object to the child who cannot see it—something that she may feel the need to get rid of as quickly as possible.

One idea is to give the child lots of opportunity to learn about objects gradually, to manipulate them, to put them gently into containers, large and small, then take them gently out again. This can often help to change the behaviour of a child whose throwing appears to be random.

Biting and sucking (for comfort)

Some children start biting and sucking their hands because they are trying to comfort or stimulate themselves. What starts as comfort behaviour can become an ingrained habit if the warmth and security they are seeking are not provided. Some suck and bite their hands so obsessively that they have no time for other activities. If they are not provided with other, legitimate, activities that they can successfully get on with by themselves, then their only stimulation will be their own bodies and the uses to which they can put them. Self-stimulation of this type is no more common in children with multisensory impairment than in other children with disabilities, but it is much more understandable if a child has no other outlets for her energies. The adverse effects of sensory deprivation are well documented, and it has been found that self-stimulation is almost inevitable if children are not engaged actively.

One idea to help the child who is biting and sucking her hands is to provide a variety of other experiences that she can take part in and that she is likely to enjoy as much as the self-stimulatory behaviour. With the young child, start by showing her how much she is loved and how thoroughly she can trust you, by close one-to-one contact, entering into her world in as gentle and reassuring a way as possible. Rocking her and very gradually moving her hands away from her mouth can help, as (if there is no contraindication) can massage on the back of the hands. Eventually some children learn to massage their own hands when they feel the need for comfort.

Biting and sucking (defensive)
The biting and sucking of hands can be a defensive mechanism. If the child has her hands in her mouth she may feel that she will not be asked to take part in activities that frighten and confuse her. This often means that when she is biting and sucking she is left alone even more, thereby perpetuating the behaviour.

One idea for changing the child's behaviour is to work towards increasing adult–child contact, so as to help her learn that she is a part of a world that can offer her exciting alternatives to occupy her hands. *But this has to happen, and you have to stick at it*—there is no point in devoting considerable time to the child, encouraging her to have trust and confidence in you, and then, when the hand-biting has faded, to withdraw from her. Plans must be made for suitable, age-appropriate activities to be on offer to her throughout her day.

Head-banging
Head-banging is often found to have a similar cause to that behind the biting and sucking of hands: that is, the child has turned inwards on herself for stimulation because she has not been presented with satisfying physical or mental alternatives. Some head-banging can be so intense that it becomes pleasurable—it is

thought that head-banging can release endorphins in the brain, causing heightened sensations and stimulation.

First, decide why the head-banging is occurring. Then, if it is felt that the aim is self-stimulation, *one idea* for decreasing the behaviour is to provide extra physical stimulation using a circuit (see page 116), which may be able to offer her almost equal sensation to that provided by the head-banging. Physical activities such as rolling, swinging, running, bouncing and jumping can offer safe and healthy exhilaration. The child will learn that this physical activity is as enjoyable and energising as her previous activity.

Withdrawing

If a child feels threatened because she is uncertain about what is happening to her, she may completely withdraw. She may demonstrate her distress by sucking or biting her hands, banging her head, totally refusing to cooperate by screaming or crying, or curling up into a ball; or she may isolate herself by withdrawing from any activity that you try to engage her in. This behaviour should not be thought to be insoluble, but it needs to be approached in a particularly careful and structured way. It is necessary to look at the child's environmental situation as a whole in order to ensure that she gains or regains, a sense of security. Everyone involved will need to give a great deal of thought to planning her programme, with a view to establishing shared responsibility for her, involving several adults.

One idea is that, if she is given every opportunity to form close relationships, and to bond, preferably with at least two people, it should be possible gradually to encourage her to interact with them in a safe, quiet, structured environment.

Eye-pressing

Eye-pressing often starts when a child is twelve to eighteen months old. Many people mistakenly believe that the child's eyes are sore or that she is tired, not realising that she is deriving stimulation, pleasure or comfort from pressing her eyes. As soon as she starts to do so, she should be taken to the ophthalmologist so as to be sure that her eyes are not hurting her and that an

Eye-pressing.

important aspect of her eye condition has not been missed. If the ophthalmologist can confirm that her eyes do not require atten- tion, then awareness that this habit may be starting will enable you to take action to eliminate it.

Further damage can be caused to the eye if it is constantly pressed. This in itself should be a good enough reason to take preventive action. Certainly, a child who constantly eye-presses may develop large, discoloured rings around her eyes, making them appear to sink back into their sockets.

One idea for trying to stop eye-pressing is to gently and without comment remove the child's hand from her eye. Talk to her, give her a toy, or play a little game with her, to divert her attention for a few minutes. It is important to remember not to draw her attention to the eye-pressing, in case she begins to regard it as an important activity that adults are bound to pay heed to, thereby increasing rather than decreasing the behaviour. Substituting pleasurable activities for a short while, thus helping her to learn

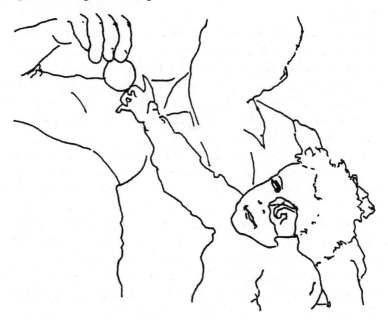

Substituting pleasurable activities to discourage eye-pressing.

that her hands can be otherwise occupied, is the best way to ensure permanent elimination.

Eye-poking

Eye-poking may occur at about the same time as eye-pressing, and may be caused by the child's attempt to get increased stimulation from a flashing-light effect in her eyes. This is often an unconscious habit that becomes more noticeable in situations such as when the child is unoccupied or anxious, or in certain lighting.

One idea is to occasionally use light to provide more stimulation. If you give the child more things to do with her hands involving light, such as teaching her to use a switch, thereby creating light, and to use a computer keyboard to activate visual-stimulation programmes, you will enable her to use her interest in light in more productive ways.

Rocking

Rocking backwards and forwards may happen when the child is seeking a rich and stimulating sensory activity because she is bored, or because she is trying to avoid situations that she finds threatening, or because she is anxious. We have to look at the reasons for the rocking before trying to eliminate the behaviour, because we shall decide how to deal with it according to the child's reason for doing it.

One idea for altering rocking backwards and forwards in the child who is bored is to provide physically stimulating activities. *An idea* for changing rocking in the child who is fearful or anxious, once we have investigated the cause of her fear or anxiety, is to offer her shared activities which include intensive interaction (see Chapter 6), with a view to showing her that her environment and the people she meets can be trusted.

Looking at the child's rocking behaviour objectively will produce ideas for its eventual elimination into more positive physical movement.

MORE THOUGHTS ABOUT BEHAVIOURAL DIFFERENCES

When looking at the behavioural differences of young children with multisensory impairment, it is important to remember that they often need not occur. With more knowledge about the value of early stimulation programmes, parents, teachers and therapists can often prevent them happening in the first place. It is always true that prevention is better than cure—and a lot easier. It is important never to overreact when trying to eliminate or prevent some mannerism or habit in a child. Overreaction usually results in the behaviour increasing rather than decreasing.

When observing any child's behaviour, you must for the child's sake consider how to work towards altering it before it becomes habitual. If the negative behaviour is such that it might make her life easier if she did not have the behaviour, then usually it is worth deciding to change it now. Some behavioural patterns may become too ingrained and time-consuming to alter later on, so getting rid of them now may make a real difference to the way the child lives. Considering whether or not her quality of life will be enhanced if this particular behaviour is altered or eliminated should help you to formulate firm plans for her.

It is also important to remember that the longer the child has had the habit, the longer it will take to eliminate. To use an analogy from our diet-conscious world—it will take very little time or effort and not a scrap of willpower to lose five pounds/ grams, but much time and effort to lose five stones/kilos.

There are, of course, children with multisensory impairment who *do not* manifest any behavioural differences at all. These children are usually able to communicate with adults and with their peers in their preferred mode and they have a rich, integrated day that provides them with enough personally satisfying activities. One factor that may be significant is the age of onset of the child's impairment. Often, children who become deafblind in later childhood will have had more experiences and more opportunities to make use of them than children who are born deafblind. Some children who have acquired deafblindness utilise and profit from memories of previous sighted or hearing experiences throughout their lives. For example, visual memory may remain in a child who becomes blind, so that when an environment is described to him he will be able to use the knowledge of height, dimension and colour that he has retained, and to apply it in appropriate situations.

There are also children with multisensory impairment whose behaviour difficulties are to do not so much with the severity of their impairment as with the way adults have reacted to them.

BENJAMIN

If the adults around him have become so used to a child's behaviour that they do not see it as needing to change, then there is no possibility of altering it. Before remedial measures can be completely successful, the cooperation of most of the adults in his life, not just some of them, will be needed.

Benjamin, aged two at the time of referral, had cortical visual impairment and a severe hearing loss. He used to 'blow raspberries', and was content to do this for much of the day until his mother decided that, unless he changed his habit, he would never want to do anything more constructive. So she worked very effec-tively at eliminating the behaviour. Unfortunately, Benjamin's father thought that blowing raspberries was amusing, and so encouraged him to carry on doing it and, in addition, got him to copy more and more peculiar sounds.

Before anything concrete can be achieved, conflict of interest in a situation, where one party is trying to eliminate an undesirable behaviour and the other is in disagreement or giving tacit approval to it, must be resolved. It is then important to ensure—as far as possible—that any agreed plans cannot be sabotaged.

Benjamin also had the habit of eye-pressing, which was described as constant, and occurred even when he was participat-ing in activities that he, his parents and his relatives enjoyed. His mother felt that she would like to eliminate this habit too. Having learnt from the raspberry-blowing experience just described, she ensured that his father knew about the need to stop the eye-pressing and that he would be included and give positive help in the campaign against it. The father had not felt that this was a problem, either. He was so used to Benjamin's behaviour that he did not notice it—although he would certainly have commented had he seen either of his other two sons pressing their eyes. He had not realised that this particular habit of Benjamin's was preventing him from fully participating in some activities, because he would only occasionally use both hands together, one hand usually being occupied in the eye-pressing.

THE IMPORTANCE OF CONCERTED ACTION

It is important to discuss the child's behaviour in some detail and to explore everyone's feelings about it. Once it has been decided that action must be taken, the next stage is to get on with planning together to do this as quickly as possible.

The first step should be to set out exactly what the behaviour is, in objective terms. Often, when the behaviour is discussed, it turns out that people think it occurs throughout the day. But when the behaviour is recorded—recording it is part of the plan—they discover that there may be a pattern to it. It often occurs as the direct result of a situation that the child would like to control, but he resorts instead to self-stimulatory or other behavioural 'displacement' activities. Benjamin's behaviour needed to change so that he would participate more in activities. The solution to his problem was simple, and writing down *exactly* what the behaviour consisted of did indeed prove very helpful to Benjamin's parents. Having carefully recorded and studied it, they were then able to formulate objectively what it was they wished to achieve with their child.

To record Benjamin's eye-pressing over one week they used a behaviour chart:

BENJAMIN

Date

Adult's name   [The adult who is going to fill in the chart]

Behaviour   Benjamin presses his left hand to his left eye. [The behaviour is written in objective terms]

Procedure   [It is important to record Benjamin's behaviour as clearly as possible. The adult's behaviour towards Benjamin remains the same during this week.]

Aim   The aim of the chart is to record Benjamin's eye pressing.

How often   [At the end of every hour, from 9 a.m. until 8 p.m., the adult records, by ticking the relevant box, the number of times Benjamin has pressed his hand to his eye during that hour.]

Recording   [If he presses his hand to his eye for the whole hour, then 'hour' is recorded. If he does not press his eye in any given hour, a nought is recorded for that hour.]

Day 1

a.m.–p.m.	9	10	11	12	1	2	3	4	5	6	7–8
	0	✓✓ ✓	0	✓✓	0	✓✓ ✓✓	0	✓✓ ✓✓	hour	✓	✓✓ ✓

A pattern begins to emerge on day one.

At the end of the week, Benjamin's chart revealed:

—that he once pressed his eye continuously for an hour

—that he often eye-pressed during mealtimes

—that he always eye-pressed when he was having his nappy changed

—that he occasionally eye-pressed when his grandmother came to the house.

Benjamin's parents now realised that the eye-pressing had occurred for good reasons. They felt that he pressed his eye during mealtimes so as to avoid eating the savoury course, when he was having his nappy changed because he felt unsure of the situation, and when his grandmother came to the house because he did not meet her regularly and so was perhaps rather fearful in this, to him, strange situation.

Having filled in their chart and analysed it objectively, Benjamin's parents were able to work towards eliminating his eye-pressing behaviour. For Benjamin's programme to be completely successful, everyone involved needed to contribute ideas towards it.

Sometimes in such a situation, even when agreement has been reached people make changes without consultation. Luckily in Benjamin's family, once agreement had been reached, everyone 'signed up' to the plan—and stuck to it. The essence of the plan was that the adults would change *their* behaviour to help Benjamin to alter *his*.

It was agreed that, since there were different reasons behind the three occasions when Benjamin most frequently pressed his eye, there would have to be different approaches for each occasion:

1　*Mealtimes*　His parents felt that if they gave Benjamin his sweet course first, so that he knew he was going to enjoy his meal, it might eliminate his eye-pressing at mealtimes. They decided that, as he always ate a good breakfast and a good supper, it was lunchtime they should target, and so they reversed the pudding and savoury courses at that meal—and the problem was solved!

2　*Nappy-changing*　The eye-pressing when Benjamin was having his nappy changed was eliminated by:

● giving him far more warning about nappy-changing times, through speech and gesture

● avoiding changing his nappy on surfaces of which he was

unsure—previously it had been done wherever in the house
he happened to be

● changing his nappy at regular intervals—for example, always
before and after a meal so that he would begin to associate
mealtimes with nappy-changing.

3 *Grandmother's visits*   It was more difficult to decide how to
eliminate the eye-pressing when his grandmother came to the
house. She would have been very hurt, had she realised that
her visits made Benjamin fearful. It was agreed that for these
occasions, certain toys and activities would be chosen that
only the two of them would share—toys and activities that
were pleasurable for both of them—so that he would associate
his grandmother with having a good time. It was also felt
that if she came to see him more often he would become
more used to her, and would thus be able to look forward to
her visit as an enjoyable event in his weekly routine. Also,
as Grandma always wore a certain type of silky scarf, she
would be encouraged to cuddle Benjamin more often, so that
he not only associated her with fun activities but also would
learn to recognise her scarves as an additional clue. The
family decided, too, that, as Grandma was rather sedentary
she would also be asked to take part in one of his least
boisterous activities—singing with him.

Benjamin's chart for the second week, taking account of the
three previous problem situations, was filled in as follows:

BENJAMIN
Date
Adult's name   [The adult who is going to fill in the chart]
Behaviour   Benjamin presses his left hand to his left eye.
Procedure   [Benjamin presses his eye during mealtimes, when his nappy is
    being changed and when his grandmother comes to the house. It should be
    discovered this week whether the strategies outlined above are successful in
    eliminating, or helping to eliminate, eye-pressing in the three situations.]
Aim   [The aim of the chart is to record the adult's behaviour, *as well as*
    Benjamin's.]
How often (lunchtime)   [Benjamin's breakfast and supper remain the same as
    before. At lunchtimes, his pudding is given to him first. At the end of
    lunchtime the adult records whether or not, and/or how often, Benjamin has
    pressed his hand to his eye.]

How often (nappy-changing) [Benjamin has his nappy changed on a surface that is familiar to him. The same tactual clues are always used to warn him that his nappy is about to be changed: it is agreed that the adult will put her hands on both sides of the nappy he is presently wearing, to warn him that nappy-changing time is starting. (As Benjamin has a hearing loss it is important to remember to speak and sign with him, using the same phrases and signs for all nappy-changing activities.) At the end of nappy-changing the adult records whether or not, and/or how often, Benjamin has pressed his hand to his eye.]

How often (Grandma's visits) [Benjamin's grandmother is asked to come to the house more often and to stay a little longer to have tea—which will be another clue for Benjamin to associate with her visit. Grandma is asked always to chat to her daughter before going to speak to Benjamin, so that he gets used to the idea that Grandma is here. He will then be readier to spend some time with her, having fun, songs and cuddles. At the end of Grandma's visit the adult records whether or not, and/or how often, Benjamin has pressed his hand to his eye.]

Recording [As the adult's behaviour is being recorded as well as Benjamin's, the emphasis has now changed. It is Benjamin's parents' responsibility to carry out the agreed strategies and to record their behaviour.]

Getting parents to analyse the child's unwanted behaviour objectively, to work towards participating fully, with the professionals involved, in planning how to alter that behaviour, and to look also at the adults' behaviour in relation to the child, are all far more useful to them and to their child than just 'offering suggestions'. Observing and discussing together can often help show all concerned that each one of them needs to change his or her behaviour—not just the child's—in order to achieve permanent success.

Taking time to think about ways of changing negative behaviour may depend on analysing several options, with all involved adults, before starting the child's plan. Behaviour such as eye-pressing can become obsessive and, as the child grows older, a real problem. The importance of eliminating it as early and efficiently as possible cannot be overemphasised.

Making notes and devising charts such as those that Benjamin's parents used are two ways of preparing for behavioural change. Another kind of chart would record the child's behaviour, describing exactly what happens:

Behaviour
What do you think caused it?
Where did it happen?
What did you do?
What happened next?

Observations (examples)
Eye-pressing
Nappy changing
Sitting-room
Carried on changing him in sitting-room
He screamed and pressed both eyes
  even more

A child's behaviour can also be recorded in a *participation chart*, which is an extremely useful tool when trying to deal with very ingrained obsessive behaviour such as, for example, rocking. The observations in the chart that follows are based on an individual experience and an individual child, whom I have called Jane:

JANE

Participation in self-selected activities

Implications for child

Participation in other, skilled activities

Skills achieved

Environment

Observations

Jane rocks most of the day.

She does not participate in other activities. She enjoys rocking.

She has no time to participate in other skilled activities.*

She is becoming more skilled in rocking, and rocks forward so that her head touches the floor.

She is in a very unstimulating environment with little adult contact.

Jane's participation chart highlights precisely what she needs—more stimulation, more contact with adults and an individual programme that puts communication at the forefront. Observing Jane permits those involved with her to set targets for her, and can help them to pinpoint the salient questions:

- What skills does Jane need to develop?
- What changes need to be made to achieve these skills?
- What must happen to achieve these changes?
- How will we know when the desired changes have occurred?

* Note that rocking can be regarded as a skill.

- How can we tell what progress Jane is making?
- How can we record that success has occurred?
- How must the adults involved with her change their working practices so as to increase Jane's chances of success?
- What further skills will her newly acquired skills lead to?

CREATING OPPORTUNITIES

Environments need to be created that will give Jane opportunities to develop and achieve new skills. If she succeeds, these new skills should be seen as a basis from which to build up more skills. If she does not succeed, it has to be assumed that the adults involved have not set realistic targets. Jane *needs* to succeed, and it is crucial that the adults take time to plan and prepare together. Focusing on her environment and the activities provided for her within that environment will be vital if success is to be achieved.

Remember that it is often the adult, or adults—as shown in Benjamin's case, for instance—who need to change more than the child. Two important questions to ask are whether it is realistic to expect the child to behave in the desired way *in difficult situations*, and whether success is possible *at this particular time*. Sometimes time-scales need to be extended, and adults need to study the child's reactions closely before they are able to set goals, whether short-term or long-term, that take her ability levels fully into account.

It cannot be overemphasised that, before starting any programme, it is essential to know everything there is to know about how the child communicates, and about her hearing, vision and physical skills. Only by going about it in this way will it be possible to tailor an individual plan to the exact specifications of the individual child.

What often works best for the child is to accept her present skill—rocking, for instance—as a positive activity, or as an element that can be retained but modified in the process of acquiring other skills. Rocking backwards and forwards can become rocking from side to side, which can lead on to rocking with a partner, dancing, trampolining and so on. In other words, it is important not to try to take away completely the skill that the

Has the child had opportunities to explore?

child has, but to incorporate it in a meaningful way in another, more constructive, activity.

As well as the child's physical abilities, visual and hearing skills, *outside influences* need to be borne in mind. Everyone's behaviour is influenced by many factors, such as:

—social experience: what is being expected of the child, and are those expectations reasonable?
—environmental experience: has she had opportunities to explore?
—tactile skills: is she sensorily defensive, or unduly accepting?
—opportunity: has she had chances to experiment?
—mobility: has she explored for herself?
—nutrition: do certain foods affect her? Does she have feeding difficulties?
—bodily functions: is she uncomfortable because she is constipated?
—health: is she well or ill, or in pain? Is she fatigued?

—medication: is she taking medication that may be making her
aroused, or sleepy?
—other people (all adults, peer group, family members): what is
their attitude to her?
—past experience: does she have preconditioned notions about
what she thinks might happen because of her behaviour?
—additional difficulties: does she have motor difficulties such
as hypotonia or hypertonia (floppiness or stiffness) that make
her feel not in control and insecure?

Some children have poor sensory integration or body image, or
limited physical skills, that may lead to exaggerated feelings of
inadequacy, anger or fear. For example, if a child's 'tilt and save'
reactions are underdeveloped, she may defend herself against
many movements because she does not like the feeling of being
off balance. Some children feel very unsettled, for instance, with
even a very small amount of jostling. None of these additional
difficulties should be overlooked when considering a child's
behaviour.

It is particularly important to consider her overall health—
many children have been mislabelled as 'difficult' when in fact
they have been in pain, intense or intermittent. Children whose
personal communication mode is not fully established or recognised may suddenly bang their faces or ears. If you see this
happen, check for toothache, middle-ear infection or glaucoma.
Solutions may be very quickly found—once the child's pain is
gone, then the face-banging will probably disappear. Behaviour
that is problematical and that challenges adults can often be
rapidly sorted out once we have realised what is bothering the
child. Other strategies should be reserved for altering behaviour
that appears to be caused by external factors.

As always, studying the child's situation in some detail will
result in better planning for long-term positive effects. Plans will
involve pooling ideas and having clear aims and objectives, as
well as methods that are easy to follow and a firm confidence in
the benefit that the child will derive from the programme. There
will also be an emphasis on objectives to be achieved by the
adult, with a view to giving the child the best possible opportunity

to reach her goals. You can usefully ask yourself these three questions:

1   What can I do to make activities more appropriate for the child?
2   What skills do I need to master to achieve more appropriate communication with her?
3   What alterations and adaptations can I make to ensure that the environment is more appropriate for her?

Before embarking on the child's plan, discuss whether to use strategies such as:

—avoiding the problematical situation
—demonstrating other skills (such as putting things in a container rather than throwing)
—helping her to anticipate what is happening
—altering the situation slightly
—changing the environment
—noticing and praising her abilities.

Beware of not noticing or inadvertently rewarding negative aspects. Above all, remember that helping the child acquire communication skills that are appropriate for her, that will permit her to make herself understood all of the time, will always be the most positive way forward.

Some of the ideas and strategies described above helped the adults involved to devise plans for James and Thomas, two children with multisensory impairment.

JAMES

At the age of ten, James, who had light perception and a moderate to severe hearing loss, had an interest in light that was completely absorbing. He had become so totally obsessed with light that he would search for it everywhere and bang his head if not allowed to be close to the brightest light source in the room. Although he was interested in food, he would ignore it completely if he was seated under a light or by a window in a sunny room.

Eye-poking and light-gazing are often associated with older

James had a total obsession with light-gazing.

children born deafblind. They are not observed so often in children who have been given attention early. Those who have taken part in appropriate early-learning intervention programmes have less need for self-stimulation; they learn age-appropriate activities that absorb them and are provided with a rich diet of sensory stimulation. Some older children, on the other hand, may be so obsessed with self-stimulation that it is very difficult to reach them and to help them relate to the outside world.

When considering the older child's behaviour, it is helpful to observe not only him but also his environment and his reactions to the adults and children within that environment. Initially, it is the adult or adults who are going to be required to modify their behaviour. We should ask ourselves what has gone wrong in the child's past, or is wrong in his present situation, to cause him to manifest this behaviour. *We need to adapt ourselves to him, as well as asking him to adapt to us.*

In James's case, it was agreed that the aim was to change his negative obsession with light-gazing and to encourage him to transfer his interest in light towards more positive activity. Strategies included:

—altering the fitments in the classroom and dining-room to emit diffuse lighting, so that James was not distracted by bright overhead light
—acquiring several torches with different types of switch and coloured bulbs, which were demonstrated coactively with him
—appreciating that James could have fun activating the torches, and making it a part of his programme at regular times each day. Acquiring this new skill gave his negative behaviour a positive outcome.

Establishing positive activities for James introduced three important new elements into his programme:

1   He could now benefit from a reward system, which involved activating torches.
2   He could now work a switch to gain his reward.
3   He could be taught to operate other switches to obtain other effects.

Choosing activities that it was felt James would enjoy, and using light to highlight them, acted as a stimulus to his participation. He was encouraged to take part in classroom and mealtime activities by always having the activity or the meal well lit by a downlight. He was rewarded for positive behaviour by being given the opportunity to play with toys that incorporated light or sound rewards. (Some recommended toys that work on a cause-and-effect principle, using switches, light and sound, are described in Chapter 10.)

THOMAS
Thomas used to bang his face, rock backwards and forwards and bang his head on any convenient hard surface. He was nine years old, and had been excluded from his school because his behaviour was so dangerous to other children as well as to his teachers. He had light perception and useful residual hearing in his left ear,

but had a severe sensorineural loss in his right ear. He lived alone with his mother, who could no longer cope with his destructive habits.

Thomas's mother described her efforts to change his behaviour as follows:

- In order to stop him from hurting himself when he banged his head, she had provided him with a mattress-covered area in his bedroom. There was a mattress on each of two adjacent walls and one on the floor, giving him a triangular area in which to bang his head.
- In order to prevent him from banging his head, she would restrain him by holding him against her body and holding his hands very tightly against his sides.
- In order to prevent him from both banging *and* rocking she would give him snacks and sweets throughout the day, because when he was occupied in eating he did not rock or bang so hard.

Carefully recording his mother's response to the behaviour and discussing it with her helped her to realise that she was constantly reinforcing it. She was giving Thomas extra opportunities to bang his head by providing the mattress-covered area, she was paying extra attention to the behaviour by restraining him and holding his hands down, and she was rewarding him by providing him with sweets and snacks as a distraction. In other words, her reactions to his destructive behaviour had increased it.

People had become afraid of Thomas, so were withdrawing from him rather than going towards him. The further they withdrew, the more negative behaviour Thomas displayed. The only person not afraid of him was his mother, and she had demonstrated this by restraining him from his dangerous and self-abusive actions, but unfortunately she was also reinforcing them.

It was vital that Thomas's mother restructure her behaviour, and to achieve this she needed to be helped to observe Thomas at a distance; it was equally vital to demonstrate to Thomas that adults were not afraid of him, and that he could find other ways of gaining attention. By making the effort to stand back from the problem, and by discussing it together, parents and co-workers were able to find ways of solving the difficulties.

A programme that would give Thomas as much caring bodily contact as possible was initiated. It was essential to demonstrate to him that there were legitimate means of using his energies. A great many children resort to violent rocking because they do not have the same outlets for their energy as their sighted–hearing peers. Rather than walking, they twirl on the spot. Rather than running, they stand and rock backwards and forwards in what appears to be a frenzied manner. They may poke their eyes, bang their heads or bite themselves in order to gain from their bodies a stimulation which they would otherwise gain from activities within the environment. Incorporating a set of structured active play and work strategies and long-term goals ensured complete success for Thomas. Elimination of negative behaviour cannot take place if the child has no legitimate stimulating activities with which to replace them and which continue to give him constant enjoyment.

Weekly goals were agreed, as well as the long-term goal of completely changing Thomas's behaviour within a year. Short-term goals, with realistic targets that are reviewed at least weekly to ensure continuity of approach, can always be set within a time-limited programme.

THOMAS'S PROGRAMME

Rocking

Thomas needed an outlet for his energies, and it was decided that it could be beneficial if an adult joined him in his rocking activities. As rocking often led to head-banging, he was not provided with mattresses, either to sit on or on the walls of his room, but instead he sat on a blanket on the floor. Appropriate musical activities were devised in the hope that this would lead to changing Thomas's negative rocking behaviour into cooperative two-way interaction. The idea was that he would be sung to as he rocked and, if he would allow it, he would hold hands with the adult and they would move together with the music.

It was agreed that the only place to be well lit would be the 'rocking blanket', on which the teacher would also sit. The rocking session lasted for as long as Thomas's interest was sustained, his teacher withdrawing close contact only *if he was self-abusive* by pinching or banging himself. The contact was *not* withdrawn if he was abusive towards his teacher. Establishing a good relationship was important, and Thomas needed to realise that if he withdrew into himself less fun activity would happen. Week by week, through these intensive interactive sessions, he began to appreciate that the adult was always there, that she would always stay close to him and always remain calm. Gradually, he began to move up to the teacher and join her in shared rocking games which depended on him interacting with his teacher.

Head-banging

Careful observation of Thomas's head-banging led his mother to conclude that he would often stop momentarily, before or after banging his head, in order to discover what the adults' reactions were going to be. It needed to be made clear to him that he would receive a great deal of attention throughout his structured sessions, but no attention at all, for ten seconds, if he banged his head.

Thomas had managed to gain much attention from his head-banging. His mother had even bought him a crash helmet to try to stop him, but when he wore it, she reported, the behaviour had increased. On one occasion he smashed his head against a window, causing a great deal of damage—and consequent attention. Using the crash helmet now appeared to his mother to have reinforced the banging.

It was decided that if Thomas banged his head, the teacher would put his hand on the part of his head that he had banged and would then take that hand and sign a clear 'Thomas, sit and wait.' They would both sit still *together*, for ten seconds. Thomas soon learned that it was far more interesting to take part in activities than to sit still for ten seconds. His head-banging gradually decreased. Other methods that helped to eliminate it were extra physically stimulating activities such as:

—rolling over a large physiotherapy ball
—running with a partner out of doors
—using a jogging machine on a very low setting
—jumping on a trampoline with a partner
—swinging and dancing with a partner

All these activities were designed to give Thomas extra sensory stimulation and movement that was fun. They were also designed to help him to understand that activities that depend on partnership and cooperation are even more fun.

Children who are visually impaired and who have other disabilities as well have less choice of activity than sighted children. They may use their bodies for pleasure or stimulation. Rocking of the head and body, movements of the hands or head, vigorous breathing, tooth-grinding, scratching and rubbing the skin, light-gazing, eye-poking, hair-twirling, screaming, outbursts of laughter—are all behaviours that can be observed in some children and adults. The reasons why these behaviours arise must be seen to be as important as the activities themselves. If the cause of the behaviour is not eliminated, the activity will continue. The causes of maladaptive behaviour include the need to seek comfort, to reduce or avoid anxiety, to increase stimulation and to gain extra attention.

Children whose main channels of information are damaged often have no other means of relating to the world; their behaviour can be seen as a reaction to the actions of others towards them, and to a world that has little meaning for them. Giving meaning, order, structure and routines can help some children towards a more engaged and active life. There are children whose behaviour has become so deeply entrenched over time that they need programmes that have been especially carefully devised and that will last for a considerable period; and some of those may never lose their negative behaviour entirely, for the longer they have been engaged in it the more difficult it will be for them to change. Some children revert to their previous negative behaviour when under stress. It is therefore vital for parents and teachers to inform each other about occasions when negative behaviour is likely to recur, in order to prevent it happening.

Establishing positive associations, strong relationships and partnership activities will usually be a fruitful means of helping children to acquire positive behaviour. Very gradual elimination techniques that involve adults making modifications to their own behaviour can make the child's life more purposeful and enjoyable.*

Very often long-term change *can* be effected through cooperative effort.

---

* It must be remembered that there are specific reasons for the behaviour of some children, related to their condition or syndrome. For example, Tourette syndrome is associated with characteristics such as twitching, blinking and nodding and can include making involuntary sounds; attention-deficit hyperactivity disorder (ADHD) is a condition that results in a child being considerably overactive; autism is associated with stereotyped behaviour. Some children are known to be very sensitive to certain sounds or other stimuli, and may withdraw if they are 'overloaded'. Others may have behavioural needs related to long periods of hospitalisation. Information about specific conditions and rare syndromes can be obtained from the *CaF Rare Syndromes Directory* (see Recommended Reading).

9 Zachary and Felicity

ZACHARY

'If I don't know where I'm going, how will I know when I've got there?'—if Zachary had had the words, this is what he would probably have said to the adults in his life.

Zachary's story is almost entirely to do with his having been neglected. From the age of eight months he had been placed in a series of ten short-term foster homes that proved emotionally disastrous for him. He is totally blind and, because of his persistent ear infections (and consequent conductive hearing loss), was completely unable to understand the activities going on around him. He responded by withdrawing into self-stimulatory behaviour. He is hypotonic.

Zachary was extremely timid, panicking if he was left alone. He quite clearly had no idea about his environment, behaved in an extremely insecure fashion and was alarmed by being moved, however gently. He was unable to sit up unsupported, neither did he reach out for a sound-making toy. He gave very few noticeable signals, although he did nestle closer to the adult who was cuddling him.

Zachary appeared to be unaware of sound, and he showed no clear anticipation of movements in any routines. He did not copy any movements, signals or sounds, even when they were directed at him repeatedly by his most familiar adult. He did not appear to listen to an adult's vocalisation, nor to a variety of sound-making toys. He would not permit his hands, feet or body to be moved over any textures. He did not explore any object with his fingers, and he did not appear to know that he could turn objects over or that his fingers belonged to him. He had no exploratory behaviour at all. He was frightened of water: he screamed when he was put in the bath, did not splash his hands in the water or appear to gain any enjoyment from the experience of being bathed. He had no tolerance of tactile materials and withdrew from all soft textures. He was entirely passive, apparently unaware that his limbs were being touched or moved, and made no discernible movements to indicate whether he enjoyed or disliked any experience. When given a selection of toys, he made no move. Taken outside, he was extremely fearful.

When, at the age of two, he was placed with foster parents, he had very significant behaviour needs.

It was essential for his foster parents to spend a great deal of time discussing with the professionals involved his need to establish bodily signals. As he had no sight, the aim had to be to work towards increasing his use of hearing and towards his acquiring communication skills. He needed to learn to associate everyday activities with pleasure rather than fear. Attention had to be paid to his need to listen to the variety of sounds that were present within his environment, and one important goal was to help him to understand where those sounds were coming from and that they all had meaning.

One of the reasons why he was so passive was that he had no understanding of his environment. Things were happening *to him* but not *with him*. He had not as yet developed the ability to listen, or to make relationships with the countless adults he had met in his short life. His defence had been to withdraw completely.

Environmental influences which impinged on his behaviour included the fact that no one had understood that, as a child with a hearing difficulty, because he was not hearing clearly he was cutting out what he did not understand or want to hear. He was unable, because of his hearing loss, to understand the words he heard indistinctly, and he had been given no opportunities to organise his use of hearing. No sound had been localised for him; he never knew who was talking to him or what was about to happen. He had no incentive to remember or to recognise, or to associate one person with another or discriminate one person *from* another. He was able neither to receive nor to give information. He had no one with whom to reciprocate, no one to interpret his world for him, no one with whom he had been able to build up a warm and trusting emotional bond. *Nothing was meaningful*. He was in an environment with boisterous children who inadvertently frightened him. He did not receive any extra help until he was two.

It was important for the foster parents to establish one-to-one interaction as far as possible. Without this, it would be impossible for Zachary to learn to trust anyone. So intensive play (see Chapter 6) was started. Gradually, it was hoped, he would learn to identify his foster parents as people who mattered, and they would then be able to engage in activities that would help to develop his auditory, tactile, motor and self-help skills. His communication skills, it was felt, would only develop if clear language was used in all exchanges with him; he needed to be given explanations, at all times, about what was happening to him. Another strategy was to allow him to dictate the content, course and pace of their interactions with him. Zachary needed to feel in charge.

As he was so passive, it was extremely important that, within his intensive-play activities, his foster parents acknowledged his bodily signals, however minute. They had to work towards instilling in him the understanding that any action of his would get a response from them. His intensive play should constantly repeat the same actions, so that he would gradually learn to expect a certain pattern of movement, which he might then react to.

Zachary turned out to be something of a mystery to his foster parents. They had never before met a child who was totally blind, nor one so hypotonic. At the age of two, he was entirely unable to move independently. His physical skills were so limited that any interactions had been to do only with his bodily functions such as toileting, bathing and dressing. This, of course, meant that no meaningful conversations had taken place.

Once his foster parents had initiated intensive play activities, a dramatic change took place. He began to giggle when his two significant adults indicated that it was time for an intensive-play session. He began to learn to sit up, propped on cushions. Over time he began to pivot on his bottom when he was sitting. He began to grasp small objects, which he would sometimes drop on purpose and then pick up. He also began to use several speech-like sounds such as 'daddee', 'babee', 'mamee' and 'a-ee'. Excited by his progress, his foster parents now introduced more strategies for improving his postural control and locomotion, and to help him acquire fine motor and communications skills.

By the age of three, still in his short-stay foster home, Zachary was engaging in some very meaningful play activities.

ZACHARY AT THREE

Motor development

Zachary could now turn when he was sitting, and hold on to furniture when standing. Much of his ability to move forwards or sideways when standing depended on his attitude towards it; his interest in food could be used as an inducement to do so. He still got very unsure of himself when asked to stand and walk

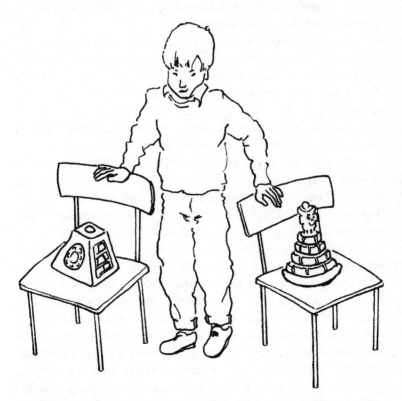

Standing between two chairs, each with an interesting sound-making toy.

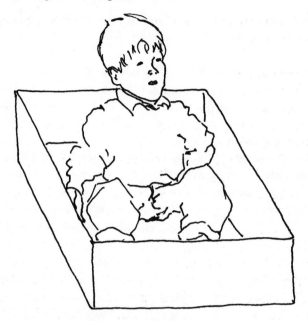

Sitting in a box feeling the perimeters.

forward. He did not have enough confidence to know that he could do it. He did not yet *want* spontaneously to pull up from sitting to standing, but he could be motivated to rise if his interest in noise-making toys was brought into play. Sometimes he would stand between two chairs, on each of which an interesting sound-making toy had been placed, and gently move his hands over the surface of the chairs, one after the other, to find the toys.

Zachary now felt much safer. He could accept the idea of standing, with furniture or an adult for support, and of playing with his toys. Over time he was able to reach further and further for them. He could sit unsupported in a large box with low sides, and was prepared to move around on his bottom to seek his toys. A box that was big enough to explore but small enough for him to find the perimeters, gave him a feeling of security. His foster parents did a great deal of work with him sitting on their knees, giving him experience of different positions, particularly rocking backwards and forwards, and in this way he was able to learn new motor skills. He could, and was prepared to, move his body in space, and could use his muscles and counteract any momentary loss of balance.

Fine motor skills

Zachary could grasp and purposely drop objects, pick them up and manipulate them, and turn them over to examine them. He could move his fingers in many directions and was prepared to hold both soft and hard objects. He did not reject materials with different textures, and was adventurous in the way he approached new objects.

He now needed to learn to handle smaller, more intricate cause-and-effect objects and materials. He could take objects out of a container, but he could not yet put them in and then take them out of the same container, or dump objects out of a container and then put them back in, or transfer things from one container to another. Posting objects into a container such as a coffee tin with a lid encouraged him to learn to take the lid off in order to get an object out such as a biscuit, and he could put the lid back again. He was encouraged to play in the water by being sat in a small baby bath, inside the family bath, thereby maintaining a feeling of security when in water. He could feel for toys in his play bath and was beginning to pour water.

Auditory skills

As well as the speech-like sounds already mentioned—'daddee', 'a-ee' and 'babee', 'mamee'—Zachary now said 'ahah', 'emem', 'mamer', 'naner' and apparently called himself 'Aki'. His foster parents responded to these babbles by imitating them right up close to him, so that he could feel their faces. He always used his left ear in preference to his right, listening to toys by holding them to that ear. He enjoyed using sound-making toys such as a drum and a xylophone, and could search for rattles and noisy bells when they were played about 45cm (18in) from his hands.

His foster parents used certain key phrases, accompanied by body signs, when addressing Zachary. The importance of always speaking to him in clear, simple sentences was emphasised. He now appeared to be using his residual hearing. As part of his play activities, his foster parents were working towards increasing his listening skills by presenting him with a variety of sound-making toys. They chose the sort that he could bang and shake, encouraging him to copy rhythms and to listen out for his favourite toys before they were given to him. At this vital stage, he was given as much auditory information as possible about all the activities and people within his environment.

Zachary continued to make very good progress, although he was still significantly delayed, particularly in his physical development. At the age of three he could not yet stand unsupported. In addition, his speech and his understanding of language were of special concern. A hearing test revealed that he had a hearing loss in both ears of approximately 65 decibels. The test revealed that there was little movement of the timpanic membrane and no measurable middle ear pressure point, which was indicative of fluid in the middle ear cavity causing a conductive hearing loss (sometimes called glue ear). It was felt that, until this medical problem was resolved, it would be very difficult to establish whether or not Zachary had an underlying sensorineural hearing impairment.

By now, the lack of bonding opportunities that had characterised all other placements had begun to be somewhat offset by the compensatory activities provided by his foster parents. At three and a half and still in the short-stay foster home, Zachary was continuing to make good progress.

ZACHARY AT THREE AND A HALF

Motor development

Zachary could now pull himself to standing, hold on to furniture and bottom-shuffle towards a sound-making toy, and he would hold on to a hand and walk with people if he felt secure. His main need, now that he was able to negotiate furniture, was to gain in confidence to move by himself. This could only be achieved through practice, and by his learning which objects were safe to hold on to and which were not. He practised the art of mobility by exploring the environment through any means he chose—and his repertoire included crawling, cruising, rolling and holding hands.

As far as his mobility was concerned, it was important that he always walk *to* someone and not *away* from him or her, and he needed to walk at someone's side with *one* hand held. He also needed practice in standing alone when occupied, by being given the opportunity to stand and play at a table. He was not expected to stand alone yet, as he was still learning to feel secure. When he was unsupported he still lost his feeling of security—perhaps because of his total blindness, but more likely because of his previous very negative experiences. He still needed to feel that he was standing near something or someone supportive that would not move away unexpectedly. One experience he now began to accept was that of moving on a safe trampoline, which gave him upward movement—something that he thoroughly enjoyed.

Zachary could overcome obstacles when he was moving, and did not mind occasionally bumping into furniture. It was important to bear in mind that he probably did not appreciate the dimensions of furniture. For example, when he was standing or walking with an adult, furniture would probably appear entirely different from when he was exploring it from the floor. He was therefore given many opportunities to explore all around and behind it so that he recognised it from all angles.

Fine motor skills
Zachary was encouraged to investigate all the toys and other objects that he encountered. He was particularly interested in toys with moving parts. He was now learning how to transfer objects from one container to another, and how to take smaller lids off. He would allow himself to be shown coactively how to manipulate or use new toys.

Self-help skills
Zachary could take off his socks, shoes, scarf and hat. He was helped coactively—from behind, hand over hand—to take off and put on his clothes. Each garment was held as he put it on, and he was praised for his efforts at dressing and undressing himself. It was very important that he only dress or undress at the appropriate times, and that he should not learn formally to dress and undress but to do it naturally whenever it was an

Transferring objects from one container to another.

appropriate time. During the summer months he had many opportunities to take off and put on his clothes when he was playing in the garden.

Zachary learned to use a sponge and began to learn to clean his teeth. He knew what a brush was, and put it on his head to try to brush his hair. He ate very well, and fed himself with a spoon independently. He needed to learn the skill of drinking from a cup and to take smaller sips rather than large gulps.

Communication

Zachary's foster parents would identify the key points in his environment at any given moment by saying, for instance, 'Zachary, the chair is here' or 'Zachary, let's open the door' or 'Zachary, let's play on the grass.' They always used his name first, so that he knew instantly that they were talking to him. He was only just learning to use his residual hearing, so they needed to get his attention and alert him to situations. Zachary needed to know everything about his environment, and, at this stage only adults could supply the information he needed.

His other main need at this point was to increase his understanding that he was communicating with others and that they could understand him. He had one clear word—'dow' for 'down'—and a range of other babbles, jargoning and wordlike sounds. It was decided that one wordlike sound, 'ye' for 'yes', should be repeated so that he knew that his foster parents understood his words—for example, 'Yes, Zachary. Yes, we'll play now. Yes, Zachary. Yes, we're going out to the garden.'

Zachary was now beginning to call himself 'Zazee'. Whenever he used this word, his foster parents would say something like 'Hello, Zachary. I can hear you, Zachary, hello.' They knew that he needed to appreciate that his wordlike sounds had meaning, and it was important for them to be identified, expanded and commented on as often as possible. It was also important to pinpoint events for him, by repeating easy-to-remember phrases such as 'Zachary is coming inside', 'Zachary is going to wash his hands', 'Zachary is going to sit down', 'Zachary is going to eat tea.' In this way he was helped to identify specific moments within the day.

His foster parents always:

- *identified him by name*—he needed to know that they were talking to him
- *identified actions and places by name*—he needed to know exactly what was happening to him
- *identified themselves and other people by name*—he needed to know who was talking to him, all the time

Zachary was being guided through speech, sign and situational clues towards further understanding. Being spoken to in clear sentences accompanied by sign or gesture; being given opportunities to learn to trust and touch; and living with people able to accept his emotional differences—all these factors gave him much more stability.

* * *

At this point Zachary was moved to a new foster home. Within a short time he lost all his confidence and became extremely vulnerable, angry and disturbed.

He began to hit and bang himself all the time, and retreated into his own world. He smacked himself when he wanted something and when he heard the word 'no', he ate in an overcompensating way, he sat on the floor and circled around aimlessly, and he pushed his fists into his eyes almost constantly. He could not, with so many self-stimulating behaviours, be left to amuse himself, even for a few minutes. He was extremely clinging and needed total attention and reassurance, but it proved impossible for his new foster parents to reassure him. He cried all day and night, and was unable to sleep for more than a few exhausted moments. He was 'labelled' as 'disturbed'.

He was moved very quickly to what turned out to be another disastrous placement—but this time, an abusive one. Zachary was unhappier than ever—and now, in addition, he needed protection. His negative behaviour was increasing daily. At one stage it was felt that he manifested so many disturbing and self-destructive habits that he might never find a permanent home. He was 'relabelled' as 'extremely disturbed'. Then, at the age of five, Zachary was adopted. Six months later, a review of his progress was made.

ZACHARY AT FIVE AND A HALF

Emotional development

When Zachary went to live with his new, adoptive parents he was in a highly disturbed state, exhibiting all the self-stimulating behaviours just described. Because they were able to provide him with a one-to-one parent–Zachary ratio at all times, those behaviours ceased (except when he felt extremely unsure—when he was in new or noisy surroundings, for example, or with a strange adult). He became happy, secure and contented with them.

The following important points, nonetheless, always had to be borne in mind:

1   He had to be in a one-to-one adult relationship.
2   He had to be with adults he knew reasonably well.
3   He could not feel in competition with other people (including children, and particularly very young ones).
4   He always functioned best in quiet, calm, undisturbed surroundings.

Zachary had begun to trust again.

Motor development
Zachary could now walk freely and confidently in the house, although there had to be someone with him to guard him from danger and to give him the constant reassurance of an adult's presence. He walked up and down stairs, one hand held. He did not walk freely outside but would follow an adult's sound directions—voice or claps—so long as that adult was only one metre away. He began to learn routes, such as from the bathroom to his room and from the swing to the slide. He also began to learn how to get down from an adult-sized dining-chair and from an adult-sized toilet (with the help of his mother only, at this stage).

Self-care skills
Feeding   Zachary fed himself competently using a teaspoon or a dessert spoon, and he ate from ordinary dishes. He finger-fed himself foods such as sandwiches and bananas, and could feel in the bag for crisps before eating them. He used any cup, with or without a handle, and could search for it on the table if it had been placed on his right-hand side.
Toileting   He was usually clean and dry throughout the day. He asked for a 'wee-wee' or a 'two-two', and said 'toilet' at the appropriate times. He used an adult-sized toilet, with a child's seat. He wore nappies at night.
Washing and dressing   Zachary enjoyed a bath and accepted the teeth-cleaning process. He tried to dry himself with a towel. He liked to be clean, although, like all children, he enjoyed getting dirty again! He made good attempts at brushing his hair. He could pull off most garments with minimal assistance, and tried to pull up his pants and trousers. He knew where his clothes were kept and could name them all.

Speech
Zachary knew at least fifteen action songs and nursery rhymes and could supply the last word in a sequence. He could name most body parts and was learning to count to ten. He knew the sounds that some common animals make and would imitate police-car or siren noises. Although his speech was understandable to his parents and advisory teachers, much of it was still

indistinct and would not be understood by strangers. He made frequent consonant reversals—'g' for 'd', 'd' for 'b', 's' for 'f'—which was more in keeping with a 'developmentally young' or hard-of-hearing child. His vocabulary increased daily, he could put together three- or four-word sequences, and he could use words learned in one situation in another, appropriate, one.

Auditory skills
Zachary was being encouraged to listen to sequences of musical sounds and rhythms.

Tactual development
He was starting to 'look' at tactile books, scanning and searching for different shapes.

Leisure activities
He was always pleased to go swimming, and was very confident in the water. He played in the garden every day and enjoyed the swing, the slide and the trampoline, but his favourite activity was pushing his trolley. He walked well—with one hand held by his mother, he had managed at least a mile.

*   *   *

Throughout his early years Zachary's hearing had remained impaired. It was not until he was placed with his adoptive parents that he received the much needed medical treatment for his middle ear problem. As soon as he went to live with them he attended an ear, nose and throat hospital and had grommets inserted to drain the fluid from his ears. The results of this minor operation were nothing short of startling. He began to babble a lot more, and it was quite clear that he was beginning to understand a great deal of speech that he had previously missed. His new parents understood that communication would be the key to all his further development, but he also needed activities designed to help him achieve more skills in the following five areas.

1   *Motor development*   Care was taken to give him plenty of

One hand held by his mother.

opportunity to form mental maps of his home environment before he was expected to explore unknown locations.

2 *Dressing, undressing, self-care, feeding and toileting skills* Most of his learning was governed by the need for coactive demonstrations with a view to achieving independence in these areas.

3 *Auditory skills* As Zachary had functioned for years as a child with a hearing loss, he needed extra help in identifying the new environmental sounds that he had begun to listen to. Activities to help him learn to listen out for sounds included going to parks, farms and other places where he would hear and meet animals.

4   *Tactual development*   Giving him experience of cause-and-effect toys was instrumental in his learning to use his hands in different ways. He did not yet explore delicately, or use finger-tip scanning, vital for learning Braille.

5   *Play activities and further learning*   These are interdependent: helped by an understanding adult, children learn, through play, to use their cognitive abilities while incorporating and strengthening their existing skills. The aim was to offer Zachary activities well within his range of skills, that would provide a foundation of experience, with a view to his understanding the environment and 'real life'.

Activities that would gradually be added to his repertoire included matching familiar everyday objects such as a dish with a spoon. He went on to learn to find two objects that were the same, gradually working towards being able to sort and sequence objects and to take part in many different games involving recognition and the naming of people, places and actions.

WHAT CAN WE LEARN FROM ZACHARY'S STORY?

Zachary was not communicating because he had been taught by circumstances not to do so. Communication only develops by being meaningful and by being used. He had been so confused that, on two separate occasions, he had had no option but to withdraw completely. The first time he withdrew, when he was in his first foster home, was because the world had no meaning for him. On the second occasion, the world had begun to have meaning but that meaning was suddenly withdrawn from him, with no explanation; he was taken from the place and the people he had learnt to trust and was expected to adapt to a new environment.

The fact that Zachary has managed to overcome his emotionally disturbing start is due to several factors. These must include, above all, the fact that his adoptive parents were able to provide a secure emotional environment for him. He needed to bond with people, and a routine had to be established that would permit him always to know exactly what was happening. It is important to bear in mind that his being entirely unable to sleep when he was younger may have been due to the fact that he never knew whether he was going to wake up in the same bed or with the same people. One of the means whereby his new parents re-established his confidence was that they always allowed him to take his own time when he was about to change activities. Over time, he learned that people and places were safe. As he improved in emotional stability, so his ability to learn other things was able to flourish.

Some extracts from a diary that his adoptive mother kept illustrate how Zachary grew and changed:

Extract 1

Today Zachary played a game of hide-and-seek with the towel. He took the towel from the towel rail and draped it over his arm, saying, 'Where's your arm, Zachary, where's your arm?', then pulled the towel off and said, 'Here it is, here it is.' He repeated this game for several minutes. After some time he elaborated on the game by hiding his 'bot-bot', his tummy, his other arm, his hands, his head and his cheeks. He finished the game by saying, 'Done, finished the towel.'
Zachary could have played this game without speech, but with *speech his mother was able to understand that it was a game of hide-and-seek and that his various actions were not random.*

Extract 2

Zachary can climb upstairs holding on to the banister, hand over hand. He's very pleased with himself, calling himself a clever boy. He is able to turn the corners by kneeling down, retaining a grip on the banister, and then standing up once he feels that his hands are round the corner.
All children need to practise the skills that they have been helped to achieve in their own way, at their own pace.

Extract 3

Zachary is beginning to be able to defer his wants. He asked to play the organ while downstairs and went through the routine formula—'Up the stairs, to the toilet, and then organ time'—without getting cross.

Zachary's parents used the same phrases for certain routines within his day. This helped him to understand that certain things would always happen, and that he could feel secure in the knowledge that if his mother had said a certain event was about to take place, this would indeed be the case.

Extract 4

Yesterday Zachary got out of bed while I was downstairs making a coffee. He had pushed the safety bars too far while playing a jumping game, and fell. When I got upstairs he said (as a cue for me), 'Whatever are you doing there, Zachary?' I repeated the phrase but omitted to say 'Zachary'; he repeated his phrase—'Whatever are you doing there, Zachary?'—which I then realised I was also expected to say, exactly. When I had said this phrase, Zachary replied, 'Pony ride', and demonstrated how he had been jumping so that I would understand how he'd got out of bed.

Zachary learned that his speech meant something to his parents, and that he could explain things to them in different ways.

Extract 5

Last night I asked Zachary whether he would like a sandwich. He appeared to say 'Night night', so I asked, 'You just want to go to sleep, you don't want a sandwich?' He then explained, 'Night night for tea tea, night night sandwiches', which I then knew meant 'Marmite sandwiches'. It is interesting to see how he is now able to explain himself if I don't quite understand.

Again, language is the key to his mother's understanding. Had Zachary been unable to speak, it would have been important that the signing which started with him when he was younger should have continued, because it would have been in this way that he would have demonstrated his needs. Zachary is now able to give clear explanations to his mother so that she can understand him. He knows what communication is.

Extract 6

When Zachary woke in the night he called me (as he always does) and then said, 'Zachary go to sleep', and fell asleep immediately—normally he waits for me to reply.

Again, see how helpful the formulae have been: because his mother had always replied in the same way—'Zachary go to sleep'—he was able to fall asleep immediately, since he knew that that was what happened during the night.

Extract 7

Zachary stays dry all morning (without nappies—just pants). He has nappies during lunch and for the rest of the day, as he tends to go out in the afternoon.

It is always important to try to maintain routines that the child will understand. It is acceptable to start toilet-training in this way: that is, without nappies in the morning, but with nappies for the rest of the day. The main thing is that the child begins to understand that for some part of the day it is up to him to stay dry. In fact, by using this method of only having pants in the morning, there was no pressure on Zachary to stay dry completely.

Extract 8

Zachary lost his beater for the xylophone while I was writing this. I told him that the beater was by his right hand and he immediately put out his right hand and found it.

The importance of being able to name body parts cannot be stressed enough. Children need to know about bodies and the ways they work. If they do not learn this skill, then their mobility may well be impaired in the future.

People's attitudes towards Zachary had a great deal to do with his changing abilities. Once he was seen as a child who was capable of learning, and it was realised that he could be helped to overcome his problems, he began to develop skills.

Zachary's story illustrates the following points:

- Early behavioural 'labelling' (without identifying causing factors) is helpful neither to the *child* nor to the *adults* who are working with him.

- Assessments depend on observational techniques, and should take place over a period of time in the environment in which the child is spending most of his waking hours—for young children, this means usually their home. (Zachary had only been assessed in an unfamiliar setting.)

- It is a difficult enough task to assess a child, but it is even more difficult to be the child who is being assessed—particularly when he is nervous or unsure and does not know who is talking to him.

- Everyone who works with a particular child should be involved in the assessment procedure. The aim of the assessment is to facilitate action being taken towards providing ongoing developmental goals. (In Zachary's case, very few people had ongoing knowledge of him and his skills.)

- Environmental circumstances and past history must be taken into account when assessing children; the way the child has been handled in his early years may affect his emotional state for a considerable time.

- Some children who have even a mild hearing loss may not always be able to function well in a strange place; they need time to become adjusted to their environment and to understand it for themselves.

- Hearing loss, caused by 'glue-ear' at an early age, can affect potential language and development and may have serious consequences for the child's educational development.

*   *   *

Zachary's and Felicity's stories are entirely different, but they each illustrate some effective approaches that help children to feel safer and more secure. When children trust adults and understand their environment, and are encouraged to progress *at their own pace*, they have better prospects for long-term success.

FELICITY

Felicity, who lives with her parents, at the age of ten was trusting and confident. She had had devised for her an eminently suitable timetable that incorporated activities, people and objects that were

entirely right for her age and stage of development. Her co-
workers had ensured that she was able to explore her own
environment within the classroom. Felicity has a severe hearing
impairment which, combined with total blindness, meant that, if
she was to access the National Curriculum, her individual education programme would need to be substantially altered and
adapted.

All Felicity's co-workers and her parents worked well together,
and everything about her placement was satisfactory. As her
programme had worked so successfully, it might have been
thought that she would need no further intervention, but everyone
involved with her realised that her next most important step,
moving to a new school, might call for a fair amount of preparation. They were all aware that it had taken Felicity some time
to learn to trust her present environment, and they had taken great
care to ensure that her classroom gave her security throughout the
day. Felicity's needs, which her immediate environment had to
supply, were:

- space
- scope for exercise
- privacy
- supervision
- company
- supplementary information
- spatial knowledge
- stimulation.

PROVIDING FOR FELICITY'S NEEDS

1   The toys provided in her special area gave her the opportu-
    nity for exploration, for gathering information and for using
    her imagination. Stimulating toys and equipment gave her
    the opportunity not only to have fun but also to learn and
    build on her skills.
2   The area of the room that provided her with quiet and privacy
    contained plants, fish and animals, which enabled Felicity

to handle and help look after living things and offered to other children reality-based experiences as well.

3   The accessibility of gross motor equipment was a challenge to Felicity and offered her the opportunity to discover more about herself and about the way she used her body in space. The same area also provided stimulating activities for the other children, which led Felicity on to learn about cause and effect within group situations.

4   An experimental area for cookery and science motivated her to experiment with many materials. Access to water gave her the chance to learn to tolerate other textures, through the experience of using water and water accessories such as buckets and funnels. Pouring, splashing and sharing, and enjoying the social activity, were all part of Felicity's day.

5   Areas of different sizes were structured in such a way as to provide safe corners with soft mats and furnishings, and had easily identifiable chairs so that Felicity and the other children could relax with books.

6   At the door of the classroom herbs in pots were an indicator that the outside play area was near. To the left of the pots the children could find equipment on which they could climb and, in particular, large equipment that promoted jumping and moving at speed. All of the equipment provided exciting whole-body activities, and was within the range and capability of each student.

7   As half of the paved outside area was covered, the children could go out in all weathers and experience the feeling of being cold, of having the wind blowing on their faces and the rain in the air, as well as the warmth of the sun.

8   Beyond the classroom was a grassy area bordered by trees and bushes. This constituted an outside information area that gave Felicity and her classmates space and opportunity to learn about the outside world.

9   Within the classroom attention had been paid to lighting, background noise and the arrangement of the furniture. There were three particularly important features:

- *a static area*, which never changed
- *a challenge area*, which sometimes changed
- *an interest area*, which often changed.

10   Felicity knew exactly where each door out of the classroom
led because markers, or referents, had been placed close to
them. Beyond the two main doors a tactile wall had been
made with different-textured papers that she could 'trail'
along towards significant areas such as the dining-room, the
soft-play room and front door of the school.

Thought had been given to the lighting provided in the room,
according to individual children's needs. Small high-density
lamps made close work easier for some, and glare had been
avoided by not having shiny surfaces, which could have been
very confusing for some children with partial sight.

Plain carpets and furnishings and uncluttered working surfaces
wherever possible were provided. Contrasting colours, particularly against door frames and steps, highlighted these possible
problem areas for children with some residual vision. Much of
the room was carpeted, which helped to damp down echoes and
made it easier for children such as Felicity to discriminate and
locate sounds. Dividing up the classroom into smaller areas by
the use of screens and furniture provided a quiet environment for
all the children, and in particular gave Felicity opportunities to
explore small spaces. Small areas that are easily defined are more
helpful for most children. Learning to move from one clearly
defined small area to another helped to make Felicity feel in
control.

At her annual review, plans were put in place to ensure that
Felicity would make a successful move from her safe and familiar
planned environment to her new school the following year. The
review made provision for Felicity to learn to operate in the
nextdoor classroom and to transfer her skills to that room, so that
when she moved to her new school she would be able to take
this ability with her.

The importance of cues and routines

It was agreed that since Felicity made good use of cues and clues within her present environment, it would be a good idea to show her that they could be useful in new places too. It had been noticed, for example:

- that when she reached the front door she always stood still. It was likely that she did this because she was aware of the different temperature in the hallway, which gave her a chance to take in the fact that the front door was close by
- that when she travelled the longer distance from the hall to the dining-room she often stood at the corner before walking the last two metres. It was assumed that she was orientating herself in her own time, deciding which way to go—she knew that if she went forward she would reach the dining-room, whereas if she turned left she would enter the soft-play room. It was realised that Felicity was also using her sense of time to signal to her which way she should go. (Of course, the smells from the dining-room were an extra clue)
- that when she moved in any direction that she knew well she never trailed her hand or searched for door markers. Her familiarity with trailing techniques and markers could, however, help her to learn that other rooms could have features in common with her old classroom, so it was agreed that the old door markers would move to the new room.

Felicity had learnt routes to the toilet and other essential areas, and it was vital to consider her continued autonomy in the toilet routine, hand-washing and so on as another feature of the move. This aspect of her programme was prioritised, so that when she moved to the new classroom she would have confidence in her toilet routine. As Felicity could not say 'toilet' and was not consistent when signing 'toilet', she was taught to hold a toilet bag containing her pants and towel when she went to the toilet.

Taking her ability to hold the toilet bag as the base-line for action, she was shown how to take the bag from a hook by the classroom door before proceeding to the toilet, then she learned that the bag could be in different parts of the room. Once she

realised this, she demonstrated the important skill of object per-
manence—i.e. she remembered where things were, she associated
the found object with an activity and she undertook the activity.
When she wanted to go to the toilet, she invariably picked up
her bag and trailed towards the toilet area. On one notable
occasion she picked up the bag when she was getting on the
school bus. This indicated to everyone that Felicity was independently 'making a statement' about going to the toilet before she
got on the bus, because hitherto she had always gone at set times
during the day.

Building on her skills, using understandable routines and
structures, allowed her to demonstrate her readiness to move on
to new environments. Planning with a view to helping her to
explore new, safe places within the school, in her own time,
helped her to change from one classroom to another. If change
is implemented gradually, with regular checks that the child is
still understanding, and if any difficult aspects are introduced
especially slowly, children like Felicity manage to function very
well in new environments. In addition, time needs to be allowed
for them to explore and consolidate their new knowledge. And
it is equally essential that established skills and routines be trans-
ferred to the new situations, new people, new classrooms and
new environments.

As noted earlier, many children with severe visual and severe
hearing impairments need extra time and opportunity to absorb
information about environments other than home and school—for
example, learning about what goes on at farms, in parks, shops
and cafés, and what it's like to travel on trains, buses and any
transport other than the family car. Children need to be able to
explore every new environment that they encounter, so that if
they go into a bookshop they are aware that books are found there,
that if they go into an electricity showroom washing machines can
be bought there, and so on.

The final essential part of the plan was to make sure that all
Felicity's new routes were consolidated, and that a feeling of
safety, security and trust continued in her new environment. This
is indeed what happened. After an appropriate spell in the new
classroom, she went on to make a successful transition to her

new school. Felicity could probably have said to the adults in her life, 'I know where I'm going, and I know when I've arrived.'

*   *   *

It is important to remember that children like Zachary and Felicity will change as they grow older, and that their horizons should broaden. Both children may need access to a rehabilitation officer trained to help them work towards maximising their independence, which will include acquiring safe and efficient independent mobility.

Knowing the routes to learning which these children have taken highlights the importance of cooperative effort between all disciplines. Ensuring the continued acquisition of further skills into adulthood will depend on sound 'future planning' on a regular basis.

10 Extending the Child's Skills

Children without disabilities absorb information from a very early stage, rapidly increasing their understanding by interaction with people, objects and environments usually doing this in well-recognised developmental sequences.

Children who have sensory impairments combined with other disabilities may have reduced motivation, lack of curiosity and delayed interaction. This delay can often be the result of confusing feedback from the distorted information that they receive. Some of these children can be helped to make the optimum use of their residual vision, hearing and other senses by adopting a collaborative approach towards extending the child's skills.

VISUAL DEVELOPMENT

There are some children who will use their remaining residual vision without intensive adult intervention. There are, however, many other children who will benefit from planned approaches to encourage use of their residual vision in the important early stages. Adjustments to methods of working, modifying some teaching approaches, working and playing within the child's particular developmental stage and incorporating daily routines, which give the child maximum opportunities to use their vision in functional situations, can all be planned. This approach is often particularly necessary for children with multisensory impairments who have learning or physical disabilities. Giving these children opportunities to use their remaining residual vision in everyday routines may involve parents, teachers and therapists working together towards planning the child's programme.

The child needs to be:

- in her best physical position (this may involve use of side-lying, prone-boards or standing-frames)
- in a clutter-free environment
- in a well-lit but glare-free room
- in a calm, friendly atmosphere without too much extraneous noise
- in a time scale which allows her to look, touch, and feel at her own pace.

All of these targets can be achieved, even in a busy nursery, classroom or home but they take time to plan for and commitment to carrying them out. All those involved need to understand the difficulties some children have in using their limited vision. These difficulties can sometimes arise from limitations imposed by their physical disabilities and positioning and a careful assessment of these physical factors should always be taken into account before plans are finalised.

Children with additional disabilities who have benefited from such a planned collaborative approach, are Christopher, Belinda-Ann, Mohammed, Shona and April. (All of the children, as well as having visual impairment, have severe communication delay and complex needs).

CHRISTOPHER
Christopher has cortical visual impairment. (Cortical visual impairment can occur either before, during or after birth. Damage to the visual cortex can result in the child being unable to interpret visual information). Christopher, at age four, spent a great deal of his school day sleeping. Common to many children with cortical visual impairment, he experienced 'sensory overload' and one way he found of coping with this was to sleep. He was completely confused by the lights and fast moving toys which were being used in order to 'stimulate' him. Unable to cope, he slept—thus protecting himself from the confusing images presented to him. Christopher could not function visually if extra/over-stimulating lights, fast moving projected images or torches were shone directly towards him. Many nurseries and schools have stimulating sensory rooms which, if poorly used, can have an adverse

effect on children like Christopher–the equipment effectively over-loading and confusing them.

Opportunities to integrate plans to help his use of vision through very careful use of a separate clutter-free area could, however, enable Christopher to gradually accept and begin to enjoy carefully monitored visual activities. Creating a clutter-free corner in a sensory room is possible through use of bland partitioning or through drawing dark green, blue or black curtains across one area. Some sensory rooms can be made either dark or white by simple modifications which enable most equipment to be stored in cupboards painted matt white or black. Appropriate curtaining can serve to provide a good, clear, contrasting background to the carefully selected visually stimulating equipment to be presented in sequence to children such as Christopher.

Dark room

Christopher first experienced visual awareness of fibre optics in a *quiet* dark room. As a child with cortical visual impairment, he could sustain more visual attention in this quiet environment. Christopher's needs included having plenty of opportunity, several times a week, to enjoy the experience of awareness of the moving fibre optics in a calm atmosphere. At this stage the emphasis was on his awareness and enjoyment of the experience. Christopher benefited from one to one time in an auditorily as well as visually clutter-free environment. In this room, work on focusing and tracking using planned routine strategies, included introducing one object at a time for him to look at. He learned to enjoy and tolerate activities which previously he found confusing, slowly showing preferences for some activities. Once Christopher was given enough **time** to become visually aware he showed different behaviours, sometimes widening his eyes and making head movements to the right and left depending on the position of the fibre optics. Adequate time to acclimatise ensured that Christopher was able to use this excellent environment to experience different activities at his own pace.

As a child with complex needs, Christopher's positioning always needed to be accounted for. Ensuring that Christopher had tasks or activities within quiet environments also made sure that his attention was completely focused. Taking in visual, tactile and auditory information at his own pace and integrating his use of all this gradually gathered information so that he had opportunity to:

- look and touch
- look and listen
- look, touch and listen

were his next goals.

BELINDA-ANN

Belinda-Ann has haemianopia affecting her left field of vision in both eyes. (Haemianopia can arise from damage to the visual cortex in the brain and affects half of the visual fields in either or both eyes. The lower, upper, left or right fields of vision may be affected. This eye condition may be present in children with cerebral palsy.) Use of Belinda-Ann's remaining vision was monitored by her physical position. Through very careful observation and systematic planning, Belinda-Ann's mother, nursery keyworker, physiotherapist and advisory teacher devised useful strategies in order to enable her to be visually aware of toys and activities. Belinda-Ann's progress in her use of visual responses ultimately helped her to make progress in other skill areas (such as communication).

Positioning

At the age of two, Belinda-Ann had often appeared not to be able to see anything until careful positioning gave her the chance to relax and 'do one thing at a time'. *Position* affected everything that Belinda-Ann achieved. It was too hard for her to 'look' in her standing-frame as she was expending a great deal of energy on concentrating on standing, appearing not to be visually aware. Once Belinda-Ann was sitting or side-lying comfortably, she could track some moving toys presented on her right side. In other words, as soon as she was given opportunities to be more comfortable, through supported upright-sitting, side-lying and use of a sloping-prone-board, she showed that she was able to use her remaining vision from different physical positions.

Presenting one thing at a time to Belinda-Ann within and across her field of vision, and giving her time to adjust to new activities, was of positive help. She needed time to integrate the specific visual information she was receiving, time to hold the toy/object, time to experience it and time to enjoy the situation.

White room

In the white room Belinda-Ann asked for 'more' by continuing to play with, or look towards, an object presented in this peaceful atmosphere. It was possible to identify the fact that she had finished with an object when she stopped playing or looking, whereas in busier rooms this was not always possible. Once she began to show different responses to selected activities—such as 'pop-up' toys, press-on toys, switch toys, activities involving mirrors, refractive toys and other visually stimulating materials— this opened up opportunities to note progress in her other skills:

- anticipation—to toys presented in the same sequence
- acceptance—of more favoured toys
- rejection—of less favoured activities
- signalling for more—of particular activities
- choice—continuing to play longer with selected toys, looking towards favoured people

When Belinda-Ann was in her side-lying board she was able to reach out for toys placed within her hand's reach—impossible for her prior to use of individual positioning strategies.

Utilising her visual skills helped Belinda-Ann to develop further potential—one developmental area influencing the way she progressed in another. She needed to get as much information as possible about the feel, sound and important visually appealing aspects of toys/objects as possible. Making sure that people approached her by moving gently towards her within her field of vision helped in her person-to-person contact and so extended her social skills. She learned to respond to adult interaction by face-turning and began to be able to gain and engage adults' attention.

Belinda-Ann's positioning was vital at all stages of development. Things and people could go out of her visual field quickly if she was not in her optimum physical position. Everyone needed to ensure that they were within her visual field before giving her objects, that the object was presented so as to engage her attention and that she had ample time to understand what the activity was, through taking in situations, clues and cues. (This was particularly important to remember in all new activities.)

MOHAMMED

Mohammed has retinopathy of prematurity (with light perception) and cerebral palsy. (Retinopathy of prematurity is retinal scarring which can occur in premature babies' eyes due to a reaction to changes in oxygen pressure. Some children may have useful residual vision, others may experience deterioration overtime or have no sight.) By age three, Mohammed was still startled by unexpected sounds. He was in a very busy, noisy classroom and was surprised by sounds which he could not understand. Sometimes, Mohammed needed a specially safe, uncluttered environment which he could use for part of the day, as it was difficult for him to function well in a noisy atmosphere. Mohammed's programme included ensuring that the environment could be made more predictable for him by using his awareness of light through:

- having a very large piece of shiny, refractive paper pinned to the wall of his well lit part of the sitting room at home, to give him the chance to be more aware of approaching this area.
- using bold primary coloured materials for him in his quiet area at school. These materials were big enough for him to lie on so that his whole body could gain experience of different textures. It was important not to put Mohammed's palms and fingers directly on top of these materials but to give him opportunity to feel, experience and hold them for himself. The brightly coloured materials were placed so that Mohammed could be aware of their presence against a well lit, contrasted background.

Using a quiet place regularly also gave him experience of using his perception of light and dark through the selection of some special pieces of equipment such as a vibrating white bubble tube. Ensuring that Mohammed could always touch or feel the vibration of the tube began to result in Mohammed having consistent responses to the vibration and, possibly, to the lights. He widened his eyes when the bubble tube was switched on and was observed, often, to change his expression during the session. Use of his perception of light within a distraction-free area, combined with very careful use of other bright/shiny equipment began to give Mohammed more consistent awareness of the presence and absence of light. Over time this awareness could be utilised when going into the well lit bathroom, giving him time to show through his expression that he realised that he was in a different place, going outside on a sunny day and so on: using situations to give meaning + utilising light perception.

SHONA

Shona has Coloboma. (Coloboma is an eye condition which develops in the child before birth. It can result in loss of visual field, decreased visual acuity and sensitivity to light (photophobia). The severity of its effect on the lens, iris or retina will depend on foetal age at the time of onset.) At age six, Shona had the ability to grasp and hold but did not look at the grasped object. She needed to learn to reach out and grasp objects within her visual field and to put her hands towards them as they were slowly brought towards her. Shona could feel tactile books whilst an adult turned the pages but seemed distressed by picture books. Close observation helped to pin-point her problem. Shona was affected by *glare*. All her picture books had been laminated so light 'bounced off' them. To avoid this problem, Shona could be seated so that books were angled and turned according to her visual/postural needs, while ensuring that the books had matt surfaces began to help her towards awareness of bold clear line drawings.

Shona's body inclined to the right and her efforts to use a battery operated toy made her head incline to the right even more when she pressed it. Her occupational therapist made suggestions for use of an adapted switch which gave Shona the ability to activate several battery operated toys which stayed within her visual field, and choice of books and activities, through use of the switch.

APRIL

Aged six, April has had cataracts removed and wears glasses, which she should wear all the time. Often her glasses slip down or off her nose because of her physical positioning. April needed someone to replace them correctly as well as to keep them clean (it was very hard for her to see anything through the dinner on the lenses!).

As a child with very delayed communication April needed consistency and constancy in order to understand situations. She changed her classroom each morning for numeracy work. When April moved from her classroom to go to the numeracy sessions she travelled in her wheelchair and she clearly became confused by the journey. Not having access to visual or environmental clues exacerbated her difficulties. Some environmental clues and adaptations to help April to understand where she was going each morning included:

- having strongly contrasted painted doors giving clear defi-nition against the walls and pushing April in her wheelchair towards them at a slow walking speed
- using lights in the corridor which reflected off the ceiling, thus causing less glare, and taking April to the same clearly defined, well lit part of the numeracy room each day
- ensuring that there was a travel system down and up the corridor so that any constant clues on walls or doors could be felt/seen/heard by all the children
- providing clues such as a distinctive shiny bell on the handle of the numeracy room at a height which could be accessed by wheelchair users
- placing a bold coloured, tactile cue landmark along the wall by the numeracy room which stood out from the clear back-ground of the uncluttered wall.

Consulting the Local Education Authority advisory teacher who monitors the progress of children with visual impairment can help to ensure that the child's individual plan is suitable. Observations of the child's responses, modifications or adaptations together with advice on ideas or activities can all be discussed. The advisory teacher will be able to discuss the implications of children's eye conditions. Advice regarding wearing and use of prescribed glasses or contact lenses can be sought from the teacher (who may consult the ophthalmologist). Low vision aids may have been prescribed for some children. It is essential to check how and where these aids should be used to ensure that all those involved are confident in their use.

Some children may be issued with sloping desktop-boards that assist in positioning their work to optimum advantage and some may need individual task lights.

The most appropriate medium to use for literacy skills may be discussed, including advice about the way work is set out. For example the optimum size of print, whether or not children will benefit (or not benefit) from having pictures or line drawings on the same page as the text, as well as text spacing, typeface and whether lines should be justified or unjustified (regular or irregular). These may all need consideration.

The child may be affected by positioning of furniture, pictures and objects in the room. Obtaining advice on how to display materials so that they can be better accessed by some children— such as highlighted borders around the pictures and diagrams, could all help the child's progress. Size of print, work materials and the child's position in using these may depend on further assessment as the child develops. Each child will have her own individual best method of working and playing which, through observation, all collaborating adults ought to be able to accommodate, planning for gradual change wherever possible.

There is no doubt that there are benefits from creating together planned opportunities to maximise use of individual children's residual vision. Everyday routines and activities as well as planned intervention strategies, give children more chance to develop their visual motor skills over time.

The development of children's skills depends on many factors, particularly chances to *do and understand* for themselves. These chances can be increased by assisting children to be more in control of their movements, by ensuring that all activities match their changing interests, pace of learning and emerging skills. Some children may not integrate all received information because they have specific sensory perceptual difficulties. Sometimes children can receive advice from a physio or occupational therapist qualified in using specific sensory integration techniques, if these techniques are thought to be individually appropriate.

Using fine motor skills will be monitored by the way the child uses her sight. Much learning, especially of the 'incidental kind' is determined by vision. Some children are able to grasp, but do not look at what they have grasped; others reach for an object but over-shoot it, then being unable to grasp it. Some will be able to look at a proffered object but will need coactive help in stretching for it in order to be able to grasp. Yet others will look and search for an object that is meaningful to them (such as sweets), but will not look and search for objects that they find less motivating. Some children will manipulate objects when they are put into their hands directly, but need encouragement to transfer things from one hand to another because they may not be aware of how their two hands function together.

It is the way the child **uses** sight that is important. The same eye condition in two different children may have two completely different usages, depending on the character of each child, the experiences to which she has been exposed—both those that limit and those that extend her ability to use vision—and her other abilities or disabilities.

Children with residual vision may have optimum focal length, and it can be common for some to lose contact with an object they are looking at so that they need help to keep it within their range of vision. The ability to track an object can mark the beginning of visual awareness in some children—when this happens, coloured lights can be usefully employed to extend the skill. Children may track from midline to the side and back again, from midline upwards, from midline downwards, from midline and then from side to side, from each side of the body to the other horizontally, then up and down, and diagonally. Tracking may lead towards being able to track objects at different distances, and then to reach forward beyond immediate grasp for objects which are presented.

Any information that can help the teacher or the parent to help the child to function at her optimum capacity is bound to be useful. For instance, does a particular colour attract her? Does she see better in certain light? Can she see all around? Does her colour vision appear to be normal? Does she need to move objects so as to get a clearer picture of them? Does she need to view objects at a particular angle, or can she sit upright in order to see clearly? Is she photophobic?

Children with visual impairment may need long-term assistance in order to achieve their own developmental sequence. (It should be noted, however, that there are some children whose visual skills may not progress in this way—careful observation and co-ordination to give these children varied experiences can still be planned for.) When considering the visual abilities of any particular child, it is her individual needs that will determine the approach we take to help her to achieve her own developmental skills. The child who is multisensory impaired can be affected by inability to compensate for impaired sight and hearing without intervention. Carefully planned intervention strategies can assist some children to maintain visual awareness and attention, to fixate and track, to turn towards a stimulus and to use these skills in functional ways: looking and touching, reaching, grasping, holding, using.

N.B. Studies of individuals show that some children with cortical visual impairment learn to perceive objects within darkened and clutter-free environments. In schools and nurseries with sensory rooms it is essential to remember that there are children who may find it very difficult to function unless only one piece of equipment is used at a time. It is essential to position lights carefully—in many sensory and dark rooms the ultraviolet lights are very badly positioned—and to make sure that, whatever equipment is used, no child is exposed to poorly positioned lights for any length of time. (Children should *never gaze* at ultraviolet light.)

See recommended reading list.

AUDITORY DEVELOPMENT

It is evident that, although all children are born with a capacity to communicate, the child who is multisensory impaired, especially if he has an additional disability, will need someone to help him to perceive that his efforts to communicate are being received. Adults must create a framework for his learning by giving him the kind of early experience that is often dependent on whole-body language, including gestures. If we observe the young child we see that the use of gestures is quite usual. Gesturing comes before speech, and accompanies babbling. Think of the imperious pointing of the young child. The interchange of a mother saying goodbye to her child will often be enhanced by the fact that her baby waves bye-bye long before he can speak. In the vital area of his understanding the environment and the situation that he finds himself in, the adult interprets for the child until she is sure that he has expressive language.

The young child learns globally. For instance, when he is taken several times a day into the bathroom to wash his hands and dry them, he will understand from tactual, visual and auditory clues, and from the whole situation, that he is expected to perform certain tasks. He knows that, when he has washed them, he is expected to dry his hands on a towel. He hears 'Now, let's dry our hands.' He sees the towel. He feels it as he dries himself. Information can be given to the child who is multisensory impaired, but will take longer to internalise and to understand in the same recurring situation. He will gain understanding from his regular visits to the bathroom through verbal, signed, tactual, visual and olfactory cues but will need repetition of the same information over again.

When considering the impact of hearing loss, it is useful to think about how the sighted deaf child compensates for his lack of hearing. He uses vision. He uses his residual hearing. He uses all means at his disposal in order to understand others, but most of all he uses his own preferred mode of communication as the key to all further learning. The extension of his skills in all areas will depend on his ability to gain and absorb information through interactions with other people.

The child with multisensory impairment may have a combination of conductive and sensorineural hearing impairment (conductive impairment is often associated with the functioning of the middle ear, 'glue ear' being the most common cause of conductive loss). Medication or minor surgery or the cessation of catarrhal colds may completely alleviate conductive hearing loss, or it may recur. Middle-ear problems sometimes go unnoticed in the child with disabilities because he has so many major difficulties to cope with. Since even a minor loss of hearing can affect the acquisition of language this should always be looked for when assessing children and planning for their individual needs.

Children who have sensorineural loss may be able to use hearing aids from an early age. Many are issued with radio aids, hearing aids that through a microphone enable adults to speak to them directly (with the result that ambient noise is reduced). Standard post-aural (behind-the-ear) aids can be prescribed for children with a severe to profound loss; but, as with all external aids, it is the wearer and his ability to use his aid which will often determine how efficiently it works for him. The type of hearing aid prescribed will depend on the degree and type of hearing loss. Some schools use a system that consists of a wire looped around the room allowing the hearing-aid user to listen directly to the desired sound source with minimal distracting background sound. The loop system is compatible with the 'T switch' kind of hearing aid.

Some children are offered cochlear implants. A cochlear implant and processor is a complex aid to hearing which by means of electrodes inserted into the cochlear, or inner ear, stimulates nerves leading to the brain, giving a sensation of hearing. Cochlear implants are *not* suitable for all types of hearing loss, but in some children they have resulted in an improved and useful awareness of sound.

Children with hearing impairment will usually be visited and monitored or advised by a teacher for the hearing-impaired. Some chlidren may be monitored whilst others will receive regular visits from the teacher. Monitoring or visiting will vary from region to region and is determined by whether children (or involved adults) need long term input and advice and other individual factors. She will explain test terms and give the necessary information to all involved parties, and can ask for auditory brain-stem response tests and otoacoustic (hearing) emission, amongst others, to be carried out. Often such teachers are involved in observational hearing assessments of children who have hearing impairment in addition to other disabilities. They can gain information of the dB levels of the varied sounds that a child responds to by using a sound-level meter, then advise on approximately what type of frequency the child has responded to. Teachers for the hearing-impaired advise on the maintenance of hearing aids and make recommendations concerning gathering information about a child's response to certain sounds. Some are able to lend auditory training units to certain children enabling them to hear amplified sounds during 'listening' sessions, and advise on their use and on any adaptations that may be necessary, as well as on activities suitable for auditory training. Offering new ideas as the child develops, giving access to the deaf world, giving support where it is needed (for instance, in the use of speech and sign), keeping parents and involved co-workers up to date and empowering them to contribute to information-gathering—all this can be encompassed in the work of advisory teachers for the hearing-impaired.

See recommended reading list.

MOTOR SKILLS

The large (gross) and fine motor skills of the multisensory impaired may be promoted by means of circuit training (see page 116) and coactive movement. Some children have a special need of the extra perception and skill of the parent or teacher to help them to understand that the environment is constant, for without this feeling of constancy they will be unwilling to step out into space, into a world that may have no order or meaning for them. This is where circuit work can prove particularly valuable—as a means of helping the child, through enjoyable activity, to practise the skills he needs to learn in a structured way, while at the same time giving him the necessary feeling of constancy within his environment. The child may also depend on an adult to show him how to manipulate objects. Some children achieve skills more successfully when they approach them coactively with the adult. For example, she may place herself behind or to the side of the child in order to demonstrate how to put on a sock. We can think of this as a series of small steps, starting with picking up the sock, then pulling it on to the foot, then up the leg so that it looks tidy. The child who does not have the motoric pattern for this skill may be able to pick up the sock, but not be able to complete the series of complicated fine-finger and hand movements to enable him to pull it up to his ankle, needing long term help to achieve the skill.

Some people find it useful to write down all the steps in a given task so that they can decide whether or not an individual child can learn the task through 'backward' or 'forward chaining'. Some children find it easier to *complete a task* and others find it easier to *start a task*. There is no definitive answer to the question of how we should approach this. All children are individual, and so all should be allowed their individual approaches and individual programmes—and, within these, the approach and the planned activities will alter as the child grows in ability and skill. With each child we need to follow five pointers which will govern our behaviour, before deciding on the way in which he will learn a specific skill:

1   Know the child.
2   Identify his abilities.
3   Identify his needs.
4   Observe him and the way he solves problems.
5   Identify the task that the child is expected to learn, and decide whether or not it is relevant to him and to his needs.

If we follow these pointers, we may find that what we thought we wanted the child to achieve is in fact slightly different from the goal we now see as appropriate. For example, we may have decided that he needs to self-feed, but when we apply the five pointers to this particular child we may discover that what he needs before self-feeding is to be able to hold his head, body, hands or arms in a particular fashion. Or we may have decided that he should spoon-feed, but then, having observed him, we may feel that it is extremely important for him to finger-feed because of his tactile needs and so on.

Constant observation of our children will prevent us from

making assumptions about their 'disabilities' and about our 'abilities' to teach them!

See recommended reading list.

FURTHER DEVELOPMENT

Children learn by doing. If they are encouraged to do things for themselves, to enjoy skills that lead them towards independence, their social and emotional development keeps pace with their awareness and their growing needs. Sometimes adaptations to our teaching methods will be necessary, or perhaps the environment will need to be modified. The toys and activities we provide will have to be more carefully chosen, and the means of communication we use will be different from those we would use with a sighted–hearing child. Our attitude towards each child will be centred on helping him to reach out towards his own personal goals. How we extend these goals will depend to a large extent on his visual, auditory, tactile and mobility skills and, within these developmental areas, we will constantly reinforce, via the child's own communication system, our pleasure in his achievements.

Remember: coact, react, interact.

In the world of the child who is multisensory impaired, nothing is left to chance. Sometimes, people feel overwhelmed by a sense of urgency when considering the needs of such a child, but it is still possible to relax and have fun together. He will derive a great deal of pleasure and satisfaction from playing and working at activities that help him to achieve his own goals.

When looked at objectively, some tasks seem quite boring and repetitive, but there are many ways of turning the acquisition of skills into games. For example, Lauren needs to learn how to fold, which is something within her capabilities; initially she will need lots of help and demonstration from her parents, but later she will be able to move on to imitating what they do. She can either learn to paper-fold as an activity in itself, or paper-folding can be linked to drawing by getting her to 'write a letter first', and then to fold her 'letter' and post it through a slit in a cardboard box. Her parents will remember to make the slit small enough for the letter to require folding a few times before it will fit.

Another game that Lauren's parents can play with their daughter, this time in order to improve her use of her distance vision, consists of taking articles that they know she can identify and hiding them in front of her: the items chosen a spoon, a small ball, a doll, her hairbrush, and her shoe are selected as she is **most** interested in these. Each object is held up in front of Lauren, and she is asked to identify it through sign before it is hidden under a cloth. Lauren has quickly learnt to find the article under the cloth and then, using the same principle, her parents move the toys and other objects further away, which intrigues their daughter and provides a great deal of fun and laughter. The aim of the game is quite serious, though: her distance vision is being utilised, her sign/communication is being practised, and all the interactions between parents and child are reinforced.

Joseph, whom we met earlier, is mobile and explorative, and now uses his partial hearing to orientate and to find things when he is in a familiar environment. His parents have been able to help him locate all the rooms in his house by using a discreet 'trail' of a dado rail along the hallway. At each door leading from the hall there are enough fixed clues for Joseph to be able to tell which room he is entering. Every time the dado rail finishes it means that he has reached a door. The first room he reaches is the bathroom which has a distinctive tiled floor, so simply by taking one step inside he knows that he has arrived at the bathroom. A similar situation applies in the garden. He has a swing at the end of the garden, and halfway up is his rabbit hutch to which he journeys twice daily to feed his pet rabbits. The space between the swing and the rabbit hutch had prevented Joseph from finding his way between the two. When his parents moved them slightly closer together, and moved his slide to the top of the garden, they created a route that he could remember as a mental map: slide, rabbit hutch, swing. His parents knew that his return journey—swing, rabbit hutch, slide—was a new experience for him. He in his own time and pace gradually got the hang of it.

- He learned the journey first.
- He consolidated his knowledge.

- He learned his return journey.
- He consolidated his knowledge.
- He now makes both journeys independently.

MAKING MUSIC TOGETHER

Singing together can either be a purely pleasurable experience in itself, or it can be used as an aid to helping the child to remember, recognise and discriminate sounds, to associate sounds with actions, actions with words, and words with meaning. Singing and other musical activities can be instrumental in helping the child to organise his hearing and to become aware of the 'sound–no sound' principle. By participating with him in musical activities and action games, opportunities can be created for him to listen out for sounds, anticipate sounds, and so on.

The child who is exposed only to meaningless auditory input, such as a constant radio or television, will very often cut out from sounds—*because* they mean nothing to him. Particularly to some children, background noise makes *everything* sound jumbled and confused. The child who is introduced carefully to the idea of selective listening, and to the enjoyment of meaningful auditory input, will often learn to localise sound sources and to imitate sound patterns and rhythms. He will *expect* to listen.

It is not enough simply to *identify* a sound as, say, coming from a car. The child should also *interpret* the sound so as to discover, for instance, that there is a road nearby, and *locate* the sound so as to know exactly where the road is. Each skill can be encouraged separately, but when you promote one you are sure to be promoting others. Practise the art of careful listening. If you sit quietly, how many different sounds can you hear that the child may be able to identify? All the sounds within his range of hearing may need to be explained to him. Experiment with making sounds together. Make a 'sound box' with jars and tins containing different things such as pebbles, rice, sand, buttons, bottle tops and sea shells. Also collect pieces of metal, wood, plastic, cardboard, paper, felt and other material, and help him to find out how to make different noises by shaking, rubbing, banging, tapping and scratching them.

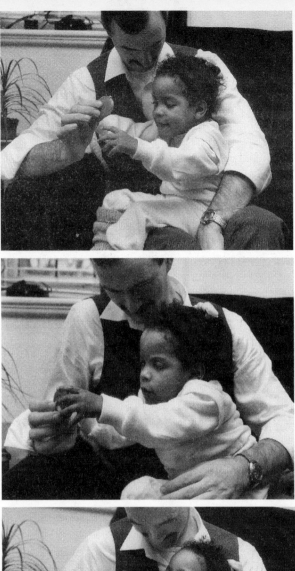

The adult extends the child's range of skills by encouraging her to move the object in a variety of ways.

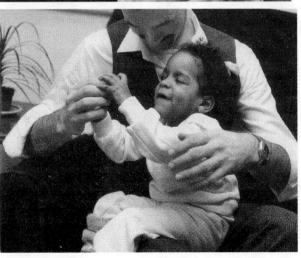

How many different sounds can you hear?

Listen together for cars, buses, lorries, vans, motorcycles, taxis and refuse lorries. Help him to interpret some of the sounds he hears by giving him experience of things and people at work, such as the refuse collectors when they carry the rubbish away and put it in the lorry, followed by the crunch of its equipment as it crushes the rubbish; and the milkman collecting the bottles from the milk float and the sound of the float as it drives away.

All the activities suggested for children in this chapter are intended to help extend their skills. We still, however, hear of children who are deafblind or have multisensory impairments 'waiting to be active and engaged', for because they have complex needs they are 'waiting for an assessment'. People who work with these children may request an assessment from a range of professionals and may delay starting a child's individual programme until they have collated all their information.

While waiting, it can be useful to make one's own observations using the following SCHEMA format:

Sight: look at the child's way of using his eyes.
Communication: decide how he receives and imparts information.
Hearing: observe the way he responds to sounds.
Environment: describe the places he appears to enjoy.
Movement: note his individual physical movements.
Activity: make observations and notes about the child's favourite activity.

The SCHEMA format is an informal way of beginning to collect information that will be very valuable when other assessments take place. Individual children tend to perform differently according to the time and place of assessment and whether or not the assessing professional is familiar to them. Informal observations are therefore a constructive way of collating and noting information that may not be available or apparent to other observers. The aim of all assessments is to provide *action and activities* that the child can undertake immediately. They should contribute information that will help the child to achieve his own ultimate goal, which is always to become as independent as he possibly can.

Using the informal observations obtained through the SCHEMA format, as well as some of the holistic approaches outlined in this book, should encourage people to get started with the child, making sense together of what he is teaching them about his needs. Any assessments that follow should enhance the information already gathered and enable an even more successful individual plan to be carried out together.

Note Hearing impairment and visual impairment in this book refer to hearing loss definitions (average hearing loss better ear) Mild: 0–40 dBHL Moderate: 41–70 dBHL Severe: 71–95 dBHL Profound: 95 dBHL and above and visual activity definitions (better eye) 6/24: slight to moderate impairment 6/60: moderate impairment 3/60: severe impairment. Children with multisensory impairment may have long standing significant need for structures and systems which ensure highest possible standards with regard to the management of their combined hearing and visual needs. The SCHEMA observation format can enable everyone to cooperate in implementing individual plans as the child's abilities change as well as acting as a 'first' observation.

TOYS AND EQUIPMENT

Many manufacturers supply a range of toys, books and equipment which children with visual and hearing impairment can enjoy. Some recommended ones include:

Tickling Mr Tickle by Golden Bear
Bounce and Tickle Me Elmo by Sesame Street
Nerf Vortex by Hasbro
Sock'Em Boppers and Powerbag by Kids International
Bumble Ball by ERTL
Butterfly Phone by Chicco
Funky 4 Sound Maracas by Wow Toys
Action Push Mower by John Deere Kids
Chicken Croquet by MB Games
Foot-to-Floor Tractor by John Deere Kids
Hightime Ball Dome Play Tent by David Halsall
Frog in a Box by Galt
Happy Sounds Ball by Tomy
Shake 'N' Light Rattle by First Years
Sleepytime Serenade by Playskool
Sleepytime Soother by Fisher-Price
Revolving Mirror Ball* by Rompa
Side Glow Fibre Optic Spray* by Rompa
Remington Whirl Foot Spa* Boots and electrical stores
BeActive Box by Suffolk Playworks
Glow Balls by Rompa
The Dawg by Rompa
My Big Book by Rompa
Tactile Sole Sensation by Rompa
Sonic Hoop by Rompa
Musical Fantasy by Mike Ayres
Koosh Balls by Mike Ayres
Rainmakers by Mike Ayres
Music Tapes by Mike Ayres

Swing Seats by TFH
Fibre Optic Plume by TFH
Inflatable Tactile Ball by TFH
Spot the Sound Sensitive Spaniel by TFH
Vibro Tube by TFH

Items marked with an asterisk in the above list work by electricity. These are not toys and require full adult supervision at all times.

As with everything else, toys should be chosen with the individual needs of the child in mind. Play should always be fun, and unless the toy is designed for two or more people the child should quickly be able to learn to activate or manipulate it for himself—sometimes discovering for himself, sometimes being shown coactively. It is also important to remember that we are thinking in terms of toys and *play* aids, not in terms of what are sometimes described as 'educational toys'. In other words, toys are for children's use at home or for those moments in school when given the opportunity to play freely. No toys have been included that come within the range of specialist toys, designed to promote auditory, visual or tactile skills, but are listed here for the element of fun and enjoyment that children can gain from them.

Some of the best and most effective toys and equipment are those that parents and professionals have made for specific children. These include tactile mats, memory quilts, large inset puzzles with customised handles, and an 'A' frame from which to hang favourite attractive toys. That extremely versatile piece of equipment, the *Resonance Board*, is in constant use at the Sense Family Centre in Ealing (see Useful Addresses). A description of how to make the board has been written by David Brown, Head of the Family Centre:

The idea for these came from a teacher in Denmark called Lilli Nielsen. The board needs the following materials:

—one piece of 6mm to 8mm thick plywood (120cms square is a good size)
—four pieces of 2.5 × 2.5cm wood (each 117.5cms long)
—superglue

—short nails (or screws)
—one large tin of furniture wax (for example, Colron).

The pieces of 2.5 × 2.5cm are superglued and nailed around the underside edges of the piece of plywood, making certain that the nails are hammered well in to leave the plywood surface safe (if screws are used, they will need to be counter-sunk). Then the upper surface of the plywood needs to be made very smooth with glasspaper. The final step is to apply at least two coats of furniture wax to the plywood with a duster (hard work!) so that the finished surface is smooth, easy to clean and nicely perfumed.

The 120cms square size is a useful one for most ages and sizes of child, though it can be a bit cumbersome to lift and carry around. We also have a 'baby'-size board which is 90cms square and has been useful with very young children, though it does not resonate as well as the larger board.

Maintenance needs depend on the amount of use: our big board is re-sanded and re-waxed every term (about three times a year). If you see parts of the surface losing its sheen and bits of frayed wood or splinters appearing, then sanding and waxing are an urgent necessity. We store our boards upright against a wall with the smooth working surface towards the wall.

Equipment to use on the board depends upon personal preferences (yours and the child's!). I like the following:

—plastic and enamel plates (various sizes)
—round tea caddies
—chains of various lengths and weights (e.g. dog choker collars)
—spinning tops
—bunches of metal keys
—bunches of plastic cutlery
—wind-up music boxes
—large, round, heavy pebbles
—plastic/metal Slinkies
—rocking toys (Roly Poly Chime Ball or Chime Bird)

For more information about the use of Resonance Boards see pp. 134 and 163.

Resonance board.

Other toys and play aids that can easily be made at home include:

1   *A feely board*   This makes use of old socks, tights or pieces of material, in which you place a variety of *safe* materials such as dried peas, wood blocks, corks. Then fill each sock with a different type of material, and attach them firmly to a board, to be played with together or separately.

2   *Feely bags*   Several can be made, in a variety of textured materials, and kept in a large bag made from material that is the same as one of the small bags or a combination of several of them, to add more interest.

3   *A feely box*   Probably the simplest play aid to make. Fill a cardboard box with all types of paper for the child to sift through and sort, or put into the box a lot of wooden spoons, saucepan lids and other interesting *safe* pieces of kitchen equipment for him to explore.

4   *Wine boxes*   Some have inside them a silver-foil bag that contains the wine. Once the wine has been drunk, you are left with a very interesting bag that you can fill with a variety of materials such as water, lentils and rice, and which you can then safely close, using the wine stopper and masking tape.

5   *Tins*   All sorts and sizes of tins can be filled with different materials, particularly dried rice, macaroni and lentils—all of these make very satisfying sounds, as do dog chains and bird toys. (Make sure the lid is safely secured.)

6   *Jars, pots and pans*   These can provide experience of learning to twist, turn and take off lids and put them back on again. You can further encourage the child to learn to twist and turn if you put a favourite toy into one of the containers. Since jars, pots and pans are usually used in the kitchen, as kitchen equipment, it is important to emphasise that kitchen containers have a use. You are trying to get across to him that specific objects have specific properties, and it may not always be desirable to give him food containers to play with in case he becomes muddled as to their usage. Cooking, or at least eating, should be the end result of opening jars containing foodstuffs.

7   *A washing-up bowl*   Put in warm water and a few things to play with, and it will give the child a great deal of pleasure and amusement. If he does not like playing with water, substitute pieces of material, or—if you know he is safe with them—split peas, lentils, etc. Remember that there are some children who do not like playing with water—this is not unusual, and should never be forced on the child. Sometimes it is a good idea to put only a minute amount of water in the bottom of the washing-up bowl, and then to place in it a favourite toy which the child will reach for, getting his hands very slightly wet as he does so. This is one small way of encouraging him to get his hands wet. Gradually you can increase the water and exchange the motivating toy for appropriate water-play toys; soap suds or fingerpaint, when the time is right.

8   *A large cardboard box*   Often makes a wonderful environment for a young child to experience. It is a safe place in which to play, and can be altered according to the child's needs. You can provide different materials for him to sit on in the box, such as an old towel or a blanket, and give him one or two toys (one favourite and one new one) to play with. Most importantly, the box gives him a feeling of security because he can feel the edges of his environment all the time.

NB It must be emphasised, though, that no child should be introduced to a box, left in one or even sat in one if there is any possibility that this might create fear. There should *never* be a lid on the box that he could pull over himself accidentally. Once he is mobile, a box is not likely to be something that he will often wish to sit in, and it should never be used as a playpen.

Many organisations, such as Sense, RNIB and RNID, can supply information about equipment for older children, including alerting devices and other useful aids:

- *Doorbells*: different types to suit all needs, ranging from louder doorbells to flashing and tactile devices.
- *Alarm clocks*: including flashing clocks and those that incorporate vibration.
- *Fire alarms and telephone alerts*: these have either flashing or vibrating devices.
- *Liquid level indicators*: placed on a mug, cup or bath, these can beep or vibrate when the desired level is reached.
- *Watches and clocks* with large numbers, raised numbers or Braille, or which 'speak'.
- *Optacon*: which enables print to be read on a tactile vibrating display.
- *Hasicom (Hearing and Sight Impaired Communication)* produce VersaBraille.
- *Mountbatten Brailler* which can translate Braille into print or display it on a computer screen.

Manufactured toys and equipment have a valuable place, but it should be remembered that the most valuable aid of all is an alert adult who can act as:

> a toy
> a climbing frame
> an interpreter
> a communicator
> a comforter
> a parent
> a teacher
> a friend.

Thank you to Sarah Walton for helping me to choose some toys

Afterword

I only know that when I touch a flower,
or feel the sun and wind upon my face,
or hold your hand in mine,
there is a brightness within
my soul that words can never trace.
I call it Life, and laugh with its delight,
though life itself be out of sound and sight.

Robert J. Smithdas, 1982
Director of Community Education,
Helen Keller National Center
for Deaf-Blind Youths and Adults,
New York.

Resources

EQUIPMENT CATALOGUES

Paul and Marjorie Abbatt Ltd., PO Box 22, Harlow, Essex CM19 5AY.

Mike Ayres & Company Ltd., Unit 1, Turnoaks Business Park, Burley Close, off Storforth Lane, Chesterfield, Derbyshire S40 2HA.

Early Learning Centre, Hawksworth, Swindon, Wiltshire SN2 1TT.

Educational Supply Association (Play Specials and Vital Years), School Materials Division, Pinnacles, Harlow, Essex.

Escor Toys Ltd., Groveley Road, Christchurch, Hampshire BH23 3RQ.

Fisher-Price Toys (Europe) Ltd., Lodge Farm Industrial Estate, Hopping Hill, Northampton NN5 7AW.

Four to Eight, Medway House, St Mary's Mills, Evelyn Drive, Leicester LE3 2BT.

Galt Educational Division, James Galt and Co Ltd., Brookfield Road, Cheadle, Cheshire SK8 2PN.

Huntercraft, ESA, PO Box 22, Harlow, Essex CM19 5AY.

Kiddicraft Ltd., Kenley, Surrey CR2 5TS.

London Music Shop, 154 Sidwell Street, Exeter EX4 6RT.

Playskool, Milton Bradley Ltd., C.P. House, 97–107 Uxbridge Road, London W5 5TL.

Rompa, Goyt Side Road, Chesterfield, Derbyshire S40 2PH.

TFH, 76 Barracks Road, Sandy Lane Industrial Estate, Stourport-on-Severn, Worcestershire DY13 9QB.

INFORMATION HANDBOOKS

Help Starts Here (for parents of children with special needs).
Free from the Voluntary Council for Handicapped Children,
National Children's Bureau, 8 Wakley Street, London
EC1V 7QE (Tel: 0207 278 9441).

The Disability Rights Handbook
Published by the Disability Alliance Educational and
Research Association, 25 Denmark Street, London WC2 8NJ
(Tel: 0207 240 0806).

CaF Rare Syndromes Directory
From Contact a Family, 170 Tottenham Court Road, London
W1P 0HA. (Tel: 0207 383 3555).

Curriculum Access for Deafblind Children
Research Report No. 1, DfEE/Sense. Available from Sense,
11–13 Clifton Terrace, Finsbury Park, London N4 3SR (Tel:
0207 272 7774).

How to Guide a Blind Person
RNIB in association with the Guide Dogs for the Blind
Association, 224 Great Portland Street, London W1N 6AA
(Tel: 0207 388 1266).

TOYS AND PLAY INFORMATION

Handicapped Persons Research Unit, Newcastle upon Tyne
Polytechnic, 1 Coach Lane, Coach Lane Campus, Newcastle
upon Tyne NE7 7TW (Tel: 01632 664061).

PLAY MATTERS/The Toy Libraries Association,
68 Churchway, London NW1 1LT (Tel: 0207 387 9592).

Toy Aids Projects, Lodbourne Farmhouse, Lodbourne,
Gillingham, Dorset SP8 4EH (Tel: 017476 2256).

British Toy and Hobby Association, 80 Camberwell Road,
London SE5 0EG (Tel: 0207 701 7271).

Fun to Learn, 3 North Street, Thame, Oxfordshire OX9 3BP
(Tel: 01844 260022).

USEFUL ADDRESSES

United Kingdom
Sense, 11–13 Clifton Terrace, Finsbury Park, London N4 3SR.
Tel: 0207 272 7774, Fax: 0207 272 6012, Minicom: 0207 272
   9848, e-mail: sense@sense.org.uk

Sense Family Centre, 86 Cleveland Road, Ealing, London
   W13 0HE.
Tel: 0208 991 0513, Fax: 0208 810 5298.

Council for the Advancement of Communication with Deaf
   People (CACDP), Durham University Science Park,
   Block 4, Stockton Road, Durham DH1 3UZ.
Tel: 0191 383 1155 (Voice and Text), Fax: 0191 383 7914,
   e-mail: durham@cacdp.demon.co.uk

Royal National Institute for the Blind (RNIB), 224 Great
   Portland Street, London W1N 6AA.
Tel: 0207 388 1266, Fax: 0207 383 4921.

Royal National Institute for Deaf People (RNID), 19–23
   Featherstone Street, London EC1Y 8SL.
Tel: 0207 296 8000, Fax: 0207 296 8199, Minicom: 0207 296
   8001, e-mail: helpline@rnid.org.uk

Royal Association in Aid of Deaf People (RAD), 27 Old Oak
   Road, London W3 7HN.
Tel: 0208 743 6187, Text: 0208 749 7561, Fax: 0208 740
   6551.

National Deaf Children's Society (NDCS), 15 Dufferin Street,
   London EC1Y 8PD.
Tel: 0207 250 0123, Fax: 0207 251 5020, e-mail:
   ndcs@ndcs.org.uk

Deafblind UK, 100 Bridge Street, Peterborough PE1 1DY.
Tel: 01733 358100 (Telephone and minicom), Fax: 01733
   358350, Helpline: 0800 132320.

ACE Centre, 92 Windmill Road, Headington, Oxford
   OX3 7DR.
Tel: 01865 763508/759800, Fax: 01865 759810, e-mail:
   info@ace-centre.org.uk

SCOPE, 6 Market Road, London N7 9PW.
Tel: 0207 619 7100, Fax: 0207 619 7399.

Contact a Family, 170 Tottenham Court Road, London
   W1P 0HA.
Tel: 0207 383 3555, Fax: 0207 383 0259, e-mail:
   info@Cafamily.org.uk

United States
American Foundation for the Blind, 11 Penn Plaza, Suite 300,
New York, NY 1001.
Tel: (212) 502-7600, e-mail: afbinfo@afb.net

John Tracy Clinic, 806W, Adams Boulevard, Los Angeles,
CA 90007.
Tel: (213) 748-5481, Fax: (213) 749-1651, e-mail:
astokes@Johntracyclinic.org

Recommended Reading

Aitken, S. and Buultjens, M. (1992). *Vision for Doing—Assessing Functional Vision of Learners who are Multiply Disabled.* Moray House Publishing, ISBN 0 901580 39 2.

Goold, L., Borbilas, P., Clark, A. and Kane, C. (1993). *An Ideas Kit.* North Rocks Press, Australia, ISBN 0 949050 03 2.

Guidelines for Assessment of Children with Complex Needs (1997). British Association of Teachers of the Deaf (BATOD), ISBN 0 903502 05 4.

José, Randall T. (ed.) (1985). *Understanding Low Vision.* American Foundation for the Blind, ISBN 0 89128 119 3.

Lewis, Vicky and Collis, Glyn M. (eds.) (1997). *Blindness and Psychological Development in Young Children.* BPS Books (British Psychological Society), ISBN 1 85433 231 7.

McInnes, J. M. and Treffrey, J. A. (1993). *Deaf-Blind Infants and Children—A Developmental Guide.* University of Toronto Press, ISBN 0 8020 7787 0.

McInnes, J. M. (ed.) (1999). *A Guide to Planning and Support for Individuals who are Deafblind.* University of Toronto Press, ISBN 0 8020 4242 2.

McCracken, Wendy and Laoide-Kemp, Siobhan (1997). *Audiology in Education,* Whurr Publishers Ltd., ISBN 1 861560 17 6.

McCracken, Wendy and Sutherland, Hilary (1991). *Deaf-Ability—Not Disability.* Multilingual Matters, Avon, ISBN 1 85359 080 0.

Morris, Jenny (1999). *Hurtling into a Void.* Joseph Rowntree Foundation, ISBN 1 84196001 2

Nielsen, Lilli (1992). *Space and Self.* Sikon, ISBN 87 503 9566 1.

Smith, Cath (1990). *Signs Make Sense*. Souvenir Press, ISBN
    0 285 65083 1.
Sonksen, Patricia and Stiff, Blanche (1991). *Show Me What my
    Friends Can See*. Institute of Child Health, London, ISBN
    0 9517526 0 X.
Stillman, R. (ed.) (1978). *The Callier Azusa Scale*. The
    University of Texas at Dallas, Callier Center for
    Communication Disorders.
Welsh, Richard L. and Blasch, Bruce B. (1983). *Foundations
    of Orientation and Mobility*. American Foundation for the
    Blind, ISBN 0 89128 093 6.
Winstock, April (1994). *The Practical Management of Eating
    and Drinking Difficulties in Children*. Winslow Press, ISBN
    0 86388 123 8.

Index

Moon 138, 158
motor skills
    fine 58, 117–18, 172–6, 219–21, 223
    gross 58–9, 112–16, 236
    self-help 186–8
movement
    coactive 100, 107, 144
    difficulties with 29, **104–35**, 161
    matching 110
    mirroring 36, 110
    programme 91
        see also interaction
movements, random hand 56, 58, 64
msi *see* impairment, multisensory
muscle problems 12, 29, 105–6, 168–70
    see also movement
music, making 111, 170–72, 258–60

Named Officer 49–50
names, use of children's 158–60
nappies, provision of 31
National Deaf Children's Society 33,
    271
National Symposium on Children and
    Youth who are Deafblind 77–8
needs of child, recognising 11–12, 16
    see also assessment of progress

occupational therapist 30, 33
older children 25–6, 130–35
ophthalmologist 32
orthoptist 32

paediatric
    Community Team 27–9
    dietitian 30–31
    occupational therapist 30
    physiotherapist 29
    speech and language therapist 30
parent-partnership schemes 22–3
parents' groups 53
physiotherapist 29, 33
play
    activities 42–3, 100, 185–6, 217–19,
        230
    aids 235, **262–7**, 269, 270
    intensive 140–41
    skills 15, 61–2, 64–6, 83–9, 146–7,
        186–8, 228

Portage 33
professional services 6–7, 10–14, 22–4,
    27–53, 78
progress *see* assessment of progress
psychologist
    clinical 30
    educational 33

reactions of other people 22, 80
real-life experiences 102–3
referents *see* STAR objects
rehabilitation workers 33
relationships, adult 9–11, 15
Resonance Board 134, 164, 263–5
RNIB (Royal National Institute for the
    Blind) 33, 271
rocking 142, 197, 204–6, 210–13
routine, importance of 60, 101–2,
    238–40
Royal National Institute for the Blind
    (RNIB) 33, 271
rubella 16, 17, **55–69**
    see also deafblind children

safety features 87, 98
scanning 249–51
SCHEMA format 261
schools 76–9, 130–3
screaming 191
seating, specialist 29, 30, 32
self-care, skills 227, 228–30
self-help, skills 38, 186–8, 223–4
SENCO (Special Educational Needs
    Coordinator) 53
Sense
    Family Centre 24–5, 33, 35, 271
Shopping, *see* skills
siblings, involvement of 18–21
sight difficulties *see* impairments, visual
signing 42, 60, 67, 144, 155–8, 182
singing 111, 170–72, 258
sitting 105–6
    see also movement; muscle problems
skills, drinking *see* skills, feeding
skills, eating *see* skills, feeding
skills, feeding 30, 41, 58, 90, 117–20,
    229
skills, shopping 130–31
skills, walking 32, 91